High-Frequency Trading

High-Frequency Trading
New Realities for Traders, Markets and Regulators

Edited by David Easley, Marcos López de Prado and
Maureen O'Hara

Risk
books

Published by Risk Books, a Division of Incisive Media Investments Ltd

Incisive Media
32–34 Broadwick Street
London W1A 2HG
Tel: +44(0) 20 7316 9000
E-mail: books@incisivemedia.com
Sites: www.riskbooks.com
      www.incisivemedia.com

© 2013 Incisive Media Investments Limited

ISBN 978-1-78272-009-6

British Library Cataloguing in Publication Data
A catalogue record for this book is available from the British Library

Publisher: Nick Carver
Commissioning Editor: Sarah Hastings
Managing Editor: Lewis O'Sullivan
Editorial Development: Sarah Hastings
Designer: Lisa Ling
Copy-edited and typeset by T&T Productions Ltd, London

Printed and bound in the UK by Berforts Group

Contents

About the Editors

David Easley is the Henry Scarborough professor of social science, professor of economics and professor of information science at Cornell University. He served as chair of the Cornell economics department from 1987 to 1993 and 2010 to 2012. He is a fellow of the Econometric Society and has served as an associate editor of numerous economics journals. David recently co-authored the book *Networks, Crowds and Markets: Reasoning About a Highly Connected World*, which combines scientific perspectives from economics, computing and information science, sociology and applied mathematics to describe the emerging field of network science.

Marcos López de Prado is head of quantitative trading and research at HETCO, the trading arm of Hess Corporation, a Fortune 100 company. Previously, Marcos was head of global quantitative research at Tudor Investment Corporation, where he also led high-frequency futures trading. In addition to more than 15 years of investment management experience, Marcos has received several academic appointments, including postdoctoral research fellow of RCC at Harvard University, visiting scholar at Cornell University, and research affiliate at Lawrence Berkeley National Laboratory (US Department of Energy's Office of Science). Marcos holds two doctorate degrees from Complutense University, is a recipient of the National Award for Excellence in Academic Performance (Government of Spain), and was admitted into American Mensa with a perfect test score.

Maureen O'Hara is the Robert W. Purcell professor of finance at the Johnson Graduate School of Management, Cornell University. Her research focuses on market microstructure, and she is the author of numerous journal articles as well as the book *Market Microstructure Theory*. Maureen serves on several corporate boards, and is chairman of the board of ITG, a global agency brokerage firm. She is a member of the CFTC-SEC Emerging Regulatory Issues Task Force (the "flash crash" committee), the Global Advisory Board of the Securities Exchange Board of India (SEBI) and the Advisory Board of the Office of Financial Research, US Treasury.

About the Authors

Robert Almgren is a co-founder of Quantitative Brokers, which provides agency algorithmic execution and cost measurement in interest rate markets. He is a Fellow in the mathematics in finance program at New York University. Until 2008, Robert was a managing director and head of quantitative strategies in the electronic trading services group of Banc of America Securities. From 2000 to 2005 he was a tenured associate professor of mathematics and computer science at the University of Toronto, and director of its Master of Mathematical Finance program. He has an extensive research record in applied mathematics, including papers on optimal trading, transaction cost measurement and portfolio construction.

E. Wes Bethel is a senior computer scientist at Lawrence Berkeley National Laboratory, where he conducts and manages research in the area of high performance visualisation and analysis. He is a member of IEEE and a Distinguished Scientist of the Association for Computing Machinery. He has a PhD in computer science from the University of California, Davis.

Alexandre Dupuis has worked at OLSEN since 2006 and is head of the quantitative research unit Romandy. His focus lies in researching and developing trading models as well as creating risk-management tools. Alex is a member of the risk-management team where he controls a third of the investment portfolio. In collaboration with universities, he supervises PhD students in the field of quantitative finance. Alex holds a PhD in computer science from the University of Geneva and has gained further research experience by working at the University of Oxford and at ETH.

Anton Golub has worked at OLSEN since the summer of 2012 as a member of the research team. He performs research in the field of market micro-structure, leveraging the methodology developed at OLSEN. Anton previously worked at the Manchester Business School as a researcher on high-frequency trading, market micro-structure and flash crashes. In 2012, he was invited to participate in an international project on computerised trading funded by the

UK Treasury. He holds a MSc degree in Financial and Business Mathematics from the University of Zagreb.

Ming Gu is a professor of applied mathematics at the University of California at Berkeley, a position he has held since 2006. Prior to joining Berkeley, he was a professor of applied mathematics at University of California Los Angeles. Ming holds a PhD in computer science from Yale University and a BS in mathematics from Nanjing University in China.

Terrence Hendershott completed his PhD at the graduate school of business at Stanford University and is the Cheryl and Christian Valentine Chair as an associate professor at the Haas School of Business at the University of California at Berkeley. His research interests include information technology's impact and role in financial markets and the structure and regulation of financial markets. His writing has appeared in national newspapers and magazines, and his academic work has been published in numerous scholarly journals. He has consulted for various financial markets and investment firms.

Charles M. Jones is the Robert W. Lear professor of finance and economics and the director of the program for financial studies at Columbia Business School, where he has been on the faculty since 1997. Charles studies the structure of securities markets, and he is particularly noted for his research on short sales, algorithmic trading, liquidity and trading costs. His published articles have won a number of best paper awards. He received an undergraduate degree in mathematics from MIT in 1987, and he completed his PhD in finance at the University of Michigan in 1994.

Michael Kearns is professor of computer and information science at the University of Pennsylvania, where he holds secondary appointments in the statistics and operations and information management departments of the Wharton School. His research interests include machine learning, algorithmic game theory, quantitative finance and theoretical computer science. Michael also has extensive experience working with quantitative trading and statistical arbitrage groups, including at Lehman Brothers, Bank of America and SAC Capital.

David Leinweber was a co-founder of the Center for Innovative Financial Technology at Lawrence Berkeley National Laboratory. Previously, he was visiting fellow at the Hass School of Business and at Caltech. He was the founder of Integrated Analytics Corporation, with was acquired by Jefferies Group and spun off as Investment Technology Group (NYSE: ITG). At First Quadrant, he was managing director, responsible for quantitative management of over US$6 billion in global equities. In 2011, he was named one of the top 10 innovators of the decade by *Advanced Trading* magazine. David holds undergraduate degrees in computer science and physics from MIT and a PhD in applied mathematics from Harvard University.

Oliver Linton holds the chair of political economy at Cambridge University and is a fellow of Trinity College. He is a Fellow of the Econometric Society, of the Institute of Mathematical Statistics and of the British Academy. His research has mostly been about econometric methodology applied to financial data. He served as an expert witness for the Financial Services Authority on a market abuse case in 2012. He was a member of the Lead Expert Group for the Government Office for Science project "The Future of Computer Trading in Financial Markets", published in November 2012.

Albert J. Menkveld is professor of finance at VU University Amsterdam, and research fellow at the Tinbergen Institute and the Duisenberg School of Finance. In 2002, he received his PhD from Erasmus University Rotterdam. He visited the Wharton School of the University of Pennsylvania in 2000, Stanford University in 2001 and New York University in 2004/5 and 2008–11. Albert's research focuses on securities trading, liquidity, asset pricing and financial econometrics. He has published in the *Journal of Finance*, *Journal of Business and Economic Statistics* and *Journal of Financial and Quantitative Analysis*, among others. He has been a member of the Group of Economic Advisors of the European Securities and Market Authority (ESMA) since 2011.

Yuriy Nevmyvaka has extensive experience in quantitative trading and statistical arbitrage, including roles as portfolio manager and head of groups at SAC Capital, Bank of America and Lehman Brothers. He has also published extensively on topics in algorithmic trading and market microstructure, and is a visiting scientist in the computer and information science department at the University of Pennsylvania. Yuriy holds a PhD in computer science from Carnegie Mellon University.

Richard B. Olsen founded OLSEN in 1985 and is chief executive officer. He oversees all portfolio investments as part of a comprehensive risk-management process and is involved in the ongoing development of trading models. Richard has written and co-authored many scientific papers and published a book, numerous articles and opinion pieces on a variety of topics. Richard's unorthodox but compelling ideas have made him a very welcome speaker at conferences around the world. His goal is "to create tools of finance that are as slick and elegant as the most sophisticated tools of technology". Richard holds a Licentiate in Law from the University of Zurich, a Masters in economics from Oxford University and a PhD from the University of Zurich. He worked as researcher and foreign exchange dealer before founding OLSEN.

Oliver Rübel is a member of the Lawrence Berkeley National Laboratory Visualization Group and a member of the NERSC Analytics team. He received his PhD in computer science in 2009 from the University of Kaiserslautern, Germany. His research has focused on high-performance data analysis and visualisation, machine learning and query-driven visualisation of multi-dimensional scientific data. During his career, Oliver has worked closely with applications including high-energy physics, climate science and biological sciences.

George Sofianos joined Goldman Sachs in 2001 and is a vice president in the firm's Equity Execution Strats group. Prior to joining Goldman Sachs, he was head of research at the New York Stock Exchange. George also worked at the Federal Reserve Bank of New York, in the financial studies department and at the open markets desk. He began his career teaching finance at the Stern Graduate School of Business, New York University. George has published research on execution strategies, trading costs, market structure, the cross-listing and trading of non-US stocks, market-maker trading behaviour, stock-price behaviour on expirations, the impact of program trading on intraday stock-price volatility and index arbitrage. He holds BSc and MSc degrees from the London School of Economics, and received his PhD in economics from Harvard University. He is an associate editor of the *Journal of Trading*.

Michael G. Sotiropoulos is the global head of algorithmic trading quantitative research at Bank of America Merrill Lynch. His group supports the global execution services business, and focuses on market microstructure and electronic trading research and development. Michael joined Bank of America in 2004 as an equity derivatives quant, after spending three years at Bear Stearns in the same role. He was head of equities quantitative research for year 2008 before moving to algorithmic trading. He has a PhD in theoretical physics from SUNY Stony Brook. Prior to joining the finance industry he taught and worked in quantum field theory and particle physics at the University of Southampton and at the University of Michigan.

Kesheng (John) Wu is director of CIFT (Computational Infrastructure for Financial Technology) at Lawrence Berkeley National Laboratory, where he works on applying high-performance computing techniques to the analysis of high-frequency trading data. He also works on a range of topics in scientific data management, data analysis and distributed computing. Examples of his work include bitmap-indexing techniques for searching large datasets, restarting strategies for computing extreme eigenvalues, and connected component labelling algorithms for image analysis. Many of these algorithms are available in open-source software packages, including FastBit indexing tool and TRLan eigenvalue tool. John earned a PhD from University of Minnesota. He is a senior member of the IEEE and a Distinguished Scientist of the Association for Computing Machinery.

JuanJuan Xiang joined Goldman Sachs in 2010 and is a vice president in the firm's Equity Execution Strats group. Prior to joining Goldman Sachs, she was a digital signal processing engineer at Starkey Laboratory. She holds BSc and MSc degrees from Huazhong University of Science and Technology, and received her PhD in electrical and computer engineering from the University of Maryland–College Park.

Jean-Pierre Zigrand is director of the ESRC-funded Systemic Risk Centre at the London School of Economics and Political Science (LSE). He is also an associate professor of finance at the LSE, a programme director at the financial markets group and the director of the executive MSc finance programme at LSE. Jean-Pierre has been a lead expert for the Foresight Project on The Future of Computer Trading in Financial Markets. He holds a PhD in economics from the University of Chicago and a BSc and MSc in economics from the Université Catholique de Louvain.

Preface

High-frequency trading (HFT) is now the norm for trading financial assets in electronic markets around the world. Be it in equities, foreign exchange, futures or commodities, high-frequency traders provide not only the bulk of volume in these markets, but also most liquidity provision. In so doing, high-frequency trading has changed how individual markets operate and how markets dynamically interact. In this book, we give a comprehensive overview of high-frequency trading, and its implications for investors, market designers, researchers and regulators.

Our view is that HFT is not technology run amok, but rather a natural evolution of markets towards greater technological sophistication. Because markets have changed, so, too, must the way that traders behave, and the way that regulators operate. Low-frequency traders (shorthand for everyone who does not have their own high-performance computers and co-located servers) need to understand how high-speed markets work in order to get effective execution, minimise trade slippage and manage risk. Regulators, who face the daunting task of crafting new rules and regulations for high-frequency environments, need to understand better how and why high-frequency markets falter. Perhaps most importantly, individual investors need to understand that high-frequency markets need not be the milieu of Terminator-like adversaries, but rather, with careful design and regulation, can be venues in which they can trade at lower costs and better prices than ever before.

The chapters in this book take on many facets of high-frequency trading, but for any of them to make sense it is important for our readers to understand some basic features of high-frequency trading. First, HFT is microstructure based, and it operates to exploit the inefficiencies in how markets operate. A market's microstructure refers to the rules and design of the trading platform. All microstructures have inefficiencies arising, for example, from tick size specifications, matching engine protocols or latency issues in sending orders both within and across markets.[1] By exploiting these inefficiencies, at its best HFT lowers transaction costs and enhances market efficiency; at its worst, HFT takes advantage of resting orders, "simple-minded" trading algorithms and pricing conventions to transfer profits from low-frequency traders to high-frequency traders. The latter outcome arises because HFT is also strategy based: it is designed to take advantage of predictable behaviours in markets. Thus, momentum ignition strategies or attempts to move quote midpoints artificially are all designed to fool and exploit "uninformed" traders, who rely on simple trading rules and strategies.

A third feature of HFT is that it uses a new type of information. Traditionally, informed traders in markets were those who had better information on asset fundamentals, but HFT information relates to the trading process and not to the asset itself. At longer time horizons, fundamental information predominates in determining asset prices, but in the very short run it is trading information that matters. Thus, information on order flows, the structure of the book or the "toxicity" of the market can all help a high-frequency trader predict where market prices are going both in a single market and across markets. This trading information is useful because of the millisecond speed at which HFT algorithms operate. Consequently, to shave a few milliseconds off order transmission, it becomes optimal to spend hundreds of millions of US dollars to lay a new cable underneath the Atlantic Ocean (as was done in Project Hibernia) or to build towers between New Jersey and Chicago (as is being done in a joint project between Nasdaq and the CME) to send orders via microwaves, thereby improving transmission speed relative to ground-based fibre-optic cables. It is only natural to question whether such expenditures are socially optimal.

It would be a mistake, however, to believe that HFT is only about speed. There have been, and always will be, some traders who are faster than others. In today's markets, distinctions are being drawn between algorithmic traders (machines that are programmed to follow specific trading instructions), high-frequency traders (also machines but typically faster than algorithmic traders and may have more complex trading behaviours) and ultra-high-frequency traders (machines that use the fastest supercomputers, lowest latency linkages, etc). Indeed, it is safe to say that the latencies of the larger broker/dealer firms are now at the levels HFT firms were at just one or two years ago. The speed differentials between different trader groups will continue to decrease, but the strategic nature of HFT will remain as an important differentiator in markets.

It would also be a mistake to assume that all HFT strategies are the same. Just as markets, and their microstructures, differ, so too do the behaviours of high-frequency traders. Strategies that are optimal in short-term interest rate futures, for example, are very different from strategies that are successfully deployed in equity markets. Moreover, these strategies are constantly evolving as high-frequency traders employ more complex and technologically advanced approaches to trade within and across markets.

These two points are the subject of the first four chapters of the book. David Easley, Marcos López de Prado and Maureen O'Hara argue in Chapter 1 that HFT is not simply faster trading, but instead represents a new paradigm for trading financial assets. This paradigm is volume-based, reflecting that machines operate not on a time basis but rather on an event basis. Recognising this new paradigm is crucial for understanding why high-frequency markets are not just the same old markets "on steroids". These authors explain how, acting strategically, high-frequency algorithms interact with exchange-matching engines to exploit inefficiencies in markets and predictabilities in other traders' behaviours. This chapter sets the stage for understanding how high-frequency trading affects low-frequency traders, and it suggests strategies that LFTs should adopt to thrive in this environment.

Chapters 2–4 then discuss in detail how high-frequency trading "works" in equity markets, fixed-income futures markets and foreign exchange markets. Their authors discuss the particular strategies used and how these strategies have evolved over time. In Chapter 2, Michael G. Sotiropoulos describes how equity trading algorithms work and how they can be structured to meet the needs of a wide variety of market participants. He discusses how trading has evolved from simple deterministic trade algorithms, such as volume weighed average price (VWAP), to new adaptive algorithms that adjust trading speeds to a variety of high-frequency indicators such as queuing time and order book imbalance. Sotiropoulos also discusses how incorporating order protection strategies into adaptive algorithms can minimise transaction costs for low-frequency traders.

In Chapter 3 Robert Almgren examines the distinctive features of trading futures on interest rate products. Fixed-income trading algorithms must have special defensive features built in to protect the trader from the shocks arising from public information events such as Treasury auction results or scheduled government data releases. Moreover, fixed-income futures are cointegrated, meaning that individual contracts are not independent of other contracts due to linkages with the term structure, varying maturities, and the like. Thus, algorithmic strategies must take account of the inherent tendency for prices to move congruently. Almgren describes analytical approaches to characterising cointegration and how this can be used for price prediction. He also highlights the role played by priority rules in affecting trading strategies.

In Chapter 4, Anton Golub, Alexandre Dupuis and Richard B. Olsen describe the unique market structure of foreign exchange (FX) trading and the main algorithms used in the industry. FX markets feature a spectrum of traders from manual traders (ie, humans using a graphical user interface) to ultra-high-frequency traders submitting (and cancelling) thousands of orders over millisecond ranges. This chapter highlights the different roles played by these traders, and in particular draws attention to the changing composition of trading during periods of market instability. Olsen *et al* also suggest a new priority rule to enhance market liquidity production and stability.

Having established the basic frameworks used in high-frequency trading, we then turn in Chapters 5 and 6 to the foundations of high-frequency trading by examining the roles of machine learning and "big data". In Chapter 5, Michael Kearns and Yuriy Nevmyvaka discuss the role that machine learning plays in developing predictive algorithms for high-frequency trading. Machine learning is an area of computer science that draws on research in statistics, computational complexity, artificial intelligence and related fields to build predictive models from large data sets. Kearns and Nevmyvaka demonstrate how techniques such as reinforcement learning can determine optimal dynamic state-based policies from data; for example, such an approach could be used to determine an optimal execution algorithm that decides whether to slow down or speed up trading depending upon current microstructure data. They also show how machine learning can use order book data to predict future price movements. This chapter, while showcasing the extensive technological sophistication underlying high-frequency trading, also makes clear the role that "human inputs" have in designing such analytical tools.

In Chapter 6, Kesheng Wu, E. Wes Bethel, Ming Gu, David Leinweber and Oliver Rübel look at another dimension of high-frequency trading: the role of "big data". Algorithmic and high-frequency trading generate massive amounts of hard-to-process data. Some of this comes from trade executions, but a much greater amount arises from the placement and cancellation of orders both within and across markets. Handling, let alone analysing, such massive databases (which can be of the order of a petabyte) is almost impossible using standard data management techniques. Wu *et al* discuss how new file formatting and computational techniques can be applied to high-frequency trading data. They use these techniques to test the predictive ability of VPIN, a measure of order toxicity, for future volatility.[2] Their results illustrate how "big data" can play a critical role in testing new risk-management tools for high-frequency markets.

The remaining four chapters focus on the implications of high-frequency trading for markets, traders and regulators. In Chapter 7, David Easley, Marcos López de Prado and Maureen O'Hara examine how volatility contagion can take place across markets. High-frequency market makers often engage in inter-market arbitrage, a strategy in which market makers "lift" liquidity by placing bids in one market and asks in another. Easley *et al* show how this results in order toxicity spreading across markets, which in turn results in volatility contagion. Using data from energy futures, they demonstrate that these contagion effects can be sizeable. These results show that the volatility process in high-frequency markets is now interdependent across markets, a result of interest to both researchers and regulators.

George Sofianos and JuanJuan Xiang consider in Chapter 8 the challenges facing low-frequency traders in markets with high-frequency traders. Trading algorithms are designed to minimise a trade's execution cost, and they generally do so by splitting orders into many smaller pieces that then have to be traded over time in the market. If high-frequency traders can detect in market data the early trades in the sequence (known as the algorithm's "footprint"), then they can front-run the subsequent trades and profit at the low-frequency trader's expense. Sofianos and Xiang discuss how feasible this is, and present an extensive empirical study to determine how easy it is to find these patterns in the data. The analysis here demonstrates how important it is for low-frequency traders to use sophisticated trading techniques in high-frequency settings.

This issue of new trading tools and techniques is also the focus of Chapter 9. Terrence Hendershott, Charles M. Jones and Albert J. Menkveld develop a new approach for measuring the effect of transitory trading costs for transaction cost analysis. The ability to measure trading costs is crucial for institutional traders, and is greatly complicated when algorithms chop orders into sequences of trades. Hendershott *et al* construct an efficient price estimator that allows an enhanced ability to compute the execution cost of a large trade. Their analysis shows the importance of temporary price effects on trading costs, and it illustrates the need to develop new analytical tools designed for high-frequency settings.

Our final chapter turns to the challenges of regulation in a high-frequency world. In Chapter 10, Oliver Linton, Maureen O'Hara and J. P. Zigrand argue that, while HFT has increased market quality on average, it has made markets more vulnerable to episodic instability. This is due, in part, to the changing nature of liquidity provision in high-frequency markets, but this vulnerability also arises because HFT has opened the door to both new forms of manipulation and market failures arising from errant technology. Linton *et al* argue for a new *ex ante* regulatory approach that relies on technology to monitor markets in real time, pre-specifies regulatory actions in the event of faltering markets and applies across, and not merely within, market settings. They also examine a variety of existing and proposed regulatory reforms in the US and Europe.

We hope this book makes the high-frequency world more accessible to our readers.

ACKNOWLEDGEMENTS

We thank our outstanding co-authors and the editors at Risk Books (particularly, Sarah Hastings) for making this book possible.

1 Latency is a measure of time delay in a system. In the context of trading financial assets, it refers to the time it takes to get orders from a trader's computer to the trading venue (and, depending on context, it may also include the time to confirm trades back to the trader). Latencies in high-frequency markets are often measured in milliseconds (thousandths of a second), or even microseconds (millionths of a second).

2 Volume-synchronised probability of informed trading (VPIN) is a measure of order imbalance and it signals when the order flow is likely to be disadvantageous, or "toxic", to market makers. High toxicity can cause market makers to withdraw from the market, and this can lead to disruptions in liquidity provision. Because of this linkage, VPIN can signal future toxicity-related volatility in markets: an issue of importance to both regulators and traders.

The Volume Clock: Insights into the High-Frequency Paradigm

David Easley; Marcos López de Prado; Maureen O'Hara

Cornell University; RCC at Harvard University; Cornell University

Legend has it that Nathan Mayer Rothschild used racing pigeons to front-run his competitors and trade on the news of Napoleon's defeat at Waterloo a full day ahead of His Majesty's official messengers (Gray and Aspey 2004). Whether this story is true or not, it is unquestionable that there have always been faster traders. Leinweber (2009) relates many instances in which technological breakthroughs have been used to most investors' disadvantage. The telegraph gave an enormous edge to some investors over others in the 1850s, perhaps to a greater extent than the advantages enjoyed today by high-frequency traders. The same could be said, for example, of telephone traders in the 1870s, radio traders in the 1910s, screen traders in the 1980s. Some traders have always been much faster than others, so what is new this time around? If there is something truly novel about high-frequency trading (HFT), it cannot only be speed.

And yet, high-frequency traders have been characterised as "cheetah traders", an uncomplimentary allusion to their speed and character. The reality is, as usual, more complex. Today's high-frequency markets are not the old low-frequency markets on steroids. To be sure, speed is an important component of high-frequency's success. However, in this chapter we shall argue that there is much more to it. We shall make the case that what lies at the heart of HFT is a change in paradigm.

THE NEW TRADING PARADIGM

The US "flash crash" of May 6, 2010, pushed HFT into the spotlight. To understand what led to the emergence of high-frequency trading, however, we have to turn the clock back five years. HFT strategies were made possible by legislative changes in the US (Regulation National Market System law of 2005, known as "Reg NMS") and Europe (the Markets in Financial Instruments Directive, or "MiFID", in force since November 2007), preceded by substantial technological advances in computation and communication. High-speed trading had been technologically possible for many years, but it was legislative action that made HFT profitable.

MiFID fostered greater competition among brokers, with the objective of improving liquidity, cohesion and depth in financial markets. It allowed new, highly technological competitors to enter the European markets, thereby introducing competition for what had been a relatively quiescent, exchange-dominated market structure. Similarly, Reg NMS encouraged competitiveness among exchanges by allowing market fragmentation. Reg NMS was wildly successful at this, as the market structure of 13 equity exchanges and 40 or more alternative venues (dark pools, dealer desks, etc) attests. Cohesion was supposedly ensured in the US through a mechanism for the consolidation of individual orders processed via multiple venues (the "National Best Bid and Offer" (NBBO)).[1] These changes, combined with decimalisation of equity markets, resulted in an "arms race" to develop the technology and quantitative methods that could extract the last cent of profitability from trading while serving the demands of market participants.

The high-frequency strategies that developed are actually very diverse. It would be a mistake, for example, to conflate the HFT strategies of cash equities and the HFT strategies of futures on equity indexes, because HFT is not particularly related to macro factors (such as asset class), but it is intimately related to market microstructural factors. While cash equity markets are fragmented and decimalised, the markets for equity futures are not, and so the first type of HFT strategies have little in common with the second.

Many high-frequency strategies model the dynamics of the double auction book. This allows HF traders to place numerous independent bets every day on the same instrument or portfolio, thus taking advantage of the multiplicative effect postulated by the "fundamental law of active management", ie, that a tiny predictive power on a sufficiently large number of independent bets yields a high information ratio and thus a profit (Grinold 1989). The goal is to exploit the inefficiencies derived from the market's microstructure, such as rigidities in price adjustment within and across markets, agents' idiosyncratic behaviour and asymmetric information. As a consequence of this higher frequency, the identification of opportunities, risk control, execution and other investment management activities must be automated. Not all algorithmic trading occurs at high frequency, but all high-frequency trading requires algorithms.

It is useful to contrast the divergent worlds of the low-frequency (LF) traders and the HF traders. Financial analysts' conferences are one milieu where LF traders converse on subjects as broad and complex as monetary policy, asset allocation, stock valuations and financial statement analysis. HFT conferences are reunions where computer scientists meet to discuss Internet protocol connections, machine learning, numeric algorithms to determine the position of an order in a queue, the newest low-latency co-location architecture, game theory and, most important of all, the latest variations to exchanges' matching engines. It could be concluded, correctly, that the LF traders and the HF traders are seemingly worlds apart.

The issues surrounding exchange-matching engines are a case in point. Economists and finance professionals often talk about the market's auctioning process as a given, but it is microstructure theorists who wade into the minutiae of how prices and volumes are actually formed. Because the devil is in the detail, understanding how exactly the order flow is handled, and thus how trades and prices are formed, allows potential profits to be made for those who can manipulate these market dynamics (Figure 1.1). Over short intervals of time, prices are not the random walks so beloved by the efficient market hypothesis, but can instead be predictable artefacts of the market microstructure. Thus, the paradox: billions are invested in HFT research and infrastructure, topics that LF traders do not even recognise as an issue.

Given their dissimilar backgrounds, it is hardly surprising that HFT professionals would operate under a different paradigm from their LFT peers. But how does this different background translate into a new investment paradigm?

Figure 1.1 Simplified depiction of a matching engine's host

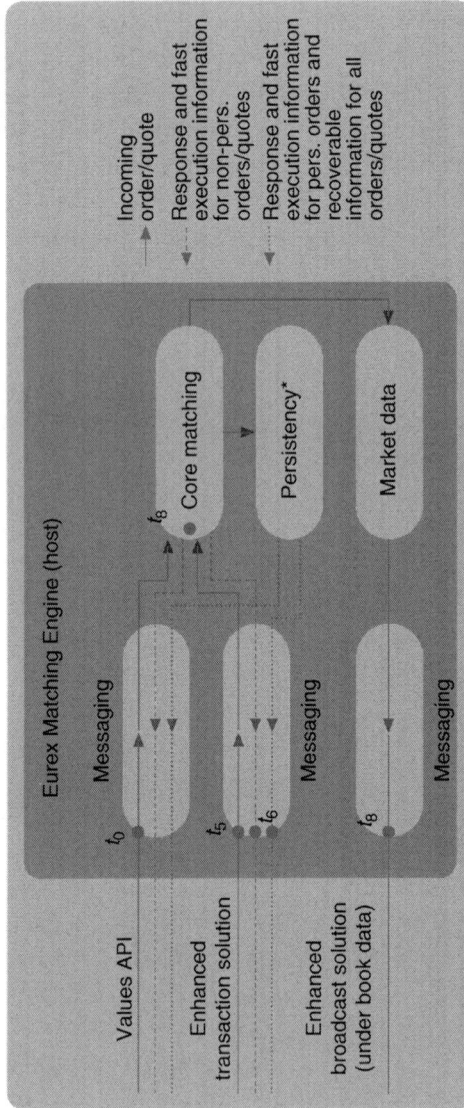

Prices and volumes are determined by the matching engine. HF traders study its design very carefully, in an attempt to uncover a structural weakness in the double auctioning process. Eurex has been particularly transparent in describing its architecture and functionality, in an attempt to level the playing field across customers. *Additional time stamps are available in messages from the persistency layer.

THE MEANING OF TIME

Time can be understood as a measuring system used to sequence observations. Since the dawn of civilisation, humans have based their time measurements in chronology: years, months, days, hours, minutes, seconds and, more recently, milliseconds, microseconds, etc. Because we have been brought up to think in terms of chronological (chrono) time, we can hardly visualise a different way of scheduling our lives. However, this is a rather arbitrary time system, arguably due to the key role played by the Sun in agrarian societies.

Machines operate on an internal clock that is not chronological, but event-based: the cycle. A machine will complete a cycle at various chrono rates, depending on the amount of information and complexity involved in a particular instruction. For the reasons mentioned earlier, HFT relies on machines; thus, measuring time in terms of events is only natural. Thinking in volume time (or any other index of activity) is challenging for humans. But for a "silicon trader", it is the natural way to process information and engage in sequential, strategic trading. For example, HF market makers may aim to turn their portfolio every fixed number of contracts traded (volume bucket), regardless of the chrono time, in an attempt to keep a certain market share.

The paradigm in this world is "event-based time". The simplest example involves dividing the session into equal volume buckets (eg, into 200,000 contract increments, or 20,000 share buckets). In fact, working in volume time presents significant statistical advantages: this time transformation removes most intra-session seasonal effects; it allows a partial recovery of normality and the assumption of independent and identical distribution; sampling in a volume-clock metric addresses the problem of random and asynchronous transactions, which is a major concern when computing correlations on high-frequency data.[2] The idea of modelling financial series using a different time clock can be traced back to the seminal work of Mandelbrot and Taylor (1967) and Clark (1970, 1973). Ané and Geman (2000) is another notable, more recent contribution. Mandelbrot and Taylor open their paper with the following assertion:

> Price changes over a fixed number of transactions may have a Gaussian distribution. Price changes over a fixed time period may follow a stable Paretian distribution, whose variance is infinite.

> Since the number of transactions in any time period is random, the above statements are not necessarily in disagreement.... Basically, our point is this: the Gaussian random walk as applied to transactions is compatible with a symmetric stable Paretian random walk as applied to fixed time intervals.

In other words, Mandelbrot and Taylor advocated for recovering normality through a transaction-based clock, moving away from chronological time. This would treat transactions of different sizes equally. Clark (1973) suggested a related variant, arguing for a volume-based clock. Mandelbrot (1973) explained the difference between them in the following terms:

> There is – as I have said – no dispute between us about the value of the concept of subordinated process. Clark's approach is an interesting and natural modification of one described by Mandelbrot and Taylor. The notion is that price change would cease to be erratic and would reduce to the familiar Brownian motion if only it were followed in an appropriate "local time" different from "clock time". Taylor and I had thought that local time might coincide with transaction time, while Clark links it with volume. He also has the merit of having investigated this hunch empirically.... However, it should be kept in mind that if price variation is to proceed smoothly in local time, then local time itself must flow at random and at a highly variable rate. Consequently, as long as the flow of local time remains unpredictable, concrete identification of the applicable local time leaves the problems of economic prediction unaffected.

Mandelbrot's rather negative conclusion regarding the role of "local time" reflected a basic reality of the markets in his day: the decisions that participants made, eg, estimating volatilities over a day or returns over a month, were all based on chronological time. Consequently, recovering normality in what he called "local time" (ie, transaction or volume time) did not seem helpful, because there is no way to translate the forecast back into chronological time. However, as we have argued, HFT operates in event-based time (such as transaction or volume), thus removing the need for this translation. HFT will monetise accurate forecasts of E-mini S&P 500 futures volatility over the next 50,000 contracts, whatever the number of (night-session) hours or (day-session) milliseconds it takes to exchange that volume. HFT market makers have little use for a model that attempts to forecast volatility over a chronological time

Figure 1.2 Partial recovery of normality through a price sampling process subordinated to a volume clock

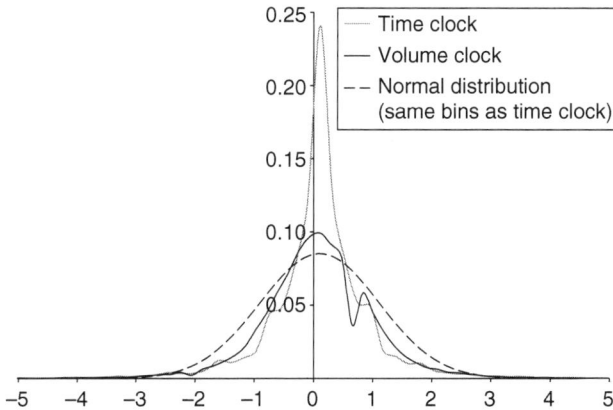

The grey line is the distribution of standardised price changes for the E-mini S&P 500 futures when we sample every minute. The black line is the equivalent if we sample every $\frac{1}{50}$ of the average daily volume. The black dashed line is the standard normal distribution. The sample goes from January 1, 2008, to October 22, 2010.

horizon, because they must keep their inventory under control in volume time (eg, by turning their inventory over for every 50,000 contracts exchanged). Being closer to actual normality and independence of observations (Figure 1.2) allows the application of standard statistical techniques, which means faster calculations, shorter cycles and thus faster reaction.

The upshot of this new paradigm is clear: even if connectivity speed ceased to be a significant edge, HFT would still exist.

MORE THAN SPEED

Easley *et al* (1996) linked liquidity to informational asymmetry by identifying how market makers adjust their bid–ask spreads to the probability of informed trading (PIN). Because informed traders monetise their superior knowledge of a security's future price by adversely selecting uninformed traders, market makers must update their quoted levels and sizes in real time in a manner that reflects their estimate of PIN. HF traders react to information leaked by LF traders in order to anticipate their actions. Direct market access (DMA) allows the deployment of this kind of strategic sequential trading logic to market venues.

To be clear, strategic sequential trading is not particular to HFT. In October 1990, sterling joined the European Exchange Rate Mechanism (ERM). Under that agreement, the Government would have to intervene in order to ensure that the exchange rate between the pound and other currencies would not fluctuate beyond a 6% band. Traders knew that, with an inflation rate three times that of Germany despite high interest rates, in addition to double digit deficits, the British Government's position was extremely vulnerable. Thus, a strategy could be devised to take advantage of that Government's predictable behaviour. On September 16, 1992 (Black Wednesday) a group of speculators launched an uncoordinated attack to force the withdrawal of the pound from the ERM (HM Treasury 1994).

What makes HFT such a great example of strategic sequential trading is its "event-based" interaction with the exchange's matching engine through DMA. Its decision-making process is synchronised with the speed at which actions take place, thus acting upon the revelation of new information.

A good metaphor for strategic sequential trading can be found in poker or chess. A chess player makes moves at different speeds during a game, depending on several factors: superiority over the adversary, stage of the game, amount of material lost, computational power, experience with the existing position, time remaining before the end of the game, etc. It would make little sense for a chess player to attempt to make moves every minute (even if that were possible). Instead, moves are made whenever the processing of the new information permits, according to the aforementioned factors. With every move, each player reveals information about their knowledge of the game, which can be used by an experienced adversary to lead the opponent to an uncomfortable situation. Once the adversary has made a move, the player has new information on the board to be cycled. Players try to anticipate each other's moves several steps ahead, and force their adversary to make an error. The next move is conditional upon the opponent's previous moves as well as their own. There are sacrifices, calculated "mistakes" and a lot of deception. All of these features are present in HFT.

Predatory algorithms constitute a very distinct species of informed traders, because of the nature of their information and the frequency of their actions. Such HFT algorithms exploit a microstructural opportunity in a way similar to that in which large speculators exploit a macroeconomic inconsistency. Rather than possessing exogenous information yet to be incorporated in the market price, they know that their endogenous actions are likely to trigger a microstructure mechanism, with a foreseeable outcome. Their advent has transformed liquidity provision into a tactical game. We now list a few examples that are discussed in the literature.

- **Quote stuffers:** these engage in "latency arbitrage". The strategy involves overwhelming an exchange with messages, with the sole intention of slowing down competing algorithms, which are forced to parse messages that only the originators know can be ignored (NANEX 2010).

- **Quote danglers:** this strategy sends quotes forcing a squeezed trader to chase a price against their interests. O'Hara (2010) presents evidence of their disruptive activities.

- **Liquidity squeezers:** when a distressed large investor is forced to unwind their position, the squeezers trade in the same direction, draining as much liquidity as possible. As a result, prices overshoot and they make a profit (Carlin *et al* 2007).

- **Pack hunters:** predators hunting independently become aware of each other's activities, and form a pack in order to maximise the chances of triggering a cascading effect (Donefer 2010; Fabozzi *et al* 2011; Jarrow and Protter 2011). NANEX (2011) shows what appear to be pack hunters forcing a stop loss. Although their individual actions are too small to raise the regulator's suspicion, their collective action may be market-manipulative. When that is the case, it is very hard to prove their collusion, since they coordinate in a decentralised, spontaneous manner.

Arnuk and Saluzzi (2008) estimate that the effect of all this toxic trading is that up to 10,000 orders are entered for every single trade in NYSE stocks. While this may be an overstatement of the problem, even the US Securities and Exchange Commission (2011, p. 13) admits that "a vast majority" of orders are now cancelled (estimates by TABB Group put this at 98%).[3]

Because of the threat posed by predators, high-frequency liquidity providers must be much more tactical (an example is given in Figure 1.3). Sometimes they may suddenly pull all orders, liquidate

Figure 1.3 Example of a tactical liquidity provision algorithm

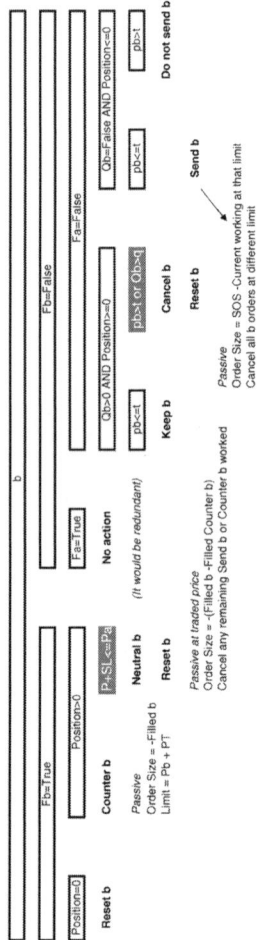

pb:= Probability of bid to be crossed (1 if already crossed)
pa:= Probability of ask to be crossed (1 if already crossed)
Pb:= price filled for Send b
Pa:= price filled for Send a
t=(0,1):= Threshold on Collapse Probability
SOS=1:= Standard Order Size
SL:= Stop Loss for single Send order
PT:= Profit Target for Send order
Fb={True,False}:= bid was filled
Fa={True,False}:= ask was filled
Qb:= Expected position in bid queue. Null if order not sent
Qa:= Expected position in ask queue. Null if order not sent
q:= Threshold on expected position in ask queue

b

Position=0 / Position>0

Fb=True

Reset b | Counter b

Passive
Order Size = –Filled b
Limit = Pb + PT

Pt+SL<=Pa

Neutral b

Reset b

Passive at traded price
Order Size = –(Filled b –Filled Counter b)
Cancel any remaining Send b or Counter b worked

Fa=True

No action

(It would be redundant)

Fb=False

Qb>0 AND Position<=0

pb<t

Keep b

pb>t or Qb>q

Cancel b

Reset b

Passive
Order Size = SOS –Current working at that limit
Cancel all b orders at different limit

Fa=False

Qb=False AND Position<=0

pb<t

Send b

pb>t

Do not send b

This algorithm would send an order at the bid (b), wait for a passive fill (Fb=True) and only then send an order at the offer (Counter b). At all times the probability of an adverse change in level is monitored (pb). However, if the order at the bid has not been filled yet (Fb=False) by the time there is an increase in the probability of adverse level change (pb > t), then the algorithm cancels the order (b). This is a typical sequential trading algorithm that conditions the provision of liquidity to a limited number of scenarios. In fact, it becomes a liquidity consumer from time to time: if the order gets filled (Fb=True) and the level drops beyond a certain stop loss threshold (SL), the algorithm competes for liquidity (grey box).

Figure 1.3 Continued

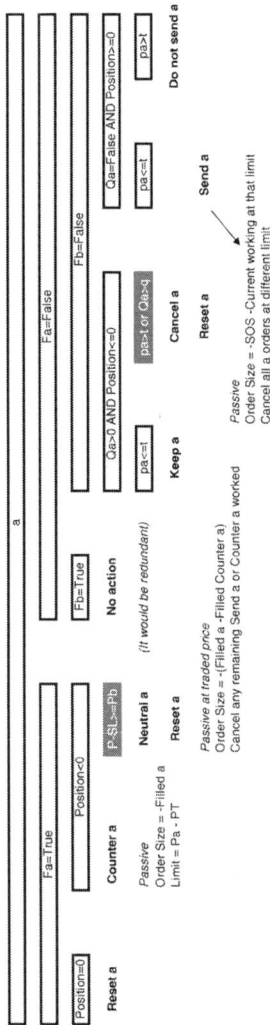

their positions and stop providing liquidity altogether. This decision has more to do with computer science and game theory than it does with valuation fundamentals. The resulting price actions may seem absurd from an economic perspective, but because the actors made their decisions applying a different rationale their behaviour is perfectly sensible.[4] Carlin *et al* (2007) model how predatory trading can lead to episodic liquidity crises and contagion.

For the HF trader, the name of the game is not to move as fast as possible, but rather to make the best possible move (before a competitor does) with the information revealed. To understand what this implies for market behaviour, consider the simple issue of trade size. Easley *et al* (2012b) report that more than 50% of trades in the S&P 500 E-mini futures contracts are now for one contract. Trade frequency quickly drops beyond sizes over 10. However, trades of size 100 are up to 17 times more frequent than trades of size 99 or 101 in the E-mini S&P 500. The reason is that many graphical user interface (GUI) traders have buttons for trade sizes in round numbers. HFT algorithms know that if many participants are operating with round numbers in a given moment of the trading session, the market is likely to behave in a particular way. Even though trading algorithms are not intelligent in the human sense (at least not yet), machine learning and game theory allow them to identify deep patterns in market activity. Predictable behaviour can then be taken advantage of by silicon traders.

Databases with trillions of observations are now commonplace in financial firms. Machine learning methods, such as nearest-neighbour or multivariate embedding algorithms, search for patterns within a library of recorded events. This ability to process and learn from what is known as "big data" only reinforces the advantages of HFT's "event-time" paradigm. It is reminiscent of "Deep Blue", which could assign probabilities to Kasparov's next 20 moves, based on hundreds of thousands of past games, or why IBM's Watson could outplay its Jeopardy opponents.

The upshot is that speed makes HF traders more effective, but slowing them down will not change their basic behaviour, that of strategic sequential trading in event time.

LIKE SHEEP AMONG WOLVES?

A number of studies have found that HFT is beneficial in many ways (Broogard 2012; Linton and O'Hara 2012; Hasbrouck and Saar 2013). Evidence suggests that HFT has added liquidity to the markets, narrowed spreads and enhanced informational efficiency. But other studies, such as Zhang (2010), find evidence that HFT heightens volatility. There are also concerns that HFT liquidity providers are too tactical in nature (they can vanish when most needed). In addition, there are clearly substantial expenses needed for LF traders to develop countermeasures against predatory algorithms. The debate regarding the social benefit of HFT is far from closed.

It appears clear that HFT cannot be un-invented, or regulated away, without some severe market effects. HFT now controls the liquidity provision process, and over 70% of all US cash equity trades involve a high-frequency counterpart (Iati 2009). HFT participation in futures is similarly important, with an estimated 50% or more transactions involving HFT. While debates rage over regulatory control, there is little consensus as to what is desirable, or even feasible. National Tobin taxes are doomed to fail, and an international agreement is unlikely. It is not even clear that these measures would do any good, other than change the rules of the game, to which HFT strategies can easily adapt.

An alternative that seems closer to the core of the HFT paradigm is a tax on FIX (Financial Information Exchange) messages (as opposed to a tax on transactions). Some exchanges and regulators have proposed charges on message traffic, but this would also affect algorithmic trading by LF traders: a form of "collateral damage" that seems undesirable. More to the point, such changes would not completely eliminate all sequential strategic behaviour. The new paradigm that underlies HFT is not really about speed, so regulatory efforts to slow "cheetah traders" miss the larger point that what is undesirable are particular manipulative strategies, not HFT *per se*.

There is no question that the goal of many HFT strategies is to profit from LFT's mistakes. Figure 1.4 shows how easy this has become. We took a sample of E-mini S&P 500 futures trades between November 7, 2010, and November 7, 2011, and divided the day into 24 hours (y-axis). For every hour, we added the volume traded at each second (x-axis), irrespective of the minute. For example, E-mini S&P 500 futures trades that occur at 20h20m01s GMT and 20h23m01s GMT are added together.[5] This analysis allows us to see the distribution of volume within each minute as the day passes, and search for LF traders executing their massive trades on a chronological time-space. The largest concentrations of volume within a minute tend to occur during the first few seconds, for almost every hour of the day. This is particularly true at 02h00–03h00 GMT (around the open of European equities), 13h00–14h00 GMT (around the open of US equities) and 20h00–21h00 GMT (around the close of US equities). This is the result of time-weighted average price (TWAP) algorithms

Figure 1.4 Percentage of E-Mini S&P 500 futures volume traded at each second of every minute

| ■ 0–1% | ■ 1–2% | ■ 2–3% | ■ 3–4% |
| ■ 4–5% | ■ 5–6% | ■ 6–7% | ■ 7–8% | ■ 8–9% |

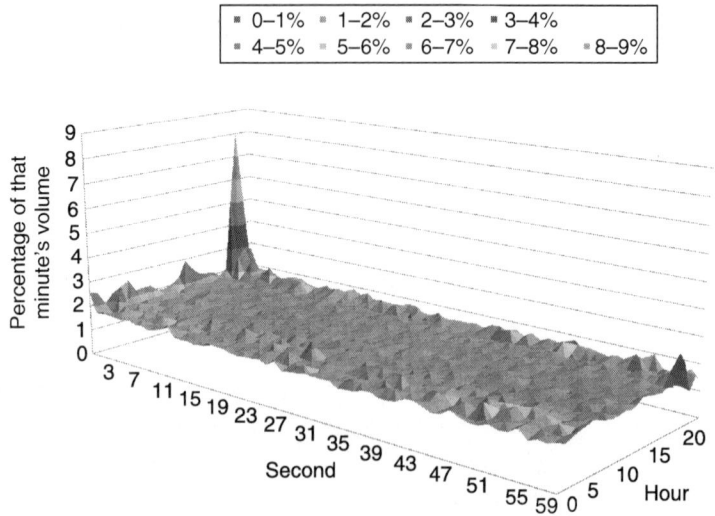

The LF trader's decisions are typically made in "chronological time", leaving footprints that can be tracked down easily. The surface above shows a large concentration of volume (over 8%) traded in the first second of every minute around the close of US equities. Because HF traders operate in the "volume clock", they can act as soon as the pattern is identified and anticipate the side and sign of LF traders' massive orders for the rest of the hour. Most academic and practitioner models have been devised in "chronological time", which means that their implementation will lead to patterns that HF traders can exploit to their advantage.

and volume-weighted average price (VWAP) algorithms that trade on one-minute slots. A mildly sophisticated HFT algorithm will evaluate the order imbalance at the beginning of every minute, and realise that this is a persistent component, thus front-running VWAPs and TWAPs while they still have to execute the largest part of the trade.

This is just one example of how vulnerable the "chronological time" paradigm has made LF traders, but there are dozens of instances like this. Easley *et al* (2012b) show that about 51.56% of E-mini S&P 500 futures trades between November 7, 2010, and November 7, 2011, were for one contract. For example, orders of size 10 were 2.9 times more frequent than orders of size 9. Size 50 was 10.86 times more likely than size 49. Because GUI traders tend to submit round order sizes, silicon traders can easily detect when there is a disproportionate presence of humans in the market and act on that knowledge. These behaviours are one likely cause of the increasing number of short-term liquidity crises over the past few years.

But just as markets have evolved, so, too, can LF traders. Part of HFT's success is due to the reluctance of LF traders to adopt (or even to recognise) their paradigm. We believe that LFT players will have to make multiple choices in order to survive in this new HFT era, including the following.

Choice #1: where possible, LFT firms should adopt the HFT "event-based time" paradigm

For issues such as portfolio selection, event-based time may not seem particularly relevant. There is an increasing awareness, however, that Alpha capture cannot be done in isolation from trading, ie, the implementation of portfolio selection requires trading, and this places it firmly in the purview of the HFT world. The best portfolio selection ability is useless if HFT algorithms can free-ride on your trades and drive up your execution costs.

Choice #2: develop statistics to monitor HFT activity and take advantage of their weaknesses

There is some evidence that "big data" is not necessarily an advantage in all instances. For example, in other work (Easley *et al* 2012b) we found that "bulk volume classification" determines the aggressor side of a trade with greater accuracy than the tick rule applied on tick data! We also showed that lower-frequency statistics (such as VPIN) can detect the toxicity in the market and determine the optimal trading horizon. Monitoring market conditions for high toxicity can be particularly beneficial for LF traders. In the US flash crash, the Waddell and Reed trader would surely have been well advised to defer trading rather than to sell, as they did, in a market experiencing historically high toxicity levels.

Choice #3: join the herd

Trade with volume bursts, such as at the opening and closing of the session, when your footprint is harder to detect. Transaction costs now largely consist of price impact costs, and astute LF traders must use transaction cost analysis products that are predictive, rather than simply reactive. Naive trading strategies are simply bait for predatory algorithms.

Choice #4: Use "smart brokers", who specialise in searching for liquidity and avoiding footprints

As we have seen, HFT algorithms can easily detect when there is a human in the trading room, and take advantage. Advanced brokers use HFT technology in a different way. Rather than attempting to identify patterns for Alpha-generation purposes, they avoid actions that may leave recognisable footprints. For example, TWAP is highly predictable and should be avoided. VWAP joins the herd, however, in a predictable way. VWAP algorithms are insensitive to the damage done to liquidity providers. A smart VWAP algorithm would incorporate a feedback mechanism that adjusts the execution horizon in real time, as it recognises the damage done by prior child orders. New algorithms by the more sophisticated brokers use volume patterns, dark executions and the like to reduce their trading footprint (see Easley *et al* (2013) for an example).

Choice #5: trade in exchanges that incorporate technology to monitor order flow toxicity

Toxic order flow disrupts the liquidity provision process by adversely selecting market makers. An exchange that prevents such disruptions will attract further liquidity, which in turn increases the corporate value of its products. One way to avoid disruptions is to make it harder for predators to operate in that exchange. Exchanges have been changing their trading systems to cater to HF traders (and the resulting liquidity they provide). But exchanges could also modify their matching engines to respond to toxicity changes that can impair liquidity provision to LF traders.

Choice #6: avoid seasonal effects

Predatory algorithms exploit humans' inclination towards predictable seasonal habits, such as end-of-day hedges, weekly strategy decisions, monthly portfolio duration rebalances and calendar rolls. Smart LFT trading will avoid these easily exploitable seasonal habits.

CONCLUSION

HFT is here to stay. The speed advantage will gradually disappear, as it did in previous technological revolutions. But HFT's strategic trading behaviour, executed by automated systems interacting directly with the exchange's double auction order book, is more robust. Strategic traders have little trouble in adapting to new rules of the game; "big data" allows them to train their algorithms before deployment. Advances in machine learning and microstructure theory will compensate for the loss of speed advantage.

Part of HF traders' success is due to LF traders' reluctance to adopt the volume-clock paradigm. However, LF traders are not completely defenseless against HF traders. Whenever a new predator makes its appearance in a habitat, there is a shock period until the hunted species adapt and evolve. There is a natural balance between HF traders and LF traders. Just as, in nature, the number of predators is limited by the available prey, the number of HF traders is constrained by the available LFT flows. Rather than seeking "endangered species" status for LF traders (by virtue of legislative action like a Tobin tax or speed limit), it seems more efficient and less intrusive to starve some HF traders by making LF traders smarter. Carrier pigeons or dedicated fibre optic cable notwithstanding, the market still operates to provide liquidity and price discovery, only now it does it very quickly and strategically.

We thank Robert Almgren, Peter Carr, David Leinweber, Riccardo Rebonato, Jamie Selway and George Sofianos for helpful comments. This chapter was originally published in the *Journal of Portfolio Management* (see Easley *et al* 2012c).

1   O'Hara and Ye (2011) present evidence that fragmentation has not degraded market quality in the US. Thus, Reg NMS accomplished its goal of creating a single virtual market with many points of entry.

2   An HFT application can be found in Easley *et al* (2012a).

3   See Patterson and Ackerman (2012).

4   US Securities and Exchange Commission Chairman Mary Shapiro made this point in her testimony before the Subcommittee on Capital Markets, Insurance and Government Sponsored Enterprises of the United States House of Representatives Committee on Financial Services (US Securities and Exchange Commission 2010).

5   We are using the GMT convention for time, as GLOBEX does.

REFERENCES

Ané, T., and H. Geman, 2000, "Order Flow, Transaction Clock and normality of Asset Returns", *Journal of Finance* 55, pp. 2259–84.

Arnuk, L., and J. Saluzzi, 2008, "Toxic Equity Trading Order Flow and Wall Street", Themis Trading LLC White Paper, December 17. URL: http://www.themistrading.com/article_files/0000/0348/Toxic_Equity_Trading_on_Wall_Street_12-17-08.pdf.

Bowley, G., 2010, "Ex-Physicist Leads Flash Crash Inquiry", *The New York Times*, September 20.

Brogaard, J., 2012, "High Frequency Trading and Volatility", SSRN Working Paper.

Brunnermeier, M., and L. H. Pedersen, 2005, "Predatory Trading", *Journal of Finance* 40(4), pp. 1825–63.

Carlin, B., M. Sousa Lobo and S. Viswanathan, 2007, "Episodic Liquidity Crises: Cooperative and Predatory Trading", *Journal of Finance* 42(5), pp. 2235–74.

Clark, P. K., 1970, "A Subordinated Stochastic Process Model of Cotton Futures Prices", PhD Dissertation, Harvard University.

Clark, P. K., 1973, "A Subordinated Stochastic Process Model with Finite Variance for Speculative Prices", *Econometrica* 41(1), pp. 135–55.

Donefer, B. S., 2010, "Algos Gone Wild: Risk in the World of Automated Trading Strategies", *The Journal of Trading* 5, pp. 31–4.

Easley, D., N. Kiefer, M. O'Hara and J. Paperman, 1996, "Liquidity, Information, and Infrequently Traded Stocks", *Journal of Finance* 51, pp. 1405–36.

Easley, D., R. F. Engle, M. O'Hara and L. Wu, 2008, "Time-Varying Arrival Rates of Informed and Uninformed Traders", *Journal of Financial Econometrics* 6(2), pp. 171–207.

Easley, D., M. López de Prado and M. O'Hara, 2011, "The Microstructure of the Flash Crash: Flow Toxicity, Liquidity Crashes and the Probability of Informed Trading", *Journal of Portfolio Management* 37(2), pp. 118–28.

Easley, D., M. López de Prado and M. O'Hara, 2012a, "Flow Toxicity and Liquidity in a High Frequency World", *Review of Financial Studies* 25(5), pp. 1457–93.

Easley, D., M. López de Prado and M. O'Hara, 2012b, "Bulk Volume Classification", Working Paper. URL: http://ssrn.com/abstract=1989555.

Easley, D., M. López de Prado and M. O'Hara, 2012c, "The Volume Clock: Insights into the High Frequency Paradigm", *Journal of Portfolio Management* 39(1), pp. 19–29.

Easley, D., M. López de Prado and M. O'Hara, 2013, "Optimal Execution Horizon", *Mathematical Finance*, forthcoming.

Fabozzi, F., S. Focardi and C. Jonas, 2011, "High-Frequency Trading: Methodologies and Market Impact", *Review of Futures Markets* 19, pp. 7–38.

Gray, V., and M. Aspey, 2004, "Rothschild, Nathan Mayer (1777–1836)", in *Oxford Dictionary of National Biography*. Oxford University Press.

Grinold, R., 1989, "The Fundamental Law of Active Management", *Journal of Portfolio Management* 15(3), (Spring), pp. 30–7.

Hasbrouck, J., and G. Saar, 2013, "Low Latency Trading", *Journal of Financial Markets*, forthcoming.

HM Treasury, 1994, "Reflections on the UK's Membership of the ERM", Report, January 5.

Iati, R., 2009, "High Frequency Trading Technology", Report, TABB Group. URL: http://www.tabbgroup.com/PublicationDetail.aspx?PublicationID=498.

Jarrow, R., and P. Protter, 2011, "A Dysfunctional Role of High Frequency Trading in Electronic Markets", Johnson School Research Paper Series No. 8.

Leinweber, D., 2009, *Nerds on Wall Street: Math, Machines and Wired Markets*. John Wiley and Sons, Chichester.

Linton, O., and M. O'Hara, 2012, "The Impact of Computer Trading on Liquidity, Price Efficiency/Discovery and Transactions Costs", in *Foresight: The Future of Computer Trading in Financial Markets. An International Perspective,* Final Project Report. The Government Office for Science, London.

Mandelbrot, B., 1973, "Comments on 'A Subordinated Stochastic Process Model with Finite Variance for Speculative Prices by Peter K. Clark'", *Econometrica* 41(1), pp. 157–59.

Mandelbrot, B., and M. Taylor, 1967, "On the Distribution of Stock Price Differences", *Operations Research* 15(6), pp. 1057–62.

NANEX, 2010, "Analysis of the 'Flash Crash'", June 18. URL: http://www.nanex.net/20100506/FlashCrashAnalysis_CompleteText.html.

NANEX, 2011, "Strange Days June 8'th, 2011 – NatGas Algo". URL: http://www.nanex.net/StrangeDays/06082011.html.

O'Hara, M., 2010, "What Is a Quote?", *Journal of Trading* 5(2), pp. 11–16.

O'Hara, M., and M. Ye, 2011, "Is Market Fragmentation Harming Market Quality?", *Journal of Financial Economics* 100(3), pp. 459–74.

Patterson, S., and A. Ackerman, 2012, "SEC May Ticket Speeding Traders", *Wall Street Journal*, February 23.

US Securities and Exchange Commission, 2010, "Testimony Concerning the Severe Market Disruption on May 6, 2010", May 11. URL http://sec.gov/news/testimony/2010/ts051110mls.pdf.

US Securities and Exchange Commission, 2011, "Regarding Regulatory Responses to the Market Events of May 6, 2010: Summary Report of the Joint CFTC-SEC Advisory Committee on Emerging Regulatory Issues", February 18. URL: http://www.sec.gov/spotlight/sec-cftcjointcommittee/021811-report.pdf.

Zhang, F., 2010, "High-Frequency Trading, Stock Volatility, and Price Discovery", Working Paper. URL: http://ssrn.com/abstract=1691679.

2

Execution Strategies in Equity Markets

Michael G. Sotiropoulos
Bank of America Merrill Lynch

In this chapter we discuss strategies, models and implementations used by large brokerage firms offering agency trading services to their clients. We focus on equities, although several of these methods and techniques are applicable or easily adaptable to other asset classes.

Information technology and regulatory changes (most notably Regulation National Market System (Reg NMS) in the US and Markets in Financial Instruments Directive (MiFID) in Europe) have drastically changed equities markets since the early 2000s. The ease and efficiency of electronic access and the opening up of liquidity provision to all market participants has led to a low latency, multi-venue marketplace, where large block trading has become rare and liquidity is always at a near critical point. This new market microstructure is the result of high-frequency algorithmic trading, defined as the execution of orders via a computerised, rules-based trading system. From a tool of automating repetitive tasks in its early days, algorithmic trading has become the dominant mode of quoting and transacting in equity markets.

Trading algorithms have very small reaction times to fluctuations in liquidity and price. Yet, the markets remain largely stable, with bounded bid–ask spread and price volatility. This is primarily due to the heterogeneous return objectives and investment horizons of the market participants. Agent heterogeneity has also created the high-frequency trading (HFT) debate about the value that low latency machine trading adds to the investment and price discovery process. Here we take the point of view that HFT is a market fact. Our objective is to understand its potential and limitations.

From the point of view of an executing broker, there are four main types of clients or market agents:

1. institutional investors, such as pension funds and asset management firms;

2. quant funds, including market makers that seek to capture the bid–ask spread or exchange rebates;

3. retail investors, driven primarily by private liquidity demand and less by proprietary signals;

4. hedgers of equity exposures, such as derivatives desks.

By using the execution services of an agency broker, all these agents realise economies of scale in

- maintaining the connectivity required in a fragmented marketplace,

- guaranteeing regulatory compliance,

- providing pre-trade advice and post-trade reporting, and

- investing in research, development and customisation of trading algorithms.

EVOLUTION OF TRADING ALGORITHMS

Every algorithm is designed to achieve optimal order execution within its feasibility space. This general statement becomes more informative once we define the control parameters and the optimality criteria. An agency trading algorithm does not have discretion over the asset, the trade direction (buy or sell), the quantity or the arrival time. These decisions are taken by the client/user. The algorithm affects the trading process in two dimensions: time and space.

- In the time dimension, the algorithm controls the speed of trading. In practice, this is achieved by slicing a client order into smaller pieces and by using a limit order model to control the aggressiveness of liquidity taking (the limit price of each slice).

- In the space dimension, the algorithm controls the allocation of each slice across several trading venues. The venues could be public exchanges with visible order books, or dark pools that match buyers and sellers at a reference price, typically the prevailing mid-quote.

Most trading systems handle the above two sets of decisions in separate components, the time dimension in the algorithmic engine and the space dimension in the smart order router.

The variability in the behaviour and even in the names used to identify algorithms comes from the plethora of trading objectives. Typically, an objective is defined by the corresponding benchmark that is to be met or exceeded. Common benchmarks are

- the fill rate, ie, proportion of the order that was actually filled,
- the fill composition, ie, proportion of transactions that were passive (filled on the bid/ask side for a buy/sell order), aggressive (crossed the spread) or dark (matched in a dark pool),
- performance or slippage versus a reference price, such as arrival price, interval volume-weighted average price (VWAP), participation-weighted price (PWP) or end-of-day closing price,
- adherence to a fixed trading speed, measured as a percentage of market volume (POV),
- compliance with preset instructions on how to speed up or slow down, based on momentum or reversion in the price path,
- the amount of price reversion against the order after the end of trading.

All of the above benchmarks are measurable quantities that are reported in a post-trade Transaction Cost Analysis (TCA). Clearly, the benchmarks are not all orthogonal or even mutually consistent. Cost-sensitive clients tend to care more about slippage, whereas information-sensitive clients mindful of HFT agents emphasise fill composition and price reversion. It is the task of execution consultants to understand the relative weights that a client assigns to the above objectives and advise on the choice of an execution algorithm and its parameters.

Algorithm generations

First generation algorithms

First generation algorithms originated in program trading desks and their objectives were rather mechanical. The most common ones are the following.

- **CLOCK:** trade at fixed rate with respect to chronological time (wall clock); at HFT timescales an order almost never gets filled uniformly, so CLOCK and similar strategies measure the speed of trading within a time aggregation interval Δt, typically of the order of minutes.

- **POV:** trade at a fixed participation rate v, with $0 \leqslant v \leqslant 1$; within the time aggregation interval Δt, the order should execute v shares for every share traded in the market.

- **VWAP:** complete the order within time interval T, such that the average execution price is equal to the market VWAP within T.

Assuming that the quantity of a fully filled client order is X asset units (shares in the case of equities), then

$$X = vT \tag{2.1}$$

This would be the case if the market traded uniformly in chronological time, or if we use the market's volume time as the clock. Either the order duration T (VWAP) or the speed of trading v (POV) needs to be specified. With variable market speed of trading we need to discretise the time interval $[0, T]$ over n steps Δt_i, and Equation 2.1 becomes

$$X = \sum_{i=1}^{n} v_i \Delta t_i \tag{2.2}$$

Therefore, executing a CLOCK or VWAP or POV strategy is a scheduling problem, ie, we are trying to enforce Equation 2.2 within each evaluation interval Δt_i while targeting a predetermined T or a variable v_i. Controlling the speed of trading v_i is a non-trivial practical problem that requires statistical models for forecasting the market volume over short horizons, as well as local adjustments for tracking the target schedule (Markov *et al* 2011). These scheduling techniques are also used in later generation algorithms.

Second generation algorithms

Second generation algorithms introduce the concepts of price impact and risk. The classic case is implementation shortfall (IS) (Perold 1988). Using the arrival price as the benchmark, high-urgency trading affects the price by moving it away from the order's side (increases the price when we buy and decreases it when we sell). Low-urgency trading creates less impact on average, but exposes

Figure 2.1 Impact–risk trade-off

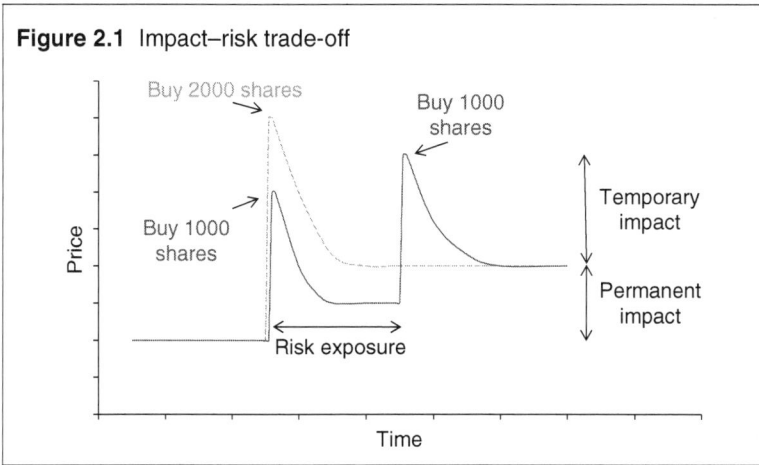

the execution to price volatility over a longer time interval. The impact–risk trade-off is illustrated in Figure 2.1 with a stylised one-versus-two-slices example.

Implementation shortfall led the field of optimal execution to a renaissance. Similar to Markowitz's classic portfolio theory, risk needs to be weighted against impact via a risk aversion parameter (Almgren and Chriss 2001). Unlike first generation algorithms, a client's risk preference affects the optimal trading schedule in IS. Moreover, the optimal schedule is affected by how price impact depends on the speed of trading, ie, it is cost-model dependent. An IS algorithm with zero risk aversion is equivalent to a VWAP strategy. The optimal balance between risk and impact traces an efficient frontier in cost–risk space as we increase risk aversion. Increasing risk aversion front-loads the schedule, achieving shorter, less risky execution at a higher impact cost.

The IS concept of risk-aware trading trajectories can be generalised in two ways. First, by reversing the time direction, we can treat, in the same framework, strategies that target the market on close (MOC) price. A risk averse client will decide to send the whole order into the closing auction in order to meet the benchmark. A less risk averse client may decide to allow the algorithm to pre-trade a portion of the order ahead of the closing auction, if there is a view on price trend (alpha) leading to the market close.

The second generalisation of IS is to apply the framework cross-sectionally for a whole portfolio of orders. It is clear that balancing risk against impact and imposing exposure constraints at the portfolio level is a more efficient method than treating each order individually. Portfolio IS algorithms rely on factor risk models for capturing intra-day return covariance and exposure, and on optimisers for creating the constituent order waves.

To summarise, the main second generation algorithms are as follows.

- IS: the classic, risk-aware extension of VWAP.

- Quantitative market-on-close (QMOC): this is IS with closing price as benchmark, used for pre-trading towards the closing auction.

- Portfolio IS (PTIS): this optimises risk versus impact cross-sectionally as well as over time.

Third generation algorithms

Third generation algorithms recognise the fact that optimal execution is a stochastic control problem conditioned on the current state and recent history of the limit order book. These algorithms are also known as adaptive or event driven. They use high-frequency trading signals to opportunistically deviate from theoretical optimal trajectories. As a result, they are much more suitable for an HFT marketplace. Below we shall use the Bank of America Instinct suite of algorithms as a representative example from this generation.

Adaptive algorithms consist of two main components:

1. an indicator function $I(t, O_t, \ldots, O_{t-h}; \theta)$;
2. a response function $R(I_t, X_t; \phi)$.

The indicator function depends on current and lagged market observables $O_t, \ldots, O_{t-h}$ and on model specific parameters θ. Examples of parameters are the window size over which we compute a moving average, a spread cut-off below which we consider the price motion as normal diffusion or an order-book imbalance ratio cut-off. The purpose of the indicator is to compute some dynamic aspect of the market and return a short-term forecast. The response function depends on the indicator I_t, the current state of the order X_t and strategy or client parameters ϕ. The purpose of the response function is to generate a trading action. Possible trading actions are:

- to increase/decrease the quantity of a child order;
- to update the limit price;

- to cross the spread;
- to cancel the child order and await further updates;
- to reallocate the posted quantities among trading venues.

These trading actions are the tactical decisions that affect the realised speed of trading v, discussed earlier. We call the combination of one indicator (or possibly several indicators) and a response function a "trading signal". Indicators and responses are typically implemented in separate components of a large trading system, in order to decouple indicator calculation and publishing from order management.

Indicator zoology

The indicators used in adaptive algorithms are the high-frequency analogues of the more popular technical indicators used for day trading. This does not mean that we can simply take a standard technical indicator, recompute it at high frequency and use it for electronic trading. Statistical relationships observed or believed to be valid for daily time series may simply be noise at millisecond timescales.

High-frequency indicators can be classified based on the statistical dependence that they aim to capture. The following is a non-exhaustive list of common indicator types.

- Trade autocorrelation: trade signs are correlated within short timescales due to algorithmic slicing of large client orders; this could lead to predictable trade direction.

- Order imbalance: the limit order book may be too heavy on one side; this could lead to predictable price movement over the next time period.

- Momentum/reversion: the price path exhibits a strong trend; momentum traders bet on the trend persisting and reversion traders bet on its reversal.

- Relative value: the traded asset is cointegrated with a sector index or another asset; this leads to predictability in the reversal of the spread between the traded and the reference asset (pairs trading).

- Volume clustering: a recent spike in trading volume may be a leading indicator of more volume spikes in the short term.

- Unexpected news: the market responds strongly to unscheduled news about a company or product; this may lead to a predictable increase in trading volume or even a predictable price trend.

- Informed trading: the presence of agents with private information may be inferred from the order flow using the probability of informed trading indicators PIN and VPIN as in Easley *et al* (2011);[1] venue toxicity can affect the trading decisions of uninformed agents.

- Venue liquidity: high activity in a certain trading venue (lit or dark) may be used to adjust the probability of getting filled across venues and reallocate quantities at the smart order router level.

All of the above can be formulated as indicator functions

$$I(t, O_t, \ldots, O_{t-h}; \theta)$$

The main effort in trading signal research is to properly calibrate the auxiliary parameters θ and identify the market regimes during which an indicator has predictive power. Techniques from machine learning are commonly used for these tasks. Once an indicator is proven useful, historical or simulation-based testing is used to adjust the response function and tune the trading engine.

It should be noted that adaptive algorithms operate on top of a baseline trading trajectory. They act as point-in-time modifiers of a default behaviour. Adaptive algorithms can easily accommodate multiple objectives. For example, they can be used as impact minimisers, but when excessive HFT activity is detected they can update minimum crossing quantities and limit prices quickly, to protect the order from being gamed or otherwise exploited. Specific examples of constructing and using HFT signals are given later, after a brief discussion of the effect of adaptive algorithms on transaction cost.

ALGORITHMS AND TRANSACTION COST

In this section we discuss transaction cost at the client order level. Although this is not a high-frequency view of the trading process, we want to understand the general properties of price impact and also provide evidence that high-frequency signals reduce the total transaction cost.

Figure 2.2 Average arrival slippage by participation rate

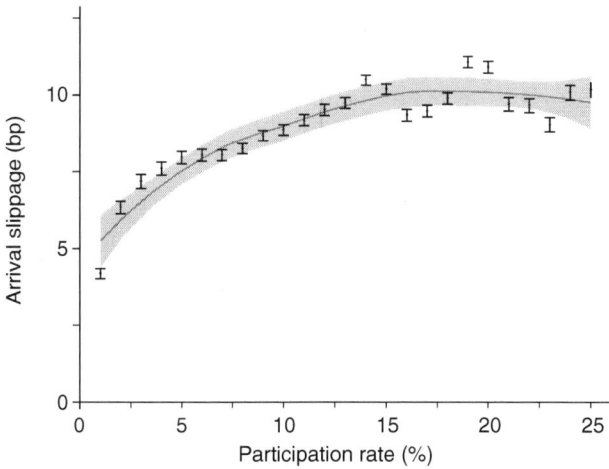

Fully filled client orders of at least 1,000 shares and duration of at least one minute were used. The continuous line and the uncertainty bands around it come from local regression.

Modelling transaction cost is an active topic of theoretical and empirical research. Every trading system implementing second and third generation algorithms needs pre-trade expectations for the cost of a client order. Most models use common explanatory variables such as the size of the order relative to the average or median daily volume, the average participation rate during the execution interval and asset-specific attributes, such as spread and volatility. Price impact is either modelled using parametric functional forms involving power laws and decay kernels (Gatheral 2010; Obizhaeva and Wang 2013) or estimated non-parametrically for various buckets of order size and participation rate. We shall not discuss in detail the structure of these models here. Instead, we shall look at the realised cost of large order samples and break it down by the algorithm used for their execution.

We shall use the arrival price as the common benchmark across all algorithms. The side adjusted arrival slippage is defined as

$$C = \eta \frac{P_x - P_0}{P_0} \tag{2.3}$$

with P_x the execution price, P_0 the arrival price and η the order sign (+1 for BUY, −1 for SELL). Positive values for C denote loss relative

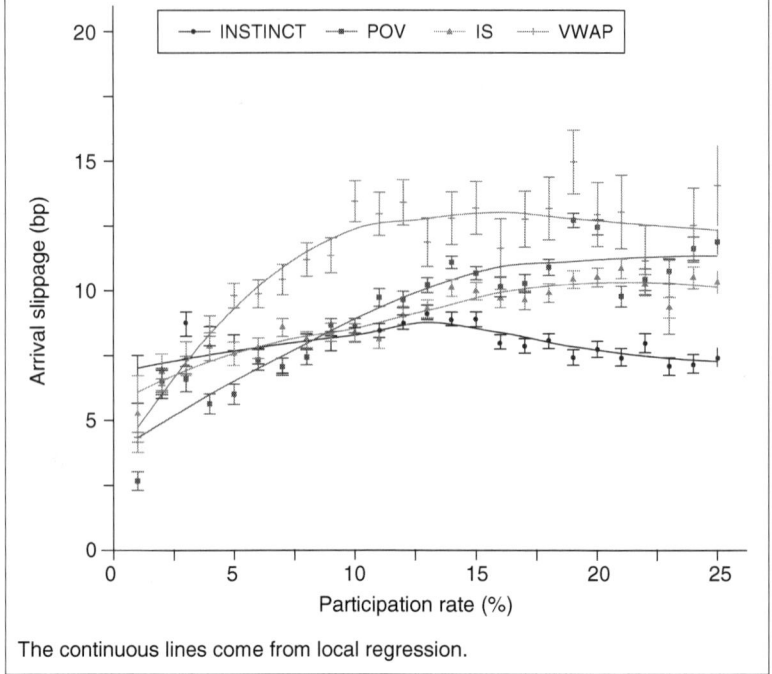

Figure 2.3 Average arrival slippage by trading strategy

The continuous lines come from local regression.

to arrival. Typical parametric models for the arrival slippage are of the form

$$C = cs + b\sigma\sqrt{T}v^{\alpha} + \epsilon \tag{2.4}$$

The explanatory variables are the asset bid–ask spread s and volatility σ, and the order duration T and participation rate v. The errors ϵ are assumed to be independent. The dimensionless coefficients c, b and the exponent α are statistically estimated by fitting large samples of historical executions.

Figure 2.2 shows the average arrival slippage as a function of participation rate. The sample used consists of client orders executed algorithmically by Bank of America Merrill Lynch throughout 2012. The standard error is computed by assuming normal residuals around the mean value for each participation rate bin. Each point in the graph is an average over all equities and order durations. There is strong evidence that the cost increases sublinearly with participation rate. The exponent α is estimated at 0.6.

In Figure 2.3 the average arrival slippage is plotted as a function of participation rate and broken down by trading algorithm. It is easy to see that for participation rates above 10% the instinct adaptive algorithm starts outperforming earlier generation algorithms. This comparison may be penalising the VWAP algorithm since its benchmark is not the arrival price but the interval VWAP. Nevertheless, it is clear that the signal-driven, adaptive strategy is more cost effective at least for medium to high trading urgency. This is the business case for execution brokers to invest in high-frequency signals development.

CONSTRUCTION OF TRADING SIGNALS

In this section we provide concrete examples of high-frequency signals that can be used in algorithmic order execution. As was stated earlier, the indicator function $I(t, O_t, \ldots, O_{t-h}; \theta)$ takes as input a recent history of the market observables $O_t, \ldots, O_{t-h}$. The first step in signal development is the choice of the time window or lag, h, and the weights to be used for summarising this history.

Timescales and weights

A simple approximation of the limit order book is a single-server queuing system. Trades arrive into the queue at random times and with average size $\bar{Q}_x$. The top of the book contains bid and ask quotes of average size $\bar{Q}_b$ and $\bar{Q}_a$. We define the queue time τ_q as

$$\tau_q := \frac{\bar{Q}_b + \bar{Q}_a}{\bar{Q}_x} \tag{2.5}$$

The queue time is the number of trades it takes on average to deplete or recycle the top of the book, independently of trade direction. It is a time interval consisting of τ_q ticks in the stochastic "trade clock".

The queue time is a stock-specific attribute. Long queue stocks have thick limit order books relative to their typical trade size. For these stocks, spread crossing is expensive (the price tick is large), so limit orders pile up at the top of the limit order book. In chronological time the price paths of long queue stocks are stepwise constant. Short queue stocks, on the other hand, have thin, fast updating limit order books, and their price paths have a lot of noisy fluctuations.

Given a stock-specific queue time τ_q, we can define the indicator time window τ_w by simply translating τ_q from trade to chronological time. Call T_{day} the duration of the trading day and N_{trd} the average number of trades per day. The quantity N_{trd}/T_{day} is the average market speed of trading. The time window τ_w is then defined as

$$\tau_w = z\frac{T_{day}}{N_{trd}}\tau_q \tag{2.6}$$

The dimensionless zooming factor $z = \mathcal{O}(1)$ allows for fine tuning of the definition. The interpretation of τ_w is clear. It is the chronological time interval to wait for τ_q trades to occur on average.

The distribution of the window size τ_w is shown in Figure 2.4 for members of the S&P 500 and Russell 3000 indexes. We note the sharp peak of the distribution between 20 and 40 seconds for the S&P 500 and between 0 and 120 seconds for the Russell 3000.

After choosing the time window τ_w as above, we summarise the observables O_t by computing an exponential moving average (EMA). An EMA is preferred over a rolling window average because it is computationally more efficient. The standard update formula of the EMA M_t of a quantity O_t is

$$M_t = wM_{t-1} + (1 - w)O_t \tag{2.7}$$

The weight w, $0 < w < 1$, is called the smoothing factor. In the limit $w \to 1$ the EMA strongly discounts the present observation O_t and the average is smooth. Conversely, in the limit $w \to 0$ the EMA tracks the present observation closely and fluctuates with it.

The weight can be dynamic, ie, a function of the observation time t. Assume that, as of t, the time of the last trade is t_{i-1}. We define the weight $w(t)$ as the exponentially decayed distance between t and t_{i-1}, measured in units of τ_w. For observation time equal to the current trade time, $t = t_i$, the weight becomes

$$w_i = e^{-(t_i-t_{i-1})/\tau_w} \tag{2.8}$$

The interpretation of w_i is easy to see in the limit of large queue times $\tau_q \gg 1$. Using the definition $\tau_w = T_{day}/N_{trd}$, and assuming that trades arrive uniformly at constant speed, $\Delta t_i = N_{trd}/T_{day}$, Equation 2.8 becomes

$$1 - w_i = 1 - e^{-1/\tau_q} \approx \frac{1}{\tau_q} \tag{2.9}$$

Figure 2.4 Distribution of the timescale τ_w for stocks in (a) the S&P 500 and (b) the Russell 3000

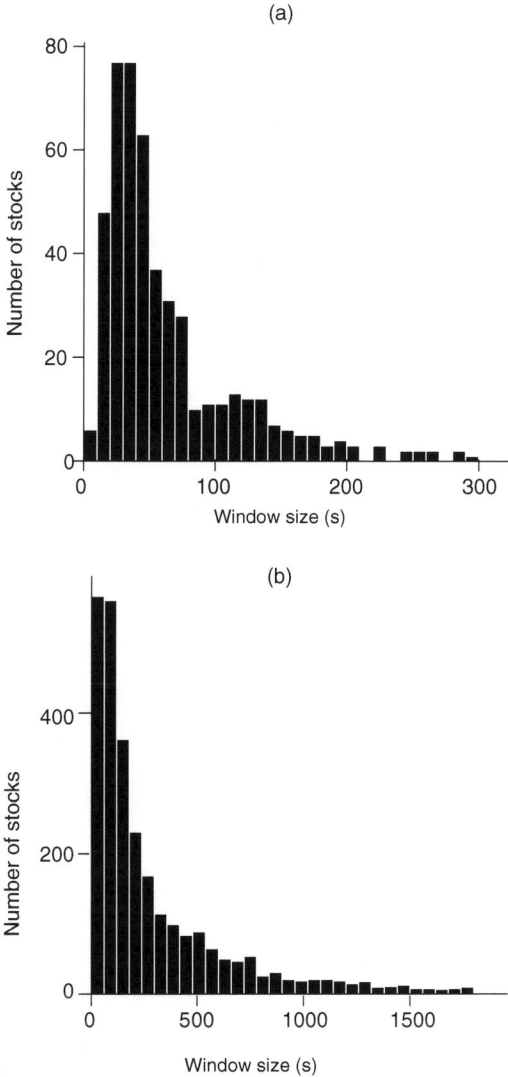

For each stock τ_w is averaged over all trading days in January 2013. The width of each bin is 10 seconds for S&P 500 and 60 seconds for the Russell 3000.

In this limit the moving average is determined by the values of the observable O_t over the last τ_q trades. In summary, we have defined a stock-specific time window τ_w and a dynamic weighting scheme

w_i for computing indicators as exponential moving averages. The next step is to choose the specific observable O_t.

Trade sign autocorrelation

The time series of trades exhibits strong autocorrelation. This can be easily demonstrated by assigning signs to every trade and computing the autocorrelation function (ACF). There are several trade sign algorithms. Here we use one of the simplest, the Lee–Ready algorithm. A trade is assigned the sign +1 (−1), meaning that the trade was buyer initiated (seller initiated) if the transaction price is above (below) the mid-price. The ACF of trade signs is plotted in Figure 2.5 for a high (Microsoft Corp symbol: MSFT) and a medium (BEAM Inc symbol: BEAM) capitalisation stock. We note significant correlation over several lags, in particular for the high capitalisation stock.

The autocorrelation of trade signs is due primarily to algorithms splitting large client orders (Tóth *et al* 2011). The log–log plot in Figure 2.5 provides evidence of a power law decay of the correlation ρ at lag h as $\rho \propto h^{-\gamma}$. We estimate the decay exponent $\gamma = 0.50$ for MSFT and $\gamma = 0.65$ for BEAM.

The predictability of the trade signs means that an indicator that measures trade arrival separately for buy and sell trades will be relatively stable. Following Almgren (2006), we generalise the trade sign from the discrete variable with ±1 values to two continuous variables, the "askness" a and the "bidness" b, both within the $[0, 1]$ range. For each trade, the variable a (b) is the distance of the transaction price from the bid (ask) measured in units of spread. Call P_x the transaction price, and P_b, P_a the bid and ask prices prevailing at the time of the trade, respectively. Then

$$a = \min\left(\left(\frac{P_x - P_b}{P_a - P_b}\right)^+, 1\right), \qquad b = \min\left(\left(\frac{P_a - P_x}{P_a - P_b}\right)^+, 1\right) \quad (2.10)$$

We use the notation x^+ for the positive part of x. The variables a and b are by construction floored at 0, capped at 1 and satisfy the constraint

$$a + b = 1 \quad (2.11)$$

A trade with a close to 1 executes near the ask, so it is buyer initiated. Likewise, a trade with b close to 1 executes near the bid, so it is seller initiated.

Figure 2.5 Log–log autocorrelation of trade signs for (a) MSFT and (b) BEAM

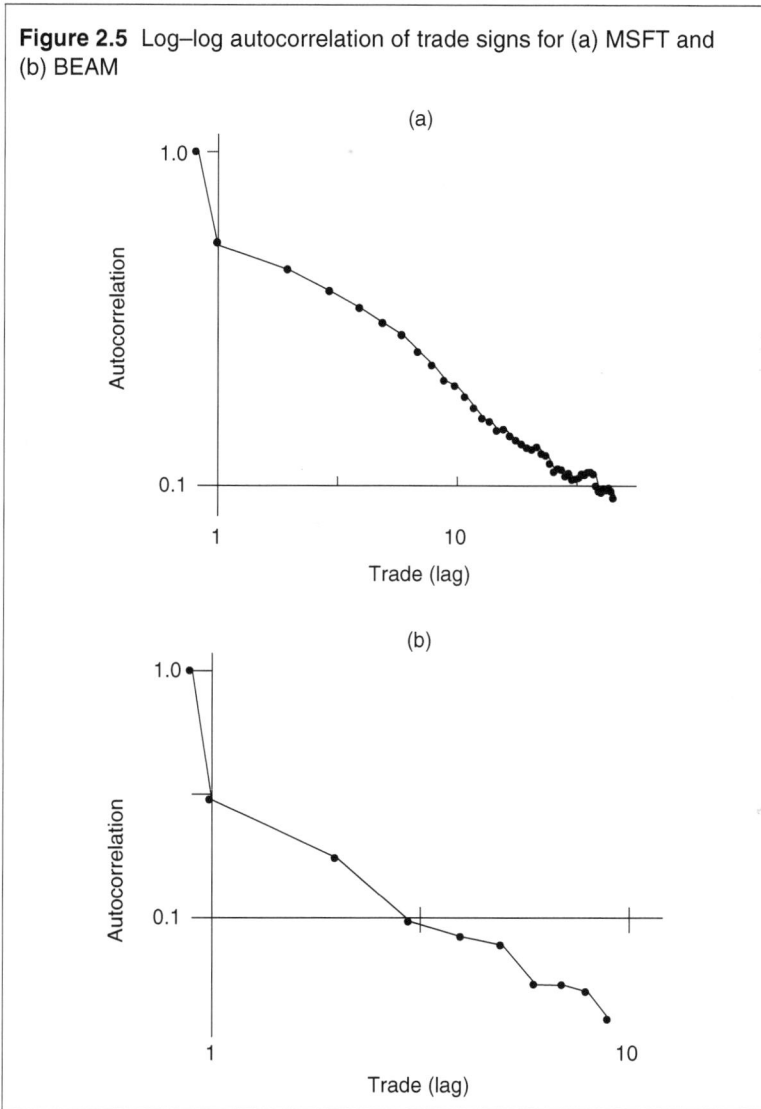

(a)

Autocorrelation

1.0

0.1

1   10

Trade (lag)

(b)

Autocorrelation

1.0

0.1

1   10

Trade (lag)

Using the timescales and weights of the previous section, we define the EMAs for a and b as

$$A_i = \frac{1}{\tau_w} a_i + w_i A_{i-1}, \qquad B_i = \frac{1}{\tau_w} b_i + w_i B_{i-1} \qquad (2.12)$$

The quantities A_i and B_i represent the local speeds at which trades arrive at the ask (bid) side of the limit order book. Finally, we normalise the EMAs by dividing by half of the average trading speed as

$$\bar{A}_i = \frac{2T_{\text{day}}}{N_{\text{trd}}} A_i, \qquad \bar{B}_i = \frac{2T_{\text{day}}}{N_{\text{trd}}} B_i \qquad (2.13)$$

If the order flow is balanced between buys and sells within the window τ_w, then $\bar{A}_i \approx \bar{B}_i \approx 1$. About half of the trades are buyer initiated and half are seller initiated.

An algorithm that is executing a BUY order at some target participation rate (say POV), may exploit the indicator $\bar{B}$, which measures the local speed of seller initiated trades. If the level of $\bar{B}_i$ is significantly higher than 1, the algorithm increases the participation rate in order to expose more of the order quantity to sellers. This is an example of a response function $R(\bar{B}_t, X_t, \phi)$, which takes as input the indicator $\bar{B}_t$, the order state variable X_t and the parameter ϕ that controls the rate of increase of the participation rate given the deviation of the indicator from the baseline value of 1. When the indicator reverts, the participation rate decreases accordingly. Similar treatment can be applied to SELL orders with the $\bar{A}$ indicator.

Figure 2.6 shows the time evolution of an order traded by an adaptive algorithm using the above signal. The order outperformed the arrival mid-quote price by 2.1 basis points, which is about one full bid–ask spread.

Order-book imbalance

Order-book imbalance as a predictor of price movement has been extensively studied in the literature (Cont and De Larrard 2011). The basic idea is that if the bid side is much heavier than the ask side, over a short time horizon the price will most likely move up because of the buy pressure. Several analytical results for the probability of price movement have been derived for the case of limit order books with Markovian dynamics (Avellaneda and Stoikov 2008; Cont *et al* 2010).

To construct a trading signal, we need an imbalance indicator and an associated response function. "Microprice" is a common imbalance indicator. It is defined as

$$P_{\text{micro}} = P_{\text{b}} \frac{Q_{\text{a}}}{Q_{\text{a}} + Q_{\text{b}}} + P_{\text{a}} \frac{Q_{\text{b}}}{Q_{\text{a}} + Q_{\text{b}}} \qquad (2.14)$$

The bid and ask prices P_{b} and P_{a} are weighted in proportion to the quantities on the opposite side, Q_{a} and Q_{b}, respectively. Therefore P_{micro} is closer to the bid level if the ask side is heavier, and becomes the mid-quote price for a balanced limit order book (Figure 2.7).

Figure 2.6 Order to sell 15,000 shares of BEAM, or 1.8% of ADV as of a day in February 2013

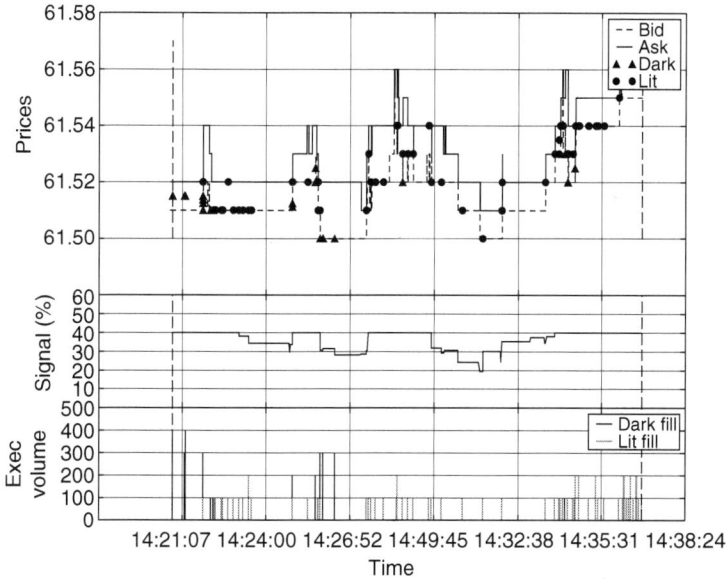

The execution duration was 16.1 minutes. Note the solid line in the second panel. This is the participation rate modulated by the signal. The third panel shows the actual fills. Grey bars are fills from lit venues and black bars are fills from dark venues.

Next comes the question of the timescale t_w, to be used for smoothing the indicator. The answer to this depends on whether P_{micro} will be used at the order scheduling layer, or as part of the limit order model, where decisions about spread crossing, cancellations and amendments are taken at high frequency. In the second case it is not necessary to average P_{micro} over its recent history. We simply read it off at each evaluation time and take an action. The response function $R(P_{\text{micro},t}, X_t, \phi)$ for a BUY order can be of the form

$$R_{\text{BUY}} = \begin{cases} \text{cross spread} & \text{if } P_{\text{micro}} > P_{\text{a}} - \phi(P_{\text{a}} - P_{\text{b}}) \\ \text{stay posted} & \text{if } P_{\text{micro}} \leqslant P_{\text{a}} - \phi(P_{\text{a}} - P_{\text{b}}) \end{cases} \tag{2.15}$$

Likewise, for a SELL order

$$R_{\text{SELL}} = \begin{cases} \text{cross spread} & \text{if } P_{\text{micro}} < P_{\text{b}} + \phi(P_{\text{a}} - P_{\text{b}}) \\ \text{stay posted} & \text{if } P_{\text{micro}} \geqslant P_{\text{b}} + \phi(P_{\text{a}} - P_{\text{b}}) \end{cases} \tag{2.16}$$

Figure 2.7 The microprice level for various top-of-book configurations

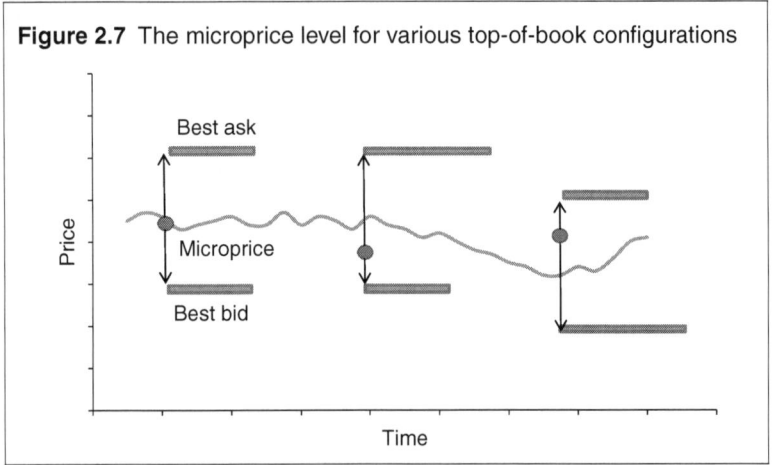

Figure 2.8 Microprice-triggered spread crossing

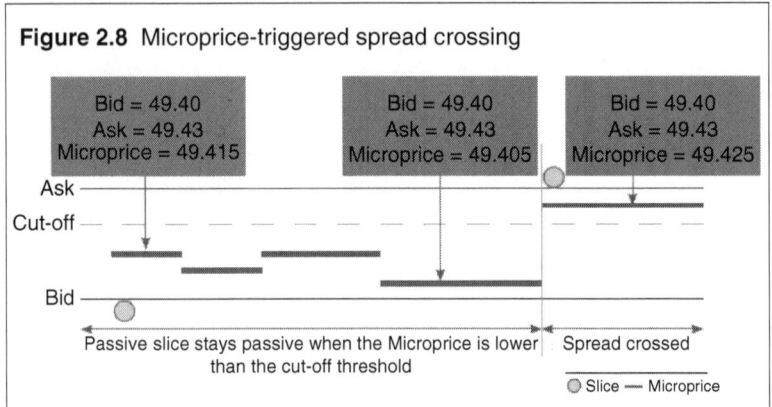

The parameter ϕ defines the distance in spread units within which P_{micro} needs to be from the opposite side for spread crossing to be triggered (Figure 2.8).

As in the case of the autocorrelation signal, the parameter ϕ needs to be carefully calibrated using historical and randomised testing. Moreover, latency effects need to be under control because they affect the performance of Microprice as well as any other HFT signal; see Stoikov and Waeber (2012) for a discussion.

FAIR VALUE AND ORDER PROTECTION

Executing orders in a high-frequency multi-venue environment creates opportunities for the faster agents. Low latency is an advantage for HFT traders and a revenue generator for exchanges that provide collocation services. To avoid explicit and implicit costs, brokers try to internalise order matching by inviting their clients to participate in dark liquidity pools. The proliferation of dark pools provides evidence for their cost benefits. There are no spread crossing or add/take fees, orders are matched at the prevailing mid-quote price and transactions occur without participating in the public price formation process. But the benefits of dark trading are limited, because dark pools cannot satisfy the liquidity demands of their clients consistently all the time. Consequently, agents end up participating in both dark and lit venues. The potential information leakage requires brokers to have mechanisms for protecting orders.

The two main threats from HFT trading are dark order detection (pinging) and sudden price movements (gaming). The first is typically intercepted by detecting the pattern of small orders that try to probe a resting order in a dark pool. Upon detection of the pinging pattern, the minimum crossing quantity is adjusted to block further attempts to infer the size of the resting order.

Sudden price movements in the lit markets and for thinly traded stocks could be suspicious. According to the standard gaming scenario, an HFT agent may have detected the size and direction (BUY/SELL) of an order resting in a dark pool or en route to an exchange. The fast agent moves the price away from the detected order (eg, buys ahead if the order wants to buy) with the intention to trade with the detected order at this new reference price (eg, sell against the buying order at an elevated mid-quote price). Such threats, real or perceived, can be mitigated by a high-frequency signal that continuously computes a reference or fair price and sets limits with respect to this price.

The "fair value" indicator is a form of VWAP over the look-back window τ_w (Equation 2.6). It is defined as the ratio of the exponentially weighted turnover divided by the exponentially weighted traded volume within τ_w. At each trade arrival time t_i we observe the transaction volume V_i and price P_i. The fair value numerator is updated as

$$N_i = w_i N_{i-1} + (1 - w_i) V_i P_i \qquad (2.17)$$

and the denominator is updated as

$$D_i = w_i D_{i-1} + (1 - w_i) V_i \qquad (2.18)$$

Figure 2.9 Fair value signal overlaid on top of a SELL order trading in dark pools

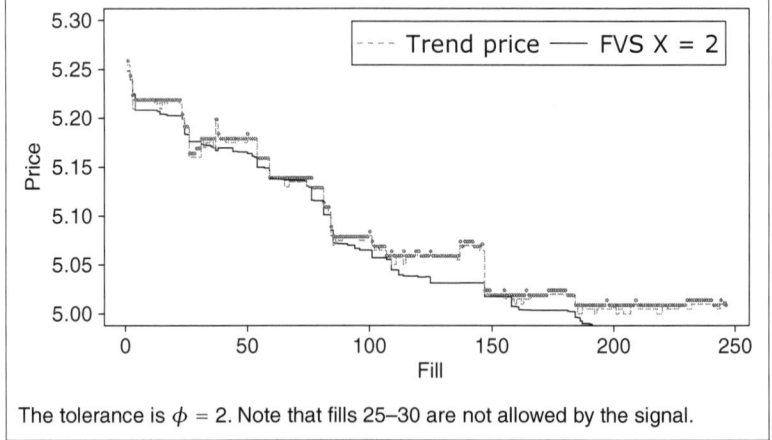

The tolerance is $\phi = 2$. Note that fills 25–30 are not allowed by the signal.

The fair value indicator $\bar{P}_i$ is then computed as

$$\bar{P}_i = \frac{N_i}{D_i} \tag{2.19}$$

By adjusting the zooming factor, z, we can shorten the window τ_w and make the indicator track the latest transaction price more closely. This is the same mechanism as in the autocorrelation signal.

The fair value response function R is parametrised by a tolerance, ϕ, which determines within how many multiples of the bid–ask spread s we allow the order to trade. The response function defines the limit price as

$$R_i = \bar{P}_i + \eta \phi s \tag{2.20}$$

with η the order sign (+1 for BUY and −1 for SELL). Figure 2.9 shows the signal in action, for a SELL order trading in the dark. The solid black line is the limit price for tolerance $\phi = 2$. Any fill below this line is not allowed by the signal.

Order protection using the fair value signal has certain advantages over a common alternative mechanism, the volatility bands. In the volatility bands method, limit prices are set a multiple of $\sigma\sqrt{T}$ away from arrival price, with σ the mid-quote volatility and T the time since order arrival. The idea here is that, according to Brownian motion scaling, price fluctuations of order $\sigma\sqrt{T}$ are diffusive (normal), whereas bigger price changes are considered jumps. Both mechanisms try to detect abnormal price jumps. The fair value signal is independent of order arrival, so it is robust under cancellations, replacements and other order amendments.

CONCLUSION

In this chapter we reviewed the evolution of trading algorithms and focused on the event-driven, adaptive generation, as this is more suitable for an HFT ecosystem. We reviewed methods of constructing trading signals and illustrated them with a few examples. Our focus was on execution strategies for large orders of predetermined size and buy/sell direction. The other large class of strategies not discussed here contains the market-making and spread-capturing algorithms of statistical arbitrage.

High-frequency trading has established a new normal mode in the equity markets and it is spreading in other asset classes. It is clear that executing orders in this environment requires fast information processing and fast action. Fast information processing leads to development and calibration of trading signals and adaptive algorithms. Fast action requires investment in computer networking and order routing technology. As experience is gained in this new environment, and as economies of scale are realised, optimal order execution in an HFT world is becoming a utility with better understood costs, benefits and trade-offs.

> The opinions in the chapter are the author's own and not necessarily those of Bank of America Corporation or any of its subsidiaries.

1   PIN denotes probability of informed trading; VPIN denotes volume-synchronised probability of informed trading.

REFERENCES

Almgren, R., 2006, "A New EMA Indicator", Banc of America Securities Technical Report.

Almgren, R., and N. Chriss, 2001, "Optimal Execution of Portfolio Transactions", *The Journal of Risk* 3(2), pp. 5–39.

Avellaneda, M., and S. Stoikov, 2008, "High-Frequency Trading in a Limit Order Book", *Quantitative Finance* 8(3), pp. 217–24.

Cont, R., and A. De Larrard, 2011, "Order Book Dynamics in Liquid Markets: Limit Theorems and Diffusion Approximations", SSRN Working Paper.

Cont, R., S. Stoikov and R. Talreja, 2010, "A Stochastic Model of Order Book Dynamics", *Operations Research* 58(3), pp. 549–63.

Easley, D., M. López de Prado and M. O'Hara, 2011, "The Microstructure of the 'Flash Crash': Flow Toxicity, Liquidity Crashes and the Probability of Informed Trading", *Journal of Portfolio Management* 37(2), pp. 118–28.

Gatheral, J., 2010, "No-Dynamic-Arbitrage and Market Impact", *Quantitative Finance* 10(7), pp. 749–59.

Markov, V., S. Mazur and D. Saltz, 2011, "Design and Implementation of Schedule-Based Trading Strategies Based on Uncertainty Bands", *Journal of Trading* 6(4), pp. 45–52.

Obizhaeva, A., and J. Wang, 2013, "Optimal Trading Strategy and Supply/Demand Dynamics", *Journal of Financial Markets* 16(1), pp. 1–32.

Perold, A. F., 1988, "The Implementation Shortfall: Paper versus Reality", *Journal of Portfolio Management* 14, pp. 4–9.

Stoikov, S., and R. Waeber, 2012, "Optimal Asset Liquidation Using Limit Order Book Information", SSRN Working Paper.

Tóth, B., I. Palit, F. Lillo, and J. D. Farmer, 2011, "Why Is Order Flow So Persistent?", Preprint, arXiv:1108.1632.

3

Execution Strategies in Fixed Income Markets

Robert Almgren

Quantitative Brokers LLC; New York University Courant Institute of
Mathematical Sciences

Reducing trading costs and slippage is a universal concern of asset managers. Although the decision of what assets to hold is still the most important aspect of investing, poor execution of trade decisions can subtract many basis points from overall return. Conversely, having an effective strategy to execute trades and to measure transaction costs can enhance returns: "A penny saved in slippage is a penny earned in alpha".

Execution techniques in equities have advanced far ahead of those in other markets, such as futures, options, foreign exchange and fixed income. Reasons for this are the overall size of the equity markets and the widespread use of active investment strategies. Another is the simplicity of the products themselves: for trading a single name of stock you need very little information beyond its price. Relationships between different stocks are at best weak. As a consequence, quant researchers in equity markets have focused intensively on the details of the execution process.

By contrast, fixed-income products are inherently complex, and quantitatively minded researchers in this area have focused on such aspects as yield curve modelling and day counts. Asset managers have not traditionally focused on measuring or managing execution costs, and have few effective tools to do so. However, the Securities Industry and Financial Markets Association (SIFMA) noted that "It is clear that the duty to seek best execution imposed on an asset manager is the same regardless of whether the manager is undertaking equity or fixed-income transactions" (SIFMA Asset Management Group 2008).

This chapter discusses some details of the fixed-income markets that present special challenges for best execution in general and automated trading in particular. The focus will be on interest rate markets and in particular on interest rates futures markets, since those are the most highly developed and the most amenable to quantitative analysis.

Following a brief overview of the markets and the products that we consider, the specific features on which we concentrate are the following.

- **Information events:** interest rates markets are strongly affected by events such as economic information releases and government auctions. In contrast to earnings releases in the equities markets, these events generally happen in the middle of the trading day and we must have a strategy for trading through them.

- **Cointegration:** interest rates products generally differ only in their position on the yield curve. Thus, they move together to a much greater degree than any collection of equities. To achieve efficient execution in a single product, we must monitor some subset of the entire universe of products.

- **Pro rata matching:** because futures products are commonly traded on a single exchange (in contrast to the fragmentation in the equities markets), the microstructural rules of trading can be much more complex. One example is pro rata matching, in which an incoming market order is matched against all resting limit orders in proportion to their size. This is in contrast to the more common time-priority matching algorithm. This change in matching algorithm has dramatic effects on the dynamics of the order book and optimal submission strategies.

FIXED INCOME PRODUCTS

The fixed-income universe is large and varied, from corporate bonds to municipal debt, mortgage-backed products and sovereign debt instruments, and includes various derived products such as swaps. Some of these products are traded only by dealers, and for some of them there is not even a central record of transactions.

We shall focus on the subset of fixed-income products that are denoted "interest rate products", that is, products for which default risk is negligible and market risk only comes from changes in the underlying interest rate. Such products are usually, though not always, sovereign debt of countries that have the ability to print the currency in which their debts are denominated. However, the short-term interest rate (STIR) products that we discuss below also fall into this category, since they are defined in terms of specific rates rather than issuers.

In particular, we shall focus on interest rate futures, since these are centrally cleared, and traded on organised exchanges for which detailed market information is easily available. Participants in all aspects of fixed-income trading use interest rate futures to hedge their rates exposure, letting them concentrate on the more idiosyncratic aspects of their preferred products. Interest rate futures are therefore a natural point of departure. As this field develops, we hope to be able to extend execution analysis to a broader range of fixed-income products.

Short-term interest rates

STIR products are instruments of very short duration. The largest product in this category is the eurodollar future. Introduced by the Chicago Mercantile Exchange (CME) in 1981, the eurodollar was the first cash-settled futures product and is now one of the most heavily traded futures contracts in the world. Each contract represents a forward bet on the London Inter-Bank Offered Rate (Libor) as of the date of expiration; the contract price is defined as 100 − Libor. The deliverable amount is three months' interest on a notional amount of US$1 million; thus, each basis point (bp) change in Libor represents a mark-to-market cash payment of US$25 per contract. The minimum price increment for a CME eurodollar (except for certain short-dated maturities) is 0.5bp, representing a cash value of US$12.50 (compared with clearing and execution costs of US$1 or less), and the bid–ask spread is almost always equal to this minimum value. Not crossing the spread becomes one of the most important aspects of trading them.

These products are thus "large-tick" in the sense of Dayri and Rosenbaum (2012), meaning among other aspects that one-tick price moves are often followed by reversals and special techniques are necessary to estimate high-frequency volatility (Large 2011).

Eurodollar futures are traded with quarterly maturities out to 10 years (plus some thinly traded "monthly" contracts that we neglect), of which at least 10–15 are active. This is in contrast to almost all other futures products, for which only the contract closest to expiration, the "front month", is active, except during the "roll". Eurodollar futures are thus inherently multidimensional.

Eurodollars trade using pro rata matching, which we discuss later (see pp. 59ff). The CME interest rates electronic markets are open 23 hours per day, with consequences that we discuss below (see pp. 46ff).

Euribor futures and short sterling, both primarily traded on the London International Financial Futures Exchange (LIFFE), are similar products, in which the underlying rate is respectively a European interbank rate and a UK rate.

Treasury futures

The other large category of interest products is more traditional futures contracts, in which the deliverable is a government debt security. For example, the CME Treasury futures complex covers products with underlying maturities from two years to twenty-five years and more. Their prices track very closely those of the underlying products, and can thus to some extent be used as proxies. These contracts also are "large-tick" because of the exchange-specified minimum price increments. They exhibit strong coupling between products, although for each, only one maturity is active at one time, except around the roll. On the CME these products, like eurodollars, trade electronically 23 hours per day.

In Europe, the analogous products are the Euro-Bund and related contracts (Bobl, Schatz and Buxl), traded on Eurex, which represent European government bonds of varying durations. The UK analogue is the long gilt contract (short and medium gilt contracts are very thinly traded).

INFORMATION EVENTS

Interest rate markets are strongly affected by information releases and economic events that happen during the day, such as US Treasury auctions, announcements by the US Federal Open Market Committee (FOMC), and releases, such as the Change in Non-farm Payrolls number from the US Bureau of Labor Statistics (BLS) on the

Figure 3.1 The 10-year US Treasury futures contract trading through the Change in Non-farm Payrolls information release at 08h30 New York time on Friday, December 7, 2012

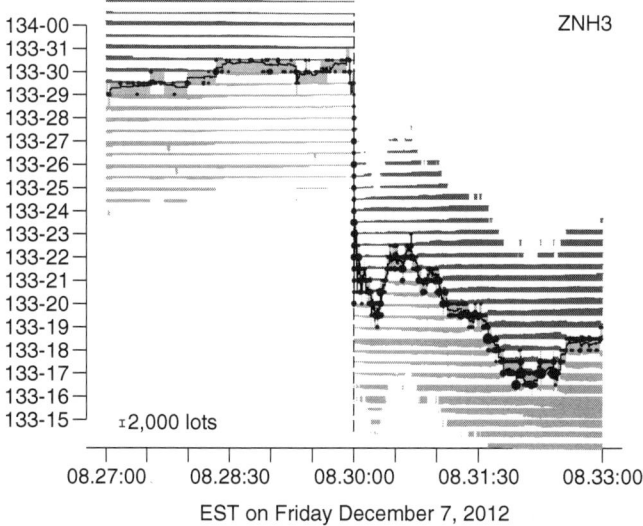

The vertical axis shows the price in dollars and 32nds; the minimum price increment for this contract is half of a 32nd. The pale grey region is bid–ask spread; black dots are trades, and shaded regions show book depth. Before the event, liquidity thins out and prices move a little. When the number is released, the price jumps and activity resumes.

first Friday of every month. These events are the analogues of earnings announcements for equities but, whereas earnings announcements are usually scheduled outside of trading hours, these events generally happen during the trading day.

Trading through information events has been specific to rates markets (and energy and foreign exchange to a lesser extent) but may be coming to other markets as round-the-clock electronic trading becomes more established. When the ICE exchange extended its hours for electronic trading of grain futures in July 2012, CME was obliged to do the same, and traders complained that "Trading now will be open during the release of most of the USDA's supply and demand reports, which will increase volatility and decrease the ability of traders to make informed decisions" (Dreibus and Wilson 2012).

Figure 3.1 shows an example of market reaction to an information event: the 10-year front-month (March 2013) Treasury futures

Figure 3.2 The 10-year US Treasury futures contract trading through a 30-year bond auction, scheduled at 13h00 New York time on Thursday, December 13, 2012

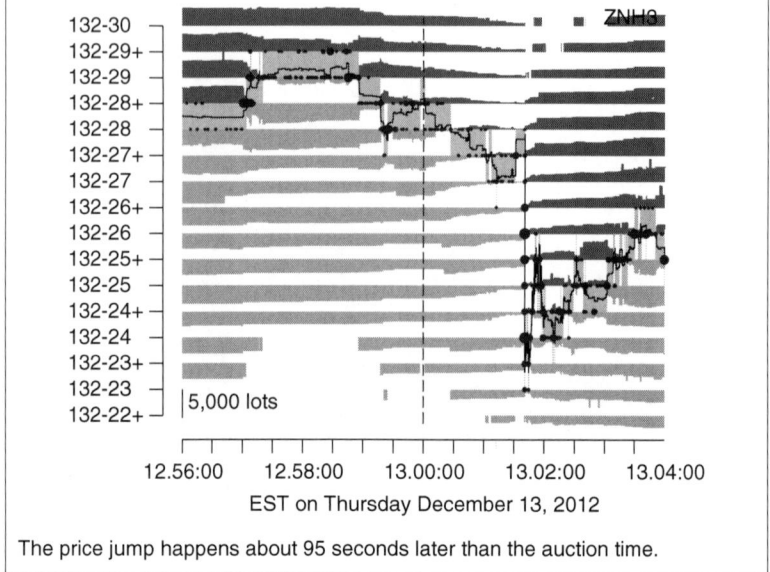

The price jump happens about 95 seconds later than the auction time.

contract trading through the Change in Non-farm Payrolls information event on December 7, 2012. (This event is one component of the Employment Situation cluster of simultaneous releases by the BLS, but it is by far the most important and most people know the cluster by this name.) This event is the most significant of all information releases, since it is the best single indicator of the health of the economy and the likely future direction of interest rates.

It is clear that this event cannot be neglected in the design of an effective trading algorithm. For any "significant" information event, the algorithm must take defensive actions before the event happens, such as removing limit orders from the book and aligning itself with the forecast schedule if the desired order type is based on a schedule. Also, all such events must be included into forecast curves for intra-day volume and volatility.

Figure 3.2 shows another example: the 10-year Treasury futures contract trading through a 30-year bond auction on December 13. The scheduled time of the auction is 13h00 New York time, but that denotes the time at which the Treasury stops accepting bids. The

Table 3.1 Events on Thursday, December 13, 2012, from Bloomberg database

NY time	Region	Event
06.00	UK	CBI trends total orders
06.00	UK	CBI trends selling prices
08.30	US	Jobless claims
08.30	US	PPI
08.30	US	Retail sales "control group"
09.45	US	Bloomberg consumer comfort
10.00	US	Business inventories
13.00	US	30-year bond auction

Not all events are significant.

market response comes approximately one and a half minutes later, when the auction results are released.

The auction is not the only event on that day: Table 3.1 shows eight events that occur on Thursday, December 13, 2012, including the 30-year bond auction. We generally look at only US, UK, EC and German events, although on this date only US and UK events occurred. If all of Western Europe and Canada are included, then there are 32 events on this day.

In order to trade through and around these events, we need to obtain quantitative answers to several questions.

- Which events are "significant"? That is, for which events should we take potentially costly action such as withdrawing orders from the book. The event database on Bloomberg shows 482 distinct events within 2012, including those in the US, Canada and Western Europe, and including government auctions and information releases. Only a small fraction of these are significant.

- When do events happen? Is the time as given by Bloomberg an accurate indication of the actual time as reflected in price action? For example, for an auction, not only is the market response a minute or two after the scheduled time, but also the uncertainty in this time is several seconds. It would be embarrassing to pull limit orders from the book several minutes before or after the actual price move.

- Do US events affect European products and vice versa?

Figure 3.3 "Event microscope" applied to the Treasury auction shown in Figure 3.2

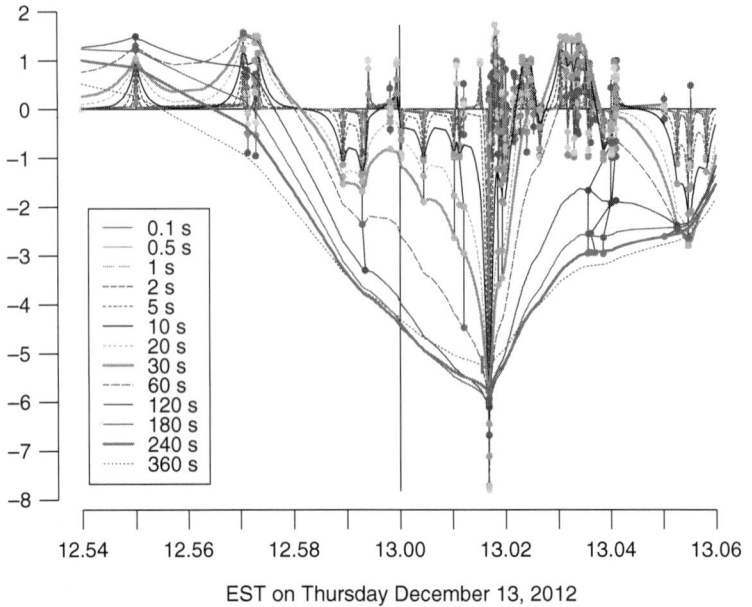

EST on Thursday December 13, 2012

The difference of moving averages identifies a price move of −8 "ticks" (minimum price increment) at a time that is 95 seconds after the event time.

Event microscope

At Quantitative Brokers, we have designed an "event microscope" to look in detail at price jumps around events. A more detailed description is given by Almgren (2012), but we give a brief summary as follows: we compute exponential moving averages of the midpoint price time series, both from the left (backward-looking) and from the right (forward-looking), with a variety of different time constants. The difference between the left-moving average and the right-moving average has a peak at the time of the event: the location and magnitude of this peak let us locate precisely the timing and significance of the event response.

Table 3.2 shows results for significant events for the US 10-year Treasury futures (ZN) and its European equivalent, the Euro-Bund (FGBL), for calendar year 2012. To generate these results, we do the analysis shown in Figure 3.3 for each instance of each different event type as given by Bloomberg (column n_e is the number of

Table 3.2 Event effects on US 10-year Treasury futures (ZN), and its European equivalent, the Euro-Bund (FGBL), for January–December 2012

Event name	Region	n_e	n	$|\Delta p|$	Δt	Rng Δt
ZN (US 10-year)						
Change in Non-farm Payrolls	US	12	12	15.5	0.2	0.4
FOMC rate decision	US	8	8	6.5	50.8	98.1
Construction and manufacturing	US	12	8	5.2	0.5	0.4
10-year notes	US	12	10	5.0	98.1	3.5
30-year bonds	US	12	9	4.6	99.0	3.0
ADP employment change	US	12	8	4.6	0.0	0.1
5-year notes	US	12	6	4.1	98.0	7.3
FGBL (Euro-Bund)						
Change in Non-farm Payrolls	US	11	11	18.2	0.3	0.6
ADP employment change	US	12	11	5.1	−0.0	0.1
PMI manufacturing	GE	24	14	5.0	−119.5	1.1
Consumer confidence	US	12	11	4.3	1.7	60.9
Consumer confidence indicator	DE	12	7	4.1	−118.4	181.7

n_e is the number of times the event occurred, eg, 12 for a monthly event. n is the number of instances that were significant for that product. $|\Delta p|$ is the median absolute price change, measured in units of the minimum price increment; this value must be at least four to be significant. Δt is the median time of the event, as an offset in seconds relative to the scheduled time. Rng Δt denotes the Q1–Q3 interquartile range of the time offset. GE, Germany; DE, Denmark; US, United States.

instances). We identify significant instances for which we detect a jump of at least twice the minimum price increment (two "ticks"), since an ordinary price change will appear as a step of one tick times the minimum price increment. We then calculate the median absolute price change across all instances, and define "significant" events to be those for which the median price change is at least four ticks.

Among significant instances, we calculate the median time offset in seconds relative to the scheduled time from Bloomberg (column Δt). We also measure the uncertainty in this time by reporting the interquartile range of jump times (rng Δt).

Table 3.3 Event effects on long-term rates futures: US 30-year Treasury futures (ZB), the CME Ultra contract (UB) and the Euro-Buxl (FGBX), for January–December 2012

Event name	Region	n_e	n	$|\Delta p|$	Δt	Rng Δt
ZB (US Bond)						
Change in Non-Farm Payrolls	US	12	12	17.3	0.3	0.5
FOMC rate decision	US	8	7	7.9	74.9	144.3
30-year bonds	US	12	11	5.9	99.0	3.2
Construction and manufacturing	US	12	8	5.9	0.5	0.9
ADP employment change	US	12	8	5.7	0.0	0.1
10-year notes	US	12	10	4.4	99.0	5.3
UB (US long-term)						
Change in Non-Farm Payrolls	US	12	12	25.6	0.5	0.6
FOMC rate decision	US	8	8	10.3	51.4	132.4
30-year bonds	US	12	12	9.9	99.0	5.0
10-year notes	US	12	11	7.0	99.4	7.0
ADP employment change	US	12	11	4.6	0.1	7.4
Goods	US	12	12	4.4	0.9	5.0
Construction and manufacturing	US	12	11	4.3	0.5	0.7
Retail sales "control group"	US	12	12	4.2	0.7	2.5
Consumer confidence	US	12	9	4.1	0.0	0.1
FGBX (Euro-Buxl)						
Change in Non-Farm Payrolls	US	11	11	13.3	0.7	1.0
FOMC rate decision	US	8	7	6.8	89.8	183.2
30-year bonds	US	12	11	5.3	96.6	70.0
ADP employment change	US	12	8	4.3	0.1	9.7
Construction and manufacturing	US	11	10	4.2	2.1	112.0
Leading indicators	US	12	9	4.2	0.5	133.4
Minutes of FOMC meeting	US	8	7	4.1	8.3	62.6

Column headings are as described in Table 3.2.

We reach the following conclusions about event effects for interest rates futures.

- Change in Non-farm Payrolls is in a class by itself in terms of significance. It consistently causes price jumps of more than 10 ticks. The time is always quite close to the scheduled time, within a fraction of a second.

- FOMC rate decision is highly significant, at least for US rates products. The time offset is a minute or more, and the uncertainty in time is several minutes.

- Treasury auctions are significant for US products. The time offset is generally 95–100 seconds, with an uncertainty of several seconds.

- A miscellaneous collection of other information events are significant for US and European products. These events generally happen near the scheduled time, though occasionally events are released with specific offsets. For example, the Purchasing Managers Index (PMI) from Markit, for which the German Manufacturing information release is shown in Table 3.2, is released on Reuters two minutes earlier than the "standard" release, and it is this pre-release that moves the market. Similarly, the Chicago Purchasing Managers' report (not shown) from the Institute for Supply Management is released to subscribers three minutes before the public release, and this offset is clearly visible in the data.

- Non-US events are almost never significant for US rates products. For European products, US events are the most important, and only a few European events rise to significance (the exact combination depends on the time period and contract). This is consistent with results found by Andersson *et al* (2009) and Cailloux (2007).

COINTEGRATION

Cointegration is a widely studied and sought-after property of financial time series; see Alexander (2001) for a broad and detailed discussion. Although strong relationships between different price series are rare in, for example, prices of different stocks, they are absolutely ubiquitous in interest rate products, since the only differences between different products concern the duration of the product and possibly the national origin. An understanding of these interrelationships is essential to obtaining effective execution. An order for even a single asset must be understood within a highly multidimensional market context.

Figure 3.4 shows an example of intra-day price motion. The contracts shown are the four primary Treasury futures contracts traded

Figure 3.4 From bottom to top, the CME 5-year Treasury (ZF), 10-year (ZN), 30-year (ZB) and Ultra (UB) futures, expiring in March 2013 (H3), from midnight to market close at 16h00 Chicago time, on December 11, 2012

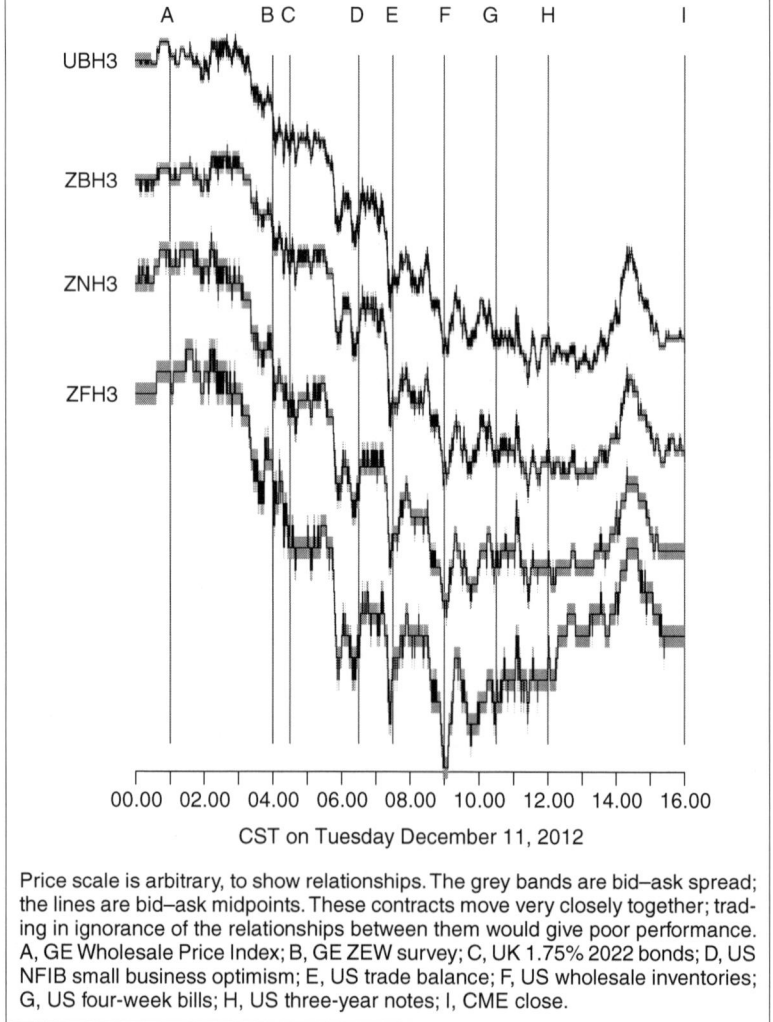

Price scale is arbitrary, to show relationships. The grey bands are bid–ask spread; the lines are bid–ask midpoints. These contracts move very closely together; trading in ignorance of the relationships between them would give poor performance. A, GE Wholesale Price Index; B, GE ZEW survey; C, UK 1.75% 2022 bonds; D, US NFIB small business optimism; E, US trade balance; F, US wholesale inventories; G, US four-week bills; H, US three-year notes; I, CME close.

on CME (the two-year contract is not shown). Since these contracts represent US interest rates at different durations ranging from five years to thirty years, they move very closely together. A cointegration model can help us identify short-term mispricings. That is, these contracts establish a relationship with each other. When that relationship

Figure 3.5 Two of the four contracts in Figure 3.4 plotted against each other: the 10-year (ZNH3, horizontal axis) and 30-year Treasury futures (ZBH3, vertical axis)

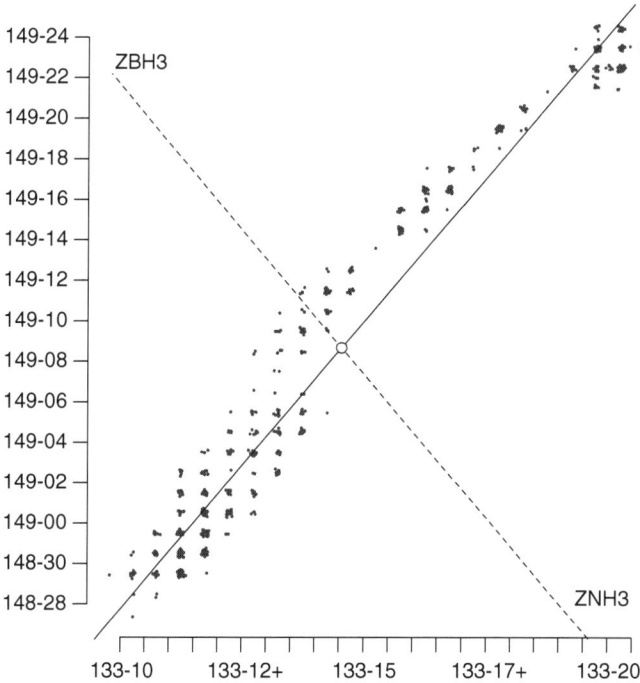

Each dot represents a one-minute sample point. Since the prices move on a grid, a small amount of random noise has been added, so that larger point clusters show larger numbers of data samples. The lines show the axes of a singular value decomposition applied to the correlation matrix of the entire day's data (this forward-looking construction is used only for an example; in practice a rolling volume-weighted average would be used).

is disturbed it is likely to re-establish itself, and that provides some amount of short-term price predictivity.

The most flexible approach to understanding cointegration is based on the principal components construction of Shintani (2001) and Chigira (2008). In contrast to the traditional approach of Johansen (1991), it does not require estimation of a discrete-time vector autoregressive model; it is extremely flexible and robust for real-time continuous market data. The construction is illustrated in Figures 3.5–3.7.

In Figure 3.5 we have extracted two of the price series shown in Figure 3.4, in order to display them against each other on the page.

In reality, we would do the analysis on the full n-dimensional price series. The relationship seen in Figure 3.5 is here reflected by the alignment of the price dots along a diagonal axis. The axes show the actual price values in US dollars and 32nds per contract. The axes have been scaled independently to accommodate each contract, but it can be seen that the 10-year contract ZNH3 moves approximately 10/32 through the course of the day (133-10 to 133-20), while the 30-year contract ZBH3 moves approximately 28/32 (148-28 to 149-24). Of course, the longer duration contract has higher volatility since its price is much more sensitively affected by changes in underlying yield (this sensitivity is the definition of "duration" for an interest rate contract), and this difference in volatility must be properly handled in the analysis.

The circle in the middle of Figure 3.5 denotes the simple mean of all the data points. The two lines denote the first and second principal components of the correlation matrix of the points, taken about this mean point. The principal components are computed using the components normalised by their variance, and are orthogonal in that scaled coordinate system. (In fact, with only two variables, each scaled, the principal vectors are $(1, 1)$ and $(1, -1)$.) Since the plot axes are also approximately scaled by standard deviation, the axes are nearly orthogonal in the plot.

In this simple example, we perform the analysis using the entire day's data. In practice this would be impossible to compute since it looks forward in time. In a real production application, both the mean and the correlation matrix would be computed as a rolling exponential average. In addition, the averages would not assign each minute equal weight, but would use some form of weighting by trade volume.

Figure 3.6 shows the price data from Figure 3.5, projected along the two principal components. The difference in the components is clear. The projection along the primary component (black line) is essentially a reflection of the overall market movements seen in Figure 3.4. In this two-dimensional example, it is merely the average of the two prices, appropriately scaled. In contrast, the projection along the secondary component – in this two-dimensional example, the difference of scaled prices – appears to fluctuate around zero. That is, deviations of this component away from zero predict a move back towards zero, and this information is extremely useful for short-term

Figure 3.6 Projection of the price series in Figure 3.5 onto the principal axes of the correlation matrix

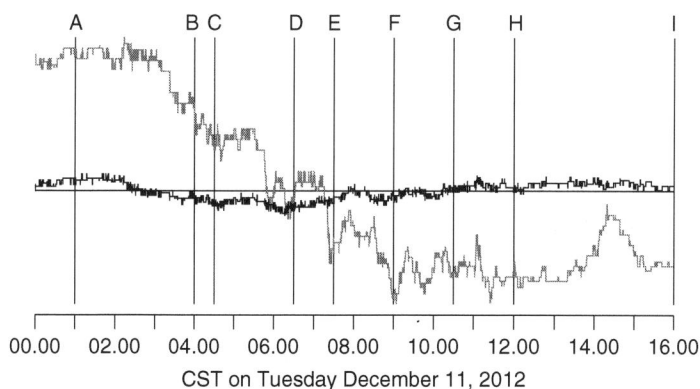

The vertical scale is arbitrary but is identical for the two components. The grey line is the projection onto the primary axis (solid line in Figure 3.5), reflecting the overall market motion (cf. Figure 3.4) and is largely unpredictable. The black line is the projection onto the secondary axis (dotted line in Figure 3.5), which shows mean reversion and is useful for prediction. A, GE Wholesale Price Index; B, GE ZEW survey; C, UK 1.75% 2022 bonds; D, US NFIB small business optimism; E, US trade balance; F, US wholesale inventories; G, US four-week bills; H, US three-year notes; I, CME close.

trading on timescales of minutes and hours. Of course, this simple graph does not constitute a rigorous test for cointegration behaviour, especially given the forward-looking construction, but it indicates the nature of the price dynamics.

Figure 3.7 shows the two price series in real time (black lines), along with the price predictor derived from the cointegration model (grey line). This price predictor is obtained by setting the secondary component to zero, in effect, projecting onto the solid line in Figure 3.5. That is, it identifies the historical relationship between the two products on an intra-day timescale, and supposes that, when they deviate from this relationship, future prices will evolve so as to restore the relationship. A systematic test of the accuracy of the cointegration prediction shows that it is far less than perfectly accurate, but still effective enough to add value to real-time trading.

Figure 3.8 shows the principal components for the full set of four price series shown in Figure 3.4. This corresponds to what would be obtained by a traditional analysis of yield curve dynamics, but here on an intra-day timescale. The first component represents the overall market motion, while the other components represent shifts

Figure 3.7 Short-term price predictor, using the projections shown in Figures 3.5 and 3.6

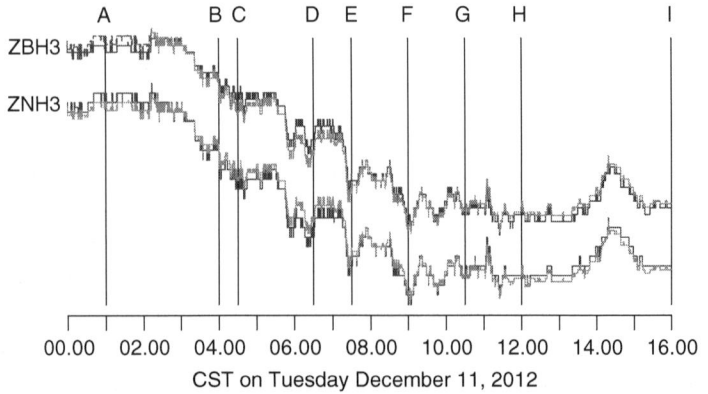

Black lines are the raw price series as in Figure 3.4. Grey lines are the forecast assuming that the secondary component in Figure 3.6 is set to zero, which is equivalent to projecting onto the solid line in Figure 3.5. This says that when the two contracts are relatively over- or under-valued relative to each other and to their historical relationship, that the contracts will return towards equilibrium. A, GE Wholesale Price Index; B, GE ZEW survey; C, UK 1.75% 2022 bonds; D, US NFIB small business optimism; E, US trade balance; F, US wholesale inventories; G, US four-week bills; H, US three-year notes; I, CME close.

Figure 3.8 Principal components for the four price series (normalised by volatilities) in Figure 3.4

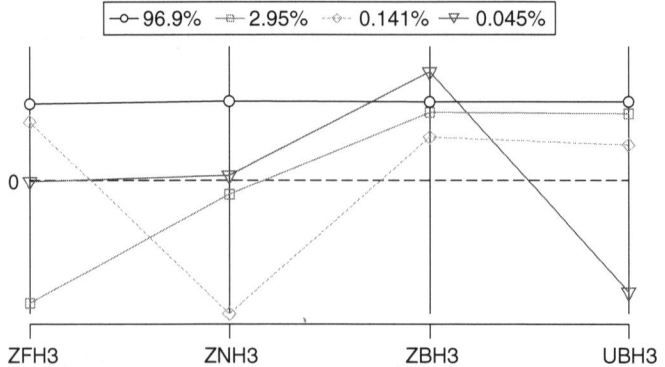

The legend shows contributions to variance. The first component, carrying 97% of total variance, is a constant component corresponding to overall price shifts. The second component, carrying nearly all of the remaining 3%, is roughly a tilt in the yield curve. The third and fourth components are negligible. Note that not until the fourth component can we distinguish the 30-year bond (ZB) from the Ultra contract (UB).

relative to equal changes. The cointegration forecast would project all components after the first to zero.

A similar equilibrium model could have been derived by considering the underlying nature of the products traded, and analysing their sensitivity to changes in interest rates. The advantage of this formulation is that it is extremely straightforward, requiring no fundamental understanding of the products.

One limitation of the cointegration formulation is that it is completely symmetric between products, and has no intrinsic way to capture whether certain components drive others by moving earlier. For example, it is a common belief that futures prices move more quickly than the underlying cash instruments. There is also some empirical evidence that interest rates futures of longer durations lead futures of shorter duration. This distinction can be extracted by careful analysis of the predictive power of the signal, which will be higher for the lagging products than for the leaders.

In practice, the models used for price prediction would be more sophisticated than this. The eurodollar complex is even more tightly coupled than the Treasuries illustrated here, and modelling their interrelationships is essential. It is debatable whether it is better to build a single model encompassing both eurodollars and Treasuries, or whether to model each asset class separately; the decision must be based on a systematic analysis of the predictive power of the regression signal. Similarly, other markets, such as Euribor, short sterling and the European Bund–Bobl–Schatz complex, may be modelled independently or together. The choice of how to group the wide range of different products is guided by a mixture of market insight and quantitative analysis.

The overall situation is not quite as simple as we have made it appear here, but cointegration is definitely a feature of interest rate markets that cannot be ignored.

PRO RATA MATCHING

The term "matching algorithm" refers to the process by which an exchange matches limit orders resting in the order book against incoming market orders. Typically, the total quantity of limit bid orders at the best bid price, say, is larger than the size of an incoming market sell order, and therefore some allocation must be made of the market order among the resting orders. The market order will be completely filled, but not all the limit orders will be. Some prioritisation must be imposed among the limit orders.

The most obvious matching algorithm, and the one that is used by the overwhelming majority of markets, is "time priority". Resting orders are maintained in a list in the order in which they were entered. The market order is matched against the earliest order; when that is filled, the remaining quantity is matched against the next earliest order, and so on. This algorithm is simple and efficient. In such a market, the traders' main concerns are to keep track of their positions in the queue, in order to have estimates of when their orders will be filled.

Interest rates futures markets, largely alone among all markets, often use some variant of pro rata matching. In pro rata matching, the incoming market order is allocated among the resting limit orders in proportion to the size of the limit order, ignoring (in a first approximation) the time sequence in which the orders were entered. That is, a large limit order will receive a large allocation, even if smaller orders were entered much earlier. Field and Large (2008) have surveyed the use of pro rata matching in futures markets, identifying its predominance in rates markets, and provide a simple model for the oversizing that we discuss below.

Pro rata matching is typically used for short duration products, most notably the CME eurodollar complex. The two-year Treasury futures contract uses a mixed time/pro rata matching algorithm. The Treasury calendar spread contracts use pro rata matching. On LIFFE, the short-term Euribor and short sterling contracts use "time pro rata", in which the allocation is weighted by preceding volume as well as by size of the individual order.

All these products have low volatility compared with the exchange-imposed minimum price increment, and as a consequence the bid–ask spread is nearly always equal to its minimum allowable value. That is, as noted above, they are "large-tick" in the sense of Dayri and Rosenbaum (2012). This means that being executed on a limit order is much more valuable than crossing the spread with a market order. Also, the bid and offer prices commonly stay at constant values for substantial lengths of time.

Figure 3.9 shows an example. The March 2015 contract is the third most heavily traded eurodollar contract on December 11, 2012 and substantial trade activity is visible (the two heaviest are March

Figure 3.9 The March 2015 eurodollar on December 11, 2012

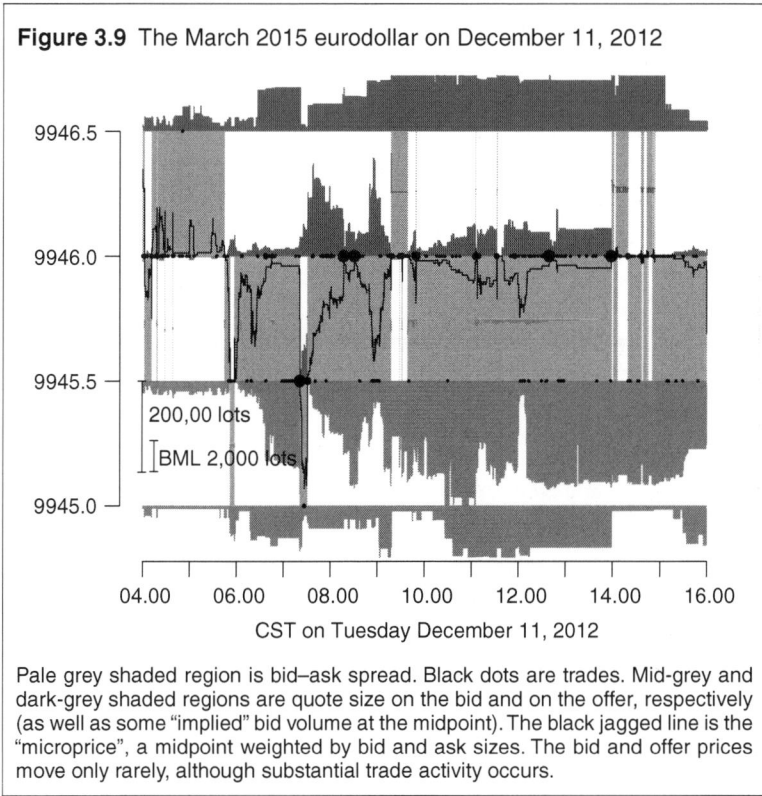

CST on Tuesday December 11, 2012

Pale grey shaded region is bid–ask spread. Black dots are trades. Mid-grey and dark-grey shaded regions are quote size on the bid and on the offer, respectively (as well as some "implied" bid volume at the midpoint). The black jagged line is the "microprice", a midpoint weighted by bid and ask sizes. The bid and offer prices move only rarely, although substantial trade activity occurs.

and June 2013, three and six months from expiration). This contract represents the Libor rate more than two years in the future. We would expect market beliefs about this quantity to change throughout the day, at least by several multiples of the minimum price increment, 0.5bp. Nonetheless, the bid and ask prices do not move at all for extended periods, for example, for a period of four hours between 10h00 and 14h00 Chicago time (though two very short flickers are visible within this interval).

When the quote prices do not move, a time priority matching algorithm would excessively weight early arrivals. If a market maker were able to capture the head of the queue with one large order on the bid, and another on the ask, then every subsequent market participant would be obliged to trade with them. Pro rata matching gives later entrants the possibility to execute.

In these markets, the dynamics of the order book is extremely volatile. Since there is no penalty for losing queue position, there is no disincentive to cancel and resubmit limit orders. This can be seen in Figure 3.9, in the substantial changes in quote volume on the bid and on the ask. The LIFFE time pro rata algorithm is an attempt to partially dampen these wild swings.

An additional consequence of pro rata matching is the "arms race" to oversize orders (Field and Large 2008). Since allocation is determined by order size, and since incoming market order volume is typically too small to satisfy the traders who are hoping for passive execution, limit order participants have incentives to post much larger quantities than they actually wish to execute. Typically, in these markets, the average volume on the bid and the ask is several hundred times a typical trade size. In Figure 3.9, the quantity on the inside quotes is in the range of 10,000–20,000 lots, whereas the average market order size for this contract is around 20 lots.

The only limitation on oversizing is the risk that a large market order will fill for much more quantity than was desired, but such large orders are rare (Arora 2011). Balancing the risk of overfilling if we do oversize against the certainty of underfilling if we do not oversize is our central concern when trading in a pro rata market.

CONCLUSION

Traders in fixed-income and interest rates markets have just as much need for effective execution and transaction cost management as their counterparts in the equities markets, although the latter markets have received vastly more quantitative attention. Several features of interest rates futures markets in particular are substantially different from these other markets, and must be taken proper account of in order to achieve good execution results.

REFERENCES

Alexander, C., 2001, *Market Models: A Guide to Financial Data Analysis*. New York: John Wiley & Sons.

Almgren, R., 2012, "High-Frequency Event Analysis in European Interest Rate Futures", Technical Report, Quantitative Brokers, October.

Andersson, M., L. Jul Overby and S. Sebestyén, 2009, "Which News Moves the Euro Area Bond Market?", *German Economic Review* 10(1), pp. 1–31.

Arora, R., 2011, "An Analysis of Large Trades in Eurodollar Futures", Technical Report, Quantitative Brokers.

Cailloux, J., 2007, "What Moves the European Bond Market? Market Responses to Surprises in Main Economic Indicators", Technical Report, The Royal Bank of Scotland.

Chigira, H., 2008, "A Test of Cointegration Rank Based on Principal Component Analysis", *Applied Economics Letters* 15, pp. 693–6.

Dayri, K., and M. Rosenbaum, 2012, "Large Tick Assets: Implicit Spread and Optimal Tick Size", Preprint, arXiv:1207.6325 [q-fin.TR].

Dreibus, T. C., and J. Wilson, 2012, "Grain-Pit Traders Squeezed Out as CME Expands to Match ICE Hours", Bloomberg, July.

Field, J., and J. Large, 2008, "Pro-Rata Matching and One-Tick Futures Markets", Preprint.

Johansen, S., 1991, "Estimation and Hypothesis Testing of Cointegration Vectors in Gaussian Vector Autoregressive Models", *Econometrica* 59(6), pp. 1551–80.

Large, J., 2011, "Estimating Quadratic Variation when Quoted Prices Change by a Constant Increment", *Journal of Econometrics* 160, pp. 2–11.

Shintani, M., 2001, "A Simple Cointegrating Rank Test without Vector Autoregression", *Journal of Econometrics* 105, pp. 337–63.

SIFMA Asset Management Group, 2008, "Best Execution Guidelines for Fixed-Income Securities", SIFMA Asset Management Group, White Paper.

4

High-Frequency Trading in FX Markets

Anton Golub, Alexandre Dupuis, Richard B. Olsen
Olsen Ltd

This chapter provides an overview of the landscape and the basic mechanics of the foreign exchange (FX) markets and their organised exchanges. We explain algorithmic trading in the foreign exchange and analyse trading frequencies of different types of market partici- pants. We continue with an overview of the key insights of academic literature of the impact of high-frequency (HF) traders in the foreign exchange market and discuss actual market events where there have been short-term price disruptions. We focus on the behaviour of the high-frequency traders involved.

There is definite empirical evidence of the path dependency of the price trajectory; a black swan event may be triggered at any time due to microstructure effects that are not linked to fundamental factors. Organised trading venues are exploring ways to prevent microstruc- ture effects distorting price action, though without reaching a sat- isfactory solution so far. This chapter proposes a new method to achieve price stability. We suggest that the queuing system of limit order books rewards market participants by offering competitive two-way prices; model simulations presented here indicate that this might well enhance market stability.

THE CURRENCY MARKET

This section describes the currency market from a high-frequency trading (HFT) perspective. We give an overview of the overall landscape of the market and the relationships between the major

Figure 4.1 Structure of the venues in the currency market

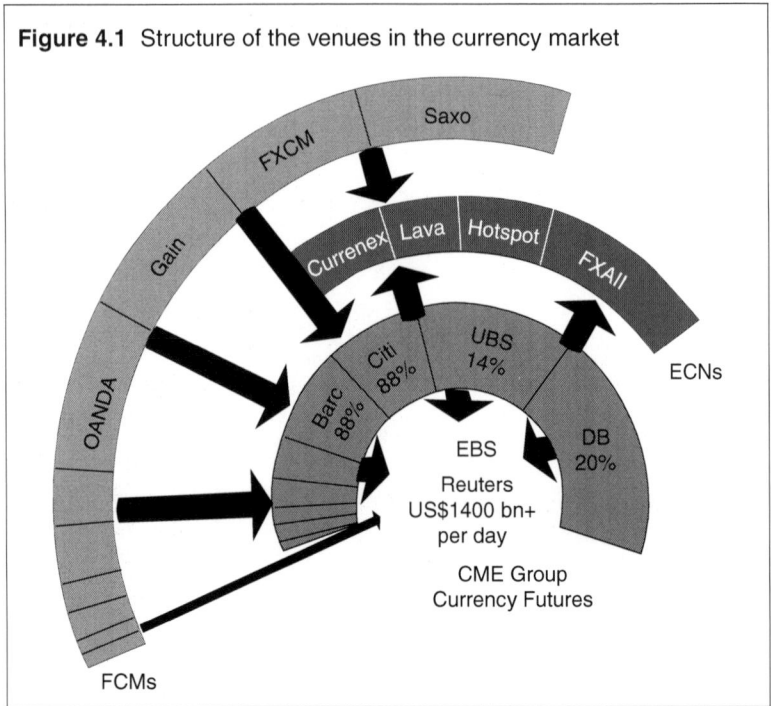

players. The dynamics is illustrated by discussing their technical details. Then we review the trading algorithms that are used in the industry and, based on Schmidt (2011) and Masry (2013), we assess their impact on market microstructure.

Market venues

The currency market is a complex system of organised exchanges. At the centre of the market there are two inter-dealer electronic broking platforms: Electronic Broking Services (EBS) and Reuters. These platforms, described in some detail below, act as a source of interbank liquidity in the FX market and they are the place where large HFT players trade. The requirement of a minimum ticket size of one million units has created a business opportunity to build alternative trading venues for retail and other market participants. Currenex, for example, has built a multi-bank electronic communication network (ECN) and there is a similar platform available by Hotspot. These new ECNs provide their customers with more sophisticated tools for market making, such as full anonymity (Bank for International Settlements 2011), where the counterparty making a trade does not know who is taking the other side; this is not the case with EBS and Reuters. Retail aggregators have reshaped the market by providing small-scale traders with access to the foreign exchange markets. The retail aggregators have become a significant force in the overall foreign exchange market, making up approximately 10% of spot volume. Finally, the largest currency futures market is operated by Chicago Mercantile Exchange Group, with a daily volume of US$100 billion.

Figure 4.1 depicts how the different venues interact. We observe that the structure is not hierarchical, as Futures Commission Merchant (FCM) firms trade with large banks and possibly on EBS and Reuters. It is also interesting to note that Figure 4.1 is dynamic, and players may change their behaviour and reposition themselves within the foreign exchange market. An example is EBS, which has decided to decrease the minimal ticket size to 100,000 units for selected major currency pairs in order to attract smaller-scale traders.

We now give some detail about some of the main venues from Figure 4.1.

EBS

EBS is the main venue for all the USD, EUR, GBP, CHF and JPY crosses. EBS provides two data feeds, one with time-sliced snapshots of the order book every 250 milliseconds[1] and a premium feed, EBS Live, which sends snapshots every 100 milliseconds. The snapshots were concurrently changed from showing the top level and two lower aggregated levels to showing ten levels of the limit order book. The minimum tick size was one pip, but was reduced to one tenth of a pip. That experiment proved to be unsuccessful; as of November 2012 the minimum tick size for most pairs reverted to one pip or half a pip. As already mentioned, EBS has a minimum ticket size of one million units and attracts large institutional traders. At the time of writing, they do not allow traders to modify orders or to have the last-look provision.[2] All quotes are pre-screened for credit, meaning that quotes will only be received from a given counterparty if the prime broker who actually clears the trade has the required credit line with the other counterparty or their prime broker. Most of the main pairs have a minimum quote lifetime (MQL) of 250 milliseconds, meaning that an order cannot be cancelled until 250 milliseconds have elapsed from the time it was added to the book. Ticks are not sent out on the data feed in a real-time manner, but are instead time-sliced to show an aggregate of the traded size at the best traded price over the interval. Filled quotes are reported immediately to the involved parties, before the rest of the market. Finally, we note that EBS has a multi-matching-engine architecture located in New York, London and Tokyo, and all engines operate independently but update one another when the order book is modified.

Reuters

Reuters is the main venue for all the crosses for Commonwealth currencies and Scandinavian currencies. Their rules are very similar to those at EBS summarised above. Reuters does not have multiple engines, and operates a single engine in London.

Currenex and Hotspot

Currenex has a fast architecture, which allows for streaming of order-based feeds and timely confirmations and executions. It does not provide an MQL feature, and no minimum ticket size is imposed. At Currenex, traders have the ability to modify orders instead of cancelling and replacing them, and to use conditional orders, execution algorithms and pegged orders. The tick size is 0.1 pips. Currenex does have some liquidity providers who use last-look provision. Hotspot is similar to Currenex, except that the minimum ticket size is 50,000 units and ticks are delayed by one second.

Hotspot does have liquidity providers who use last-look provision, though quotes from these traders can be filtered out. However, relative to the Currenex non-last-look feed, Hotspot's is relatively wide, suggesting the feature of allowing market participants to have a "last look" undermines liquidity and leads to wider spreads.

Oanda

Oanda is one of the major FCMs and one of the original FX dealers on the Internet.[3] The company's focus has been to build a highly scalable platform that executes transactions at minimum cost. In addition to the major currencies, Oanda offers trading in exotic exchange rates, precious metals and contracts for difference[4] of stock indexes and US Treasuries. Transaction prices are identical for tickets as small as US$1 and as large as US$10 million, and the same across different market segments. Interest is paid on a second-by-second basis. Unlike traditional trading venues, Oanda offers firm quotes to its clients and hedges excess exposure with institutional market makers. Oanda's main revenue is generated from market making; it earns the spread between bid and ask prices at which its customers trade.

CME

The largest currency futures market is operated by the Chicago Mercantile Exchange (CME) Group,[5] with an average daily notional volume of approximately US$100 billion, most of it is being traded electronically. Similar to other futures products, currency futures are traded in terms of contract months with standard maturity dates typically falling on the third Wednesdays of March, June, September and December. The CME Group offers 49 currency futures contracts; the crosses of the G10 countries (ie, AUD, CAD, CHF, EUR, GBP, JPY, NOK, NZD, SEK, USD) as well as crosses of emerging markets, such as BRL, KRW and RMB. The minimum tick size is one pip, and the ticket size is US$125,000. Since 2010, CME Group has offered trading in selected E-micro FX futures, which are one-tenth of the standard size. In most cases, traders will offset their original positions before the last day of trading. Less frequently, contracts are held until the maturity date, at which time the contract is cash-settled or physically delivered, depending on the specific contract and exchange. Only a small percentage of currency futures contracts are settled in the physical delivery of foreign exchange between a buyer and a seller. The CME is responsible for establishing banking facilities in each country represented by its currency futures contracts, and these agent banks act on behalf of the CME and maintain a foreign currency account to accommodate any physical deliveries.

Unlike the FX spot market, CME provides a centralised pricing and clearing service, ie, the market price and the order book information for a currency futures contract will be the same regardless of which broker is used, and the CME guarantees each transaction. CME Group ensures that self-regulatory duties are fulfilled through its Market Regulation Department, including market integrity protection by maintaining fair, efficient, competitive and transparent markets.

Trading algorithms

We distinguish between two classes: algorithmic execution and algorithmic decision-making. The first addresses the automated execution of large orders in small tickets with the objective of minimising the price impact and/or ensuring the anonymity of execution. The second class groups the automated algorithms designed to generate Alpha.

When do we classify a trading algorithm as belonging to the class of high-frequency traders? Is the decisive criterion the number of trades? Or are there additional criteria? To shed some light on these questions, we follow Gomber *et al* (2011), who consider HFT as a subset of algorithmic trading (AT). HFT and AT share common features: pre-designed trading decisions, used by professional traders; observing market data in real-time; automated order submission; automated order management, without human intervention; use of direct market access. Gomber *et al* suggest criteria that only AT fulfil: agent trading; minimising market impact (for large orders); achievement of a particular benchmark; holding periods of possibly days, weeks or months; working an order through time and across markets.

Finally, we list criteria that only HFT satisfy: very high number of orders; rapid order cancellation; proprietary trading; profit from buying and selling; no significant positions at the end of day; very short holding periods; very low margins extracted per trade; low latency requirement; use of co-location/proximity services and individual data feeds; a focus on highly liquid instruments.

Indeed, as pointed out by Gomber *et al* (2011), HFT is not a trading strategy as such.

Algorithmic execution

The main idea of these strategies is to minimise the impact on price movement of buying or selling a large order. The algorithms at hand basically slice up the order into smaller orders and select appropriate times to transact in the hope that the average price will be close to the current price, that the impact will be low and that the trades will go unnoticed.

The basic algorithm is called time-weighted average price and slices time in an equal manner given a time horizon. This algorithm is not clever in the sense that it does not follow market activity and is easily detectable. An alternative is to define time as buckets of volume and allow the algorithm to trade a quantity when a given volume has been transacted in the market; in this case we talk about volume-weighted average price. Various improvements have been proposed to make these algorithms more adaptive to market activity and to include the effect of news. More details, as well as a classification, can be found in Almgren (2009) and Johnson (2010).

Algorithmic decision-making

We list the most common trading strategies designed to generate profit; in general they are believed to contribute to market liquidity (Chaboud *et al* 2012). The complexity of the algorithms and the large number of decisions that need to be taken implies that these algorithms need to be computerised and cannot be generated by hand. The algorithms are not discretionary decisions, as all of the responses of the trading model are predetermined. Depending on their implementations, these strategies can be classified either as HFT or not.

Market-making strategies are designed to offer temporary liquidity to the market by posting bid and ask prices with the expectation of earning the bid and ask spread to compensate for losses from adverse price moves. In some trading venues, these types of strategies are incentivised with rebate schemes or reduced transactions fees. We shall explain later (see pp. 80ff) how such incentives can be used to make price discovery more robust and contribute to price stability.

Statistical arbitrage strategies are a class of strategies that take advantage of deviations from statistically significant market relationships. These relationships can, for example, be market patterns that have been observed to occur with some reasonable likelihood.

Mean reversion strategies assume that the price movement does not persist in one direction and will eventually revert and bounce back. This hypothesis is derived from the fact that positions eventually need to be closed, triggering a price reversal. An example of an automated strategy is described in Dupuis and Olsen (2012).

There exist arbitrage strategies to take advantage of price differences across platforms or take advantage of information ahead of delays. Traders embark, for example, on triangular arbitrage (eg, if buying x units of EUR/USD and selling x units of EUR/GBP, and selling the appropriate units of GBP/USD leads to an instantaneous and risk-free profit).

Liquidity detection strategies are used to spot large orders in the market and/or to trigger a particular behaviour by other market

Table 4.1 Approximation of the percentage of filled trades per trading frequencies expressed in trades per day on EBS (Schmidt 2011)

Type	Frequency	Percentage
MT	—	1.9
Slow AI	<500	1.5
HFT	500–3000	2.3
Ultra-HFT	>3000	4.2

MT, manual trader; AI, automated interface.

participants. These kinds of strategy are at the borderline of what is deemed ethical; examples are pinging (small orders to possibly hit hidden orders), quote stuffing (entering and immediately cancelling a large amount of orders to blur out the real state of the limit order book) or momentum ignition, where orders are placed to exacerbate a trend. These strategies are equivalent to spamming in the Internet; there is a need for subtle mechanism to minimise this type of abuse. We discuss such a mechanism below (see pp. 80ff).

Trading frequencies

To draw the landscape of the trading frequencies, we report on the results of Schmidt (2011) and Masry et al (2012), which have analysed transaction data from the currency market and provide the profile of the high-frequency traders with the durations of their positions.

Schmidt (2011) investigates transaction data from EBS, where, we recall, trading takes place through a limit order book and where the minimal order size is of US$1 million, which makes it a trading venue for large players. The study by Masry et al (2012) analyses transaction data from the market maker Oanda that, in contrast to EBS, has largely retail and some institutional investors; all traders have the same price terms for transactions from US$1 up to US$10 million.

Schmidt (2011) describes in detail the composition of the traders at EBS based on transaction data during the six months between May 2011 and the end of November 2011. The study defines two types of traders: manual traders (MTs), who use a graphic-user-interface-based (GUI-based) based access, and automated traders, who use an automated interface (AI) for trading. AI trading is further subdivided into three subcategories: "Slow AI" at less than 500 trades

Table 4.2 Percentages of trades that were executed at various frequencies f on the Oanda platform, as computed by Masry *et al* (2013)

Frequency	Percentage
$f \leqslant 50$	27.7
$50 < f \leqslant 100$	7.9
$100 < f \leqslant 500$	12.5
$f > 500$	52.0

Frequencies f are expressed in trades per day. Transaction data spans January 2007–March 2009.

per day, "HFT" at between 500 and 3000 trades per day and "Ultra-HFT", with more than 3000 trades per day. MTs account for 75% of EBS customers and more than 90% of MTs submit on average less than 100 orders a day. For EUR/USD, the currency pair with the largest volume, the average number of daily orders submitted by EBS customers are: MT 3.7%; Slow AI 5.7%; HFT 29%; Ultra-HFT 61.6%. Other currency pairs show similar patterns. The difference between Ultra-HFT and MT appears to be massive at first sight, but this neglects the fact that high-frequency traders typically cancel a large percentage of their orders. Schmidt (2011) reports that the average fill ratio for various EBS customer groups is around 50% for MTs, and (considering only AI belonging to the professional trading community; see Schmidt 2011) 26.6% for Slow AI, 8.1% for HFT and 6.8% for Ultra-HFT. Using the above numbers, we approximate the percentage of filled trades per trading frequency and show these in Table 4.1.

Masry *et al* (2013) analyse the transactions done at Oanda between January 2007 and March 2009. The data set comprises 110 million transactions belonging to 46,000 different accounts acting in 48 different currency pairs. First Masry *et al* categorised the traders, assigning them a trading frequency by computing the average number of transactions they made per day. Note that special care was taken to differentiate between accounts with different trading frequencies. Percentage shares of the different trading frequencies are shown in Table 4.2.

Assuming that manual traders can trade at most 50 times a day, the corresponding percentage matches the one on EBS (26.6%). This proportion is suggested by Tables 4.1 and 4.2.

ACADEMIC LITERATURE

With the rapid increase of trading volume from HFT, academic studies have investigated how computerised trading affects the overall market quality. Cvitanic and Kirilenko (2011) derive theoretical distributions of transaction prices in limit order markets populated by low-frequency traders (humans) before and after the entrance of a high-frequency trader (machine). They find that the presence of a machine is likely to change the average transaction price and that the distribution of transaction prices has more mass around the centre and thinner tails. Jarrow and Protter (2011) express concern that the speed advantage of HF traders and the potential commonality of trading actions among computers may have a negative effect on the informativeness of prices. This is because computerised traders, triggered by a common signal, collectively act as one big trader, giving rise to price momentum, causing prices to be less informationally efficient. Cespa and Foucault (2012) argue that the self-reinforcing relationship between price informativeness and liquidity is a source of contagion and fragility: a small drop in the liquidity of one security propagates to other securities and can, through a feedback loop, result in a large drop in market liquidity. This leads to multiple equilibria characterised by either high illiquidity and low price informativeness or low illiquidity and high price informativeness, where the former type of equilibrium generates a liquidity crash similar to the Flash Crash on May 6, 2010.

Empirical academic research has mostly focused on the effects of HFT on the market quality in equity markets. The studies have shown that, in general, computerised trading improves traditional measures of market quality and contributes to price discovery. Hendershott *et al* (2011) study the 30 largest DAX stocks on the Deutche Boerse and find that AT represents a large fraction of the order flow and contributes more to price discovery than human traders. Algorithmic traders are more likely to be at the inside quote when spreads are high than when spreads are low, suggesting that algorithmic traders supply liquidity when this is expensive and demand liquidity when this is cheap. Hendershott *et al* find no evidence that AT increases volatility. Hendershott and Riordan (2011) examine the impact AT has on the market quality of NYSE listed stocks. Using a normalised measure of NYSE message traffic surrounding the NYSE's implementation of automatic quote dissemination in

2003, they find AT narrows spreads, reduces adverse selection and increases the informativeness of quotes, especially for larger stocks. Hasbrouck and Saar (2012) measure HFT activity by identifying "strategic runs" of submission, cancellations and executions in the Nasdaq order book. They find that HFT improves market quality by reducing short-term volatility, spreads and depth of the order book. Menkveld (2012) claims a large high-frequency trader provides liquidity, and its entrance into the market leads to a decrease in spreads. Brogaard (2010) examines the impact of HFT on the US equity market using a unique HFT data set for 120 stocks listed on Nasdaq. HFT is found to add to price discovery, providing the best bid and offer quotes for a significant portion of the trading day, and reducing volatility. However, the extent to which HFT improves liquidity is mixed, as the depth high-frequency traders provide to the order book is a quarter of that provided by non-high-frequency traders.

The most detailed examination of the impact of HFT on the FX market was made by Chaboud *et al* (2012) using high-frequency trading data from EBS for the period September 2003–September 2007 in three exchange rates: EUR/USD, USD/JPY and EUR/JPY. The crucial feature of their data set is that, on a minute-by-minute frequency, the volume and direction of human and computer trades are explicitly identified, allowing explicit measurement of the impact of high-frequency traders. They find very strong evidence that computers do not trade with each other as much as predicted, concluding that the strategies used by algorithmic traders are more correlated and less diverse than those used by human traders.

Next, they investigate the effect that both algorithmic trading activity and the correlation between algorithmic trading strategies have on the occurrence of triangular arbitrage opportunities. They indicate that algorithmic trading activity is found to reduce the number of triangular arbitrage opportunities, as the algorithmic traders quickly respond to the posted quotes by non-algorithmic traders and profit from any potential arbitrage.

Furthermore, a higher degree of correlation between algorithmic trading strategies reduces the number of arbitrage opportunities. There is evidence that an increase in trading activity where computers are posting quotes decreases the number of triangular arbitrage opportunities. Algorithmic traders make prices more efficient by posting quotes that reflect new information.

Chaboud *et al* also investigate the effect algorithmic traders on the degree of autocorrelation in high-frequency currency returns: they estimate the autocorrelation of high-frequency, five-second returns over five-minute intervals. Similar to the evolution of arbitrage opportunities in the market, the introduction and growth of algorithmic trading coincides with a reduction in the absolute value of autocorrelation. On average, algorithmic trading participation reduces the degree of autocorrelation in high-frequency currency returns by posting quotes that reflect new information more quickly.

Finally, Chaboud *et al* report highly correlated algorithmic trading behaviour in response to an increase in absolute value of the autocorrelation in high-frequency currency returns; this supports the concern that high-frequency traders have very similar strategies, which may hinder the price discovery process (Jarrow and Protter 2011).

HFT during time of market stress

The availability of liquidity has been examined in equity markets; academic studies indicate that, on average, high-frequency traders provide liquidity and contribute to price discovery. These studies show that high-frequency traders increase the overall market quality, but they fail to zoom in on extreme events, where their impact may be very different. A notable exception is the study by Kirilenko *et al* (2011) that uses audit-trail data and examines trades in the E-mini S&P 500 stock index futures market during the May 6, 2010, Flash Crash. They conclude that high-frequency traders did not trigger the Flash Crash; HFT behaviour caused a "hot potato" effect and thus exacerbated market volatility.

In contrast to these studies, the following sections provide anecdotal evidence of the behaviour of computerised traders in times of severe stress in foreign exchange markets:

- the JPY carry trade collapse in August 2007;

- the May 6, 2010, Flash Crash;

- JPY appreciation following the Fukushima disaster;

- the Bank of Japan intervention in August 2011 and Swiss National Bank intervention in September 2011.

While each of these episodes is unique in terms of the specific details and they occurred at different stages of the evolution of high-frequency traders, these events provide valuable insight into how computerised traders behave in periods of large price moves.

August 2007 yen appreciation

The August 16, 2007, USD/JPY price rise was the result of the unwinding large yen carry-trade positions; many hedge funds and banks with proprietary trading desks had large positions at risk and decided to buy back yen to pay back low-interest loans. Chaboud *et al* (2012) provide details of this event, and report that the event had one of the highest realised volatilities and the highest absolute value of serial correlation in five-second returns. The yen appreciated sharply against the US dollar at around 06h00 and 12h00 (New York time). The two sharp exchange rate movements happened when trading algorithms, as a group, aggressively sold dollars and purchased yen; at the other side of these trades were human traders, not other algorithms. Human traders were selling and buying dollars in almost equal amounts. The orders initiated by computers were more correlated than the than those of humans. After 12h00, human traders, in aggregate, began to buy dollars fairly aggressively, and the appreciation of the yen against the dollar was partly reversed.

Flash Crash, May 6, 2010

On May 6, 2010, the US stock market experienced one of its biggest price drops, with the Dow Jones Industrial Average (DJIA) index losing 900 points in a matter of minutes. It was the second largest intraday point swing, 1010.14 points, and the biggest one-day point decline, of 998.5 points. Such a large swing raised concerns about the stability of capital markets, resulting in a US Securities and Exchange Commission (SEC) investigation (US Securities and Exchange Commission and the Commodity Futures Trading Commission 2010). This report claimed that the crash was triggered by a sell algorithm of a large mutual fund executing a US$4.1 billion sell trade in the E-mini S&P 500 futures, and while HFT did not spark the crash, it does appear to have created a "hot potato" effect contributing to the crash. Nanex (2010) reported that quote saturation and NYSE Consolidated Quotation System (CQS) delays, combined with negative news from Greece together with the sale of E-mini S&P 500 futures "was the beginning of the freak sell-off which became known as the Flash Crash". Menkveld and Yueshen (2013) analysed the May 6, 2010, Flash Crash using public and proprietary trade data on E-mini S&P 500 futures and S&P 500 Exchange Traded Fund (ETF) and found that the large mutual fund, whose E-mini trading reportedly contributed to the crash, was relatively inactive during the period of the crash, as its net selling volume was only 4% of the total E-mini net sells.

Sharp price movement was also witnessed in the FX market. Analysing the data from EBS, Bank for International Settlements (2011) showed that algorithmic execution comprised about 53.5% of total activity, versus 46.5% manual, which was higher than on average (45% algorithmic, 55% manual for 2010), suggesting that algorithmic participants did not reduce activity, as was the case for traditional market participants. The price movement is compared against two additional measurements, the ratio of algorithmic investor order submissions on May 6 to average algorithmic investor order submissions for the prior period, and the ratio of manual investor order submissions on May 6 to average manual investor order submissions for the prior period. Both manually and algorithmically submitted orders were in fact much higher than the average of the prior period. The share of algorithmic activity generated by the professional trading community (PTC) as a share of total algorithmic activity was higher than the average, suggesting that the increased contribution of algorithmic participants was driven largely by the increased activity of PTC participants.

March 2011 yen appreciation

Early in the morning of March 17, 2011, in the days following the Fukushima Daiichi earthquake, the USD/JPY declined by 300 pips, from around 79.50 to below 76.50 in just 25 minutes, between 05h55 and 06h20 Tokyo time (16h55–17h20 New York time on March 16, 2011). This price movement was triggered by stop-loss trades of retail FX margin traders (Bank for International Settlements 2011). The margin calls that the retail aggregators executed on behalf of their traders set off a wave of USD selling in a thin market. Many banks withdrew from market making and others widened their spreads so much that their bids were far below the last prevailing market price. This created a positive feedback loop of USD/JPY falling and leading to even more stop-losses until the pair hit 76.25 at around 06h20.

The exchange rate recovered in the next 30 minutes to 78.23 as hedge funds and new retail investors began to build up fresh long positions. Banks, having withdrawn from making prices during the most volatile period, resumed market making. The USD/JPY dropped again at around 07h00, to reach 77.10, coinciding with another round of automated stop-outs, executed this time by the FX margin-trading brokers that participate on a particular trading platform on the Tokyo Futures Exchange. When the system restarted at 06h55, numerous compulsory stop-out orders were generated over five minutes to the six market makers that have obligations to provide prices to this platform (an estimated US$2 billion of USD/JPY selling). During this episode, both high-frequency traders and traditional market makers withdrew from the market.

The episode suggests that, even in trading venues with designated market makers, there is no guarantee of the quality of the quotes, as some market makers with formal obligations to quote prices widened their bid–offer spread considerably during that time.

Central bank interventions

This section discusses the behaviour of high-frequency traders during central banks interventions. We focus on two events: the Bank of Japan (BOJ) intervention on August 4, 2011, following the Fukushima Daiichi earthquake, and the Swiss National Bank (SNB) intervention on September 6, 2011, following a strong appreciation of Swiss franc. As mentioned previously (see page 73), Schmidt (2011) separates traders into manual traders, who use EBS's proprietary GUI access for order management, and automated traders, who use AI for trading (slow AI users, high-frequency traders and ultra-high-frequency (UHF) traders). Two liquidity measures are calculated: the percentage of time that traders of each group provide two-sided liquidity, and bid–offer spread compiled on a one-second grid and averaged over 10-minute time intervals, with USD/JPY, EUR/JPY currency pairs for BOJ intervention, and EUR/CHF, USD/CHF currency pairs for SNB intervention.

The BOJ intervention at 01h00 GMT on August 4, 2011, caused a sharp jump in the USD/JPY exchange rate that did not disrupt the two-sided market. MTs provided liquidity 100% of the entire intervention time, while HF traders and slow AI failed to provide two-sided liquidity only for two seconds and eight seconds, respectively. UHF traders provided only intermittent liquidity during first the 10 minutes after intervention and withdrew from the market for several minutes around 02h40 GMT. The spread was always determined by HFT, while the spread formed by slow AI users after the intervention was wider than that of MT users, implying slow AI may be even more risk averse than MTs.

The SNB intervention on September 6, 2011, lasted for 30 minutes, from 08h00 to 08h30 GMT. Liquidity provided by slow AI users for the USD/CHF exchange rate had notable gaps prior to the SNB intervention. The intervention briefly decreased the percentage of time for which all customer groups quoted two-way prices. HF traders were the quickest, while UHF traders were the slowest in restoring the two-sided market. HF traders were the most active in setting the bid–offer spread during and after the intervention. For the EUR/CHF exchange rate, MTs and HF traders were the best liquidity providers during the SNB intervention. While the SNB intervention affected the EUR/USD exchange rate, its liquidity was not impaired.

These two events suggest that high-frequency traders can be valuable contributors to market liquidity during dramatic price moves of exchange rates, such as during central bank interventions. In other scenarios, HF traders can also destabilise price action, because they may be forced to close out positions all of a sudden, thus triggering an avalanche. In the next section, we shall discuss how organised exchanges can improve price discovery and reduce the likelihood of a "flash crash".

ALTERNATIVE LIMIT ORDER BOOK

Price action in financial markets is at times erratic, because second-by-second transaction volume is a mere trickle, and minor market orders can trigger a price spike that can set off a large price move due to margin calls. Price movements are spurious and respond in a non-linear fashion to imbalances of demand and supply. A temporary reduction in liquidity can easily result in significant price moves, triggering stop losses and cascades of position liquidations. High-frequency traders now account for a large share of total transaction volume; if these traders are taken by surprise and close out their positions in one go, then this can trigger a massive sell-off, akin to the May 6, 2010, Flash Crash.

In response to the Flash Crash and other similar events, regulators have introduced several rules to ensure orderly functioning of capital markets. Market-wide circuit breakers, the so-called "Limit Up–Limit Down", have been put in place in US equity markets, to halt trading in the case of violent price moves (US Securities and Exchange Commission 2012). European regulators went a step further and burdened trading firms that use HFT with several new trading obligations (European Commission 2011). First, high-frequency traders are required to provide two-sided liquidity on a continuous basis, regardless of the prevailing market conditions. Second, all orders submitted by high-frequency traders will be obligated to stay in the order book for at least 500 milliseconds. Orders placed in the order book cannot be cancelled or changed during that predefined time frame. Exchanges cap the number of orders that high-frequency traders can submit or charge them additional costs. The most extreme form of regulation is the so-called Tobin Tax, a small fee on transactions of financial securities. France is the first European country to impose such a transaction tax, which amounts to 0.2%, to be paid on all transactions by companies headquartered in France. Becchetti *et al* (2013) analysed the impact of the introduction of the French Tobin tax on volume, liquidity and volatility of affected stocks and documented that the tax has a significant impact in terms of reduction in transaction volumes and intraday volatility.

High-frequency traders are required to invest in superior technology and sophisticated trading models, risking their own capital, while providing ample liquidity and performing valuable service to market participants. Regulators and operators of organised exchanges have imposed additional costly obligations on high-frequency traders; there has been little discussion on what incentives are necessary to induce liquidity providers to stay in the market during stressful periods. We believe that the limit order queuing mechanism needs to reward competitive two-sided limit orders and give them preferential queuing status over one-sided limit orders.

Therefore, in the rest of this section we propose an order book mechanism that combines price ranking with spread ranking to queue limit orders, which we call spread/price–time priority. We use the agent-based model by Bartolozzi (2010) to analyse the benefits of the aforementioned priority mechanism. The simulations provide evidence that the spread/price–time priority is successful in increasing the overall market quality.

Spread/price–time priority

Most modern trading venues operate under a price–time priority mechanism. Price-time priority determines how limit orders are prioritised for execution. The primary priority is price: the lowest sell limit order (offer) is the first to receive execution against market buy orders, while the highest buy limit order (bid) is the first to receive execution against market sell order. The secondary ranking attribute is the time at which a limit order has been submitted to the order book. We propose an order queuing mechanism based on spread/price–time priority, where the ranking mixes the price ranking and the spread ranking according to a parameter $\alpha \in [0,1]$.

Liquidity providers submit limit orders and those limit orders can be either one sided (ie, a submitted limit order is either a buy or sell limit order) or two sided, in which case the trader simultaneously submits a buy and a sell limit order. The limit order is assigned with a rank, $\text{rank}(\alpha)$.

We propose an alternative set-up. We want to reward market participants, who reveal information not only about the trade that they want to do, but also about the other side of the trade. If a trader wants to sell, we do not rank their order only on the basis of their sale price, but also on the size of the spread: how far away the trader sets the ask. This is valuable information for price discovery; if the spread is narrow, then the market maker has a balanced expectation; if the spread is wide, then their expectation is skewed.

The queuing of limit orders within the order book is done according to a weighted average between a price contribution (weight α) and a spread contribution (weight $1 - \alpha$). In other words, the rank of an limit order equals

$$\text{rank}(\alpha) = \alpha \times \text{price} + (1 - \alpha) \times \text{spread}$$

The buy/sell limit order with lowest rank receives the highest priority for execution against sell/buy market orders. The price rank of limit orders is computed as the price difference from the currently resting limit order with best price. If the price of the newly submitted limit order sets the new best price, then the price rank of limit order will equal zero. Limit orders resting on the same side will update their price rank according to the newly set best price.[6] In other words, price ranking of a submitted limit order equals

$$price = \begin{cases} ask - ask^{best}, & \text{sell limit order} \\ bid^{best} - bid, & \text{buy limit order} \\ 0, & \text{new best buy/sell price} \end{cases}$$

where ask^{best} and bid^{best} are the best selling price and best buying price of resting limit orders. The spread ranking of two-sided limit order is computed as the difference between the price of buy limit order and sell limit order. One-sided limit orders have the same spread ranking as the resting two-sided limit order with worst spread. In other words

$$spread = \begin{cases} ask - bid, & \text{two-sided limit order} \\ spread^{max}, & \text{one-sided limit order} \end{cases}$$

where $spread^{max}$ is the largest spread of currently resting two-sided limit order. Therefore, the spread ranking of one-sided limit orders are "at par" as spread ranking of resting two-sided limit order with worst spread. Finally, if the limit orders have the same rank, rank(α), time priority determines the queuing position. We note that the parameter α is used to "tune" the significance of spread versus price for primary ranking. For instance, decreasing the α parameter puts more weight to ranking based on spread, therefore providing a bigger incentive for traders to submit two-sided limit orders to the order book as these limit orders will have greater priority for execution. On the other hand, increasing the α parameter puts more weight to ranking based on price, therefore providing incentive for traders to submit price competitive limit orders. Note that setting $\alpha = 1$ reduces the limit order queuing mechanism to price–time priority, while setting $\alpha = 0$ reduces the limit order queuing mechanism to spread–time priority, where the price plays no role at all in queueing limit orders. Finally, we note that it is possible for buy and sell limit orders to "cross" or "lock" in price, for parameter α larger than zero.[7]

Agent-based model

We have used the agent-based model by Bartolozzi (2010) to evaluate the impact of spread/price–time priority ranking of limit orders on the market quality. The agent-based model has shown to be able to reproduce several empirical features of the high-frequency dynamics of the market microstructure: negative autocorrelation in returns, clustering of trading activity (volatility, traded volume and bid–ask spread), non-linear response of the price change to the traded volume, as well as average shape of the order book and volume imbalances. We shall briefly present the model; for the details we refer the reader to Bartolozzi (2010).

The market model evolves in discrete time steps, during which agents may undertake a certain action or just wait for a more profitable opportunity, ie, cancellation or active trading, the latter including both limit and market orders. All decision steps are based on dynamical probabilities, which are functions of private and public information. At each step, specifications for each order, such as type (limit or market), price (for limit orders) and volume are decided. The agents have access to the current state of the limit order book: all of the smoothed indicators are derived by this knowledge, such as the exponential midpoint price or volatility, and are classified as public information. Private information is represented by a simple Gaussian process, independent for each trader, with zero mean and standard deviation proportional to the volatility of the market. The limit order is automatically removed if it has not been executed in a certain number of time increments, or according to a strategic decision based on the current market condition, whereas it is more likely to cancel the limit order in a more volatile market. Agents with no orders in the order book evaluate the possibility of entering the market and their decision is based on a stochastic variable that represents the "level of confidence" in their price forecast, ie, market sentiment, which relates the public and the private information. The market sentiment can be thought of as the convolution between the agents, their trading strategies, the private information and the risk factors evaluated via the public information: the stronger the signal, the more likely it is that the trader takes a decision. If the agent enters the market, the type of the order is decided based on its relative position to the best prices: if the resulting submission price is greater than the ask price and the order is long (or lower than the bid price and the trade is short), then this is interpreted as a market order, while all the other orders are considered limit orders.

Our contribution to the agent-based model is the spread/price–time priority ranking of limit orders and the ability of traders to post two-sided limit orders, ie, to be market makers. If the trader decides to post a limit order, they will post a two-sided limit order with probability $p \in [0, 1]$, or they will a post one-sided limit order with probability $1 - p$. In the case when the trader decides to post a two-sided limit order, they will do so by maintaining a spread of at most 10 ticks (in real life, this amounts to a spread of at most 10 pips). Therefore, the agent-based model has two degrees of freedom that are left for user input: the parameter α, determining the primary ranking rank(α) in spread/price–time priority, and parameter p, determining the probability of submitting a two-sided limit order.

Results and conclusion

In this section we present the results of the agent-based model simulations, claiming that spread/price–time priority ranking is suitable for decreasing the market volatility, while not affecting the overall volume (this effect on volume is likely to occur with a brute-force mechanism such as a Tobin tax). Therefore, spread/price–time priority ranking provides benefits to both short- and long-term traders: high-frequency traders would keep their source of revenue from market making, while long-term investors would be able to operate in a stable market environment.

The agent-based model has two degrees of freedom: the parameter $\alpha \in [0, 1]$ determining the primary ranking rank(α), and the parameter $p \in [0, 1]$ determining the probability of submission of two-sided limit orders. Both of these parameters are chosen on a linear grid of nine values, ranging from 0.1 to 0.9. Each simulation has 1,000 iterations and, running it for all pairs of parameters (α, p), we obtained a total of 81 simulation runs. Our primary concern was to analyse if the spread/price–time ranking was successful in decreasing the price volatility while not reducing the overall volume.

We compute price volatility as an average of price volatilities computed at smaller and larger scales. In other words, price volatility σ is an average of the price volatility for 1, 2, 5, 10, 15, 20, 25 and 50 time steps, δt

$$\sigma = \frac{\sigma_{\delta t} + \sigma_{2\delta t} + \sigma_{5\delta t} + \sigma_{10\delta t} + \sigma_{15\delta t} + \sigma_{20\delta t} + \sigma_{25\delta t} + \sigma_{50\delta t}}{8} \quad (4.1)$$

Figure 4.2 (a) Average volatility and (b) average volume of agent-based model for a linear grid of probabilities (p = 10–90%) and parameter α

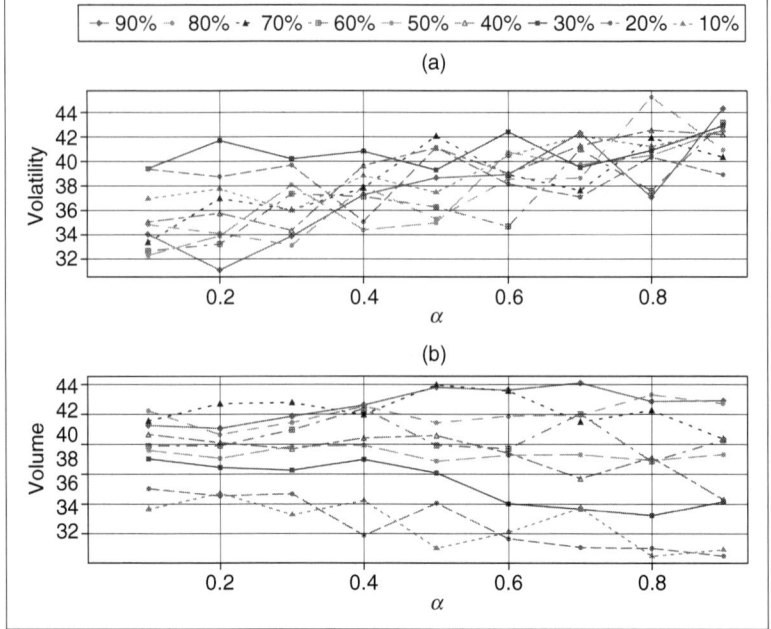

where $\sigma_{n\delta t}$ is the standard deviation of returns computed after $n\delta t$ iterations. In this manner we have included timescales of interest to both high-frequency and low-frequency traders. The total volume is computed as the total turnover in a simulation run.

Figure 4.2 shows the average price volatility and total volume. Part (a) shows the price volatility, while part (b) shows the total volume, both as a function of α determining priority ranking rank(α) and as a function of p determining the probability of submitting a two-sided limit order. Figure 4.2 indicates that decreasing α, ie, putting more weight on the spread, results in lower volatility regardless of the probability p of submitting a two-sided order. Furthermore, it is clear that the total volume is highly dependent on parameter p determining the probability of submitting a two-sided limit order, where the higher probability will result in greater turnover of volume. On the other hand, there does not seem to be an obvious relationship between the resulting volatility and turnover of volume. In summary, the lower volatility obtained with spread/price–time does not necessarily lead to a loss of volume.

CONCLUSION

The foreign exchange market with a daily spot transaction volume of US$1.4 trillion is at the core of the global economy; the foreign exchange market sets the exchange rates between countries and is decisive for the health of the economic system. Today, there is significant evidence that the spuriousness of price action can cause a major price cascade in the foreign exchange markets, akin to the flapping of the wings of a butterfly causing a tornado. These price distortions do not wash out with the other economic uncertainties. A price crash in the foreign exchange market can destabilise the economic system even further. We review clear evidence that high-frequency trading provides liquidity in dramatic events, acknowledging that some trading practices are on the verge of being unethical. To minimise the occurrence of such practices, we have suggested an alternative queuing system for organised exchanges that rewards market makers for revealing private information and providing liquidity on an ongoing basis. The simulations indicate that price quality improves significantly, without the dramatic impact on volume that might well occur with the introduction of Tobin tax. There remain many open questions in the detailed mechanics of how price shocks are propagated. Researchers need access to comprehensive data sets so that they can study in detail the market mechanics and get a deeper understanding of the complex feedback processes. It is necessary to discuss and analyse alternative queuing systems in order to develop market mechanisms that are robust and ensure consistent pricing, independent of random variations of supply and demand. Financial markets are the equivalent of bridges in a transport system; they need to be stable and robust to rapidly changing buy and sell flows to be optimal for the economic system as a whole.

1   One millisecond is one thousandth of a second.

2   The last-look provision is a waiting period of several hundred milliseconds in which the liquidity provider has an option to fill or pass the incoming market order.

3   See http://www.oanda.com.

4   Contract for difference is a financial derivative that allows traders to speculate on price movement of the underlying instrument, without the need for ownership of the instrument.

5   Smaller currency futures markets are present worldwide, including NYSE Euronext, the Tokyo Financial Exchange and the Brazilian Mercantile and Futures Exchange.

6 The updating process will manifest as adding a constant to ranks of all limit orders resting on the same side, ie, $\mathrm{rank}(\alpha)_i = \mathrm{rank}(\alpha)_i + \mathrm{const}$, $i = 1, \ldots, n$, and it will not change the queuing of resting limit orders regardless of the parameter $\alpha \in [0,1]$.

7 Crossed quotes occur in a given security when the best buying price is higher than the best selling price. Locked quotes occur when the best buying price is equal to the best selling price.

REFERENCES

Almgren, R., 2009, "Quantitative Challenges in Algorithmic Execution", Presentation, http://www.finmath.rutgers.edu/seminars/presentations/Robert%20Almgren_37.pdf.

Bank for International Settlements, 2011, "High-Frequency Trading in the Foreign Exchange Market", Report, September.

Becchetti, L., M. Ferrari and U. Trenta, 2013, "The Impact of the French Tobin Tax", CEIS Research Paper 266, March.

Bartolozzi, M., 2010, "A Multi Agent Model for the Limit Order Book Dynamics", *The European Physical Journal B* 78(2), pp. 265–73.

Brogaard, J., 2010, "High Frequency Trading and Its Impact on Market Quality", Technical Report, July.

Cespa, G., and T. Foucault, 2012, "Illiquidity Contagion and Liquidity Crashes", Working Paper, May.

Chaboud, A., E. Hjalmarsson, C. Vega and B. Chiquoine, 2012, "Rise of the Machines: Algorithmic Trading in the Foreign Exchange Market", Technical Report, October.

Cvitanic, J., and A. A. Kirilenko, 2011, "High Frequency Traders and Asset Prices", Technical Report, March.

Dupuis, A., and R. B. Olsen, 2012, "High Frequency Finance: Using Scaling Laws To Build Trading Models", in J. James, I. W. Marsh and L. Sarno (eds), *Handbook of Exchange Rates*. Chichester: Wiley Finance.

European Commission, 2011, Markets in Financial Instrument Directive 2. Technical Report, October.

Gomber, P., B. Arndt, M. Lutat and T. Uhle, 2011, "High-Frequency Trading", Technical Report Commissioned by Deutsche Boerse Groupe.

Hasbrouck, J., and G. Saar, 2012, *Low-Latency Trading*, Johnson School Research Paper Series no. 35-2010, December.

Hendershott, T., and R. Riordan, 2011, "Algorithmic Trading and Information", Technical Report, June.

Hendershott, T., C. M. Jones and A. J. Menkveld, 2011, "Does Algorithmic Trading Improve Liquidity?" *The Journal of Finance* 66(1), pp. 1–33.

Jarrow, R., and P. Protter, 2011, "A Dysfunctional Role of High Frequency Trading in Electronic Markets", Technical Report, Cornell University Working Paper, June.

Johnson, B., 2010, *Algorithmic Trading and DMA: An Introduction to Direct Access Trading Strategies*. London: 4Myeloma Press.

Kirilenko, A. A., A. S. Kyle, M. Samadi and T. Tuzun, 2011, "The Flash Crash: The Impact of High Frequency Trading on an Electronic Market", Technical Report, May.

Masry, S., 2013, "Event Based Microscopic Analysis of the FX Market", PhD Thesis, University of Essex.

Menkveld, A., 2012, "High Frequency Trading and the New-Market Makers", Technical Report, February.

Menkveld, A. J., and B. Z. Yueshen, 2013, "Anatomy of the Flash Crash", SSRN Working Paper, April.

Nanex, 2010, "May 6th 2010 Flash Crash Analysis: Final Conclusion", August, http://www.nanex.net/FlashCrashFinal/FlashCrashAnalysis_Theory.html.

Schmidt, A., 2011, "Ecology of the Modern Institutional Spot FX: The EBS Market in 2011", Technical Report, Electronic Broking Services.

US Securities and Exchange Commission, 2012, "SEC Approves Proposals to Address Extraordinary Volatility in Individual Stocks and Broader Stock Market", Press Release, June.

US Securities and Exchange Commission and the Commodity Futures Trading Commission, 2010, "Finding Regarding the Market Events of May 6", Technical Report, September.

5

Machine Learning for Market Microstructure and High-Frequency Trading

Michael Kearns and Yuriy Nevmyvaka

University of Pennsylvania

In this chapter, we give an overview of the uses of machine learning for high-frequency trading (HFT) and market microstructure data and problems. Machine learning is a vibrant subfield of computer science that draws on models and methods from statistics, algorithms, computational complexity, artificial intelligence, control theory and a variety of other disciplines. Its primary focus is on computationally and informationally efficient algorithms for inferring good predictive models from large data sets, and thus it is a natural candidate for application to problems arising in HFT, for both trade execution and the generation of Alpha.

The inference of predictive models from historical data is obviously not new in quantitative finance; ubiquitous examples include coefficient estimation for the capital asset pricing model (CAPM), Fama and French factors (Fama and French 1993) and related approaches. The special challenges for machine learning presented by HFT generally arise from the very fine granularity of the data – often microstructure data at the resolution of individual orders, (partial) executions, hidden liquidity and cancellations – and a lack of understanding of how such low-level data relates to actionable circumstances (such as profitably buying or selling shares or optimally executing a large order). Whereas models such as CAPM and its variants already prescribe what the relevant variables or "features" (in the language of machine learning) are for prediction or modelling (excess returns, book-to-market ratios, etc), in many HFT problems we may have no prior intuition about how, if at all, the distribution of liquidity in the order book (say) relates to future price movements. Thus, feature selection or feature engineering becomes an important process in machine learning for HFT, and is one of our central themes.

Since HFT itself is a relatively recent phenomenon, there are few published works on the application of machine learning to HFT. For this reason, we structure this chapter around a few case studies from our own work (Ganchev *et al* 2010; Nevmyvaka *et al* 2006). In each case study, we focus on a specific trading problem we would like to solve or optimise, the (microstructure) data from which we hope to solve this problem, the variables or features derived from the data as inputs to a machine learning process and the machine learning algorithm applied to these features. The cases studies we shall examine are the following.

- **Optimised trade execution via reinforcement learning (Nev-myvaka *et al* 2006).** We investigate the problem of buying (respectively, selling) a specified volume of shares in a specified amount of time, with the goal of minimising the expenditure (respectively, maximising the revenue). We apply a well-studied machine learning method known as "reinforcement learning" (Sutton and Barto 1998), which has its roots in control theory. Reinforcement learning applies state-based models that attempt to specify the optimal action to take from a given state according to a discounted future reward criterion. Thus, the models must balance the short-term rewards of actions against the influences these actions have on future states. In our application, the states describe properties of the limit order book and recent activity for a given security (such as the bid–ask spread, volume imbalances between the buy and sell sides of the book and the current costs of crossing the spread to buy or sell shares). The actions available from each state specify whether to place more aggressive marketable orders that cross the spread or more passive limit orders that lie in the order book.

- **Predicting price movement from order book state.** This case study examines the application of machine learning to the problem of predicting directional price movements, again from limit order data for equities. Using similar but additional state features as in the reinforcement learning investigation, we seek models that can predict relatively near-term price movements (as measured by the bid–ask midpoint) from market microstructure signals. Again, the primary challenge is in the engineering or development of these signals. We show that such prediction is indeed modestly possible, but it should be treated with caution, since the midpoint is a fictitious, idealised price, and, once we account for trading costs (spread-crossing), profitability is more elusive.

- **Optimised execution in dark pools via censored exploration (Ganchev *et al* 2010).** We study the application of machine learning to the problem of smart order routing across multiple dark pools, in an effort to maximise fill rates. As in the first case study, we are exogenously given the number of shares to execute, but, unlike the first case, where the order was split across time, here we must split it across venues. The basic challenge is that, for a given security at a given time, different dark pools may have different available volumes, thus necessitating an adaptive algorithm that can divide a large order up across multiple pools to maximise the volume executed. We develop a model that permits a different distribution of liquidity for each venue, and a learning algorithm that estimates this model in service of maximising the fraction of filled volume per step. A key limitation of dark pool microstructure data is the presence of censoring: if we place an order to buy (say) 1,000 shares, and 500 are filled, we are certain only 500 were available; but if all 1,000 shares are filled, it is possible that more shares were available for trading. Our machine learning approach to this problem adapts a classical method from statistics, known as the Kaplan–Meier estimator, in combination with a greedy optimisation algorithm.

Related work

While methods and models from machine learning are used in practice ubiquitously for trading problems, such efforts are typically proprietary and there is little published empirical work. But the case studies we examine do have a number of theoretical counterparts that we now summarise.

Algorithmic approaches to execution problems are fairly well studied, and often apply methods from the stochastic control literature (Bertsimas and Lo 1998; Bouchaud *et al* 2002; Cont and Kukanov 2013; Guéant *et al* 2012; Kharroubi and Pham 2010). The aforementioned papers seek to solve problems similar to ours, ie, to execute a certain number of shares over some fixed period as cheaply as possible, but approach it from another direction. They typically start with an assumption that the underlying "true" stock price is generated by some known stochastic process. There is also a known impact function that specifies how arriving liquidity demand pushes market prices away from this true value. Having this information, as well as time and volume constraints, it is then possible to compute the optimal strategy explicitly. This can be done either in closed form or numerically (often using dynamic programming, the basis of reinforcement learning). There are also interesting game-theoretic variants of execution problems in the presence of an arbitrageur (Moallemi *et al* 2012), and examinations of the tension between exploration and exploitation (Park and van Roy 2012).

There is a similar theoretical dark pool literature. Laruelle *et al* (2011) starts with the mathematical solution to the optimal allocation problem, and trading data comes in much later for calibration purposes. There are also several extensions of our own dark pool work (Ganchev *et al* 2010). In Agarwal *et al* (2010), our framework is expanded to handle adversarial (ie, not independent and identically distributed) scenarios. Several brokerage houses have implemented our basic algorithm and improved upon it. For instance, JP Morgan (2012) adds time to execution as a feature and updates historical distributions more aggressively, and Maglaras *et al* (2012) aims to solve essentially the same allocation/order routing problem but for lit exchanges.

HIGH-FREQUENCY DATA FOR MACHINE LEARNING

The definition of high-frequency trading remains subjective, without widespread consensus on the basic properties of the activities it encompasses, including holding periods, order types (eg, passive versus aggressive) and strategies (momentum or reversion, directional or liquidity provision, etc). However, most of the more technical treatments of HFT seem to agree that the data driving HFT activity tends to be the most granular available. Typically this would be microstructure data that details every order placed, every execution and every cancellation, directly from the exchanges, and that thus permits the faithful reconstruction (at least for equities) of the full limit order book, both historically and in real time.[1] Since such data is typically among the raw inputs to an HFT system or strategy, it is thus possible to have a sensible discussion of machine learning applied to HFT without committing to an overly precise definition of the latter; we can focus on the microstructure data and its uses in machine learning.

Two of the greatest challenges posed by microstructure data are its scale and interpretation. Regarding scale, a single day's worth of microstructure data on a highly liquid stock such as AAPL is measured in gigabytes. Storing this data historically for any meaningful period and number of names requires both compression and significant disk usage; even then, processing this data efficiently generally requires streaming through the data by only uncompressing small amounts at a time. But these are mere technological challenges; the challenge of interpretation is the most significant. What systematic signal or information, if any, is contained in microstructure data? In the language of machine learning, what "features" or variables can we extract from this extremely granular, lower-level data that would be useful in building predictive models for the trading problem at hand?

This question is not specific to machine learning for HFT, but seems especially urgent there. Compared with more traditional, long-standing sources of lower-frequency market and non-market data, the meaning of microstructure data seems relatively opaque. Daily opening and closing prices generally aggregate market activity and integrate information across many participants; a missed earnings target or an analyst's upgrade provide relatively clear signals about the performance of a particular stock or the opinion of a particular individual. What interpretation can be given for a single order placement in a massive stream of microstructure data, or to a snapshot of an intraday order book, especially considering the fact that any outstanding order can be cancelled by the submitting party any time prior to execution?[2]

To offer an analogy, consider the now common application of machine learning to problems in natural language processing (NLP) and computer vision. Both of them remain very challenging domains. But, in NLP, it is at least clear that the basic unit of meaning in the data is the word, which is how digital documents are represented and processed. In contrast, digital images are represented at the pixel level, but this is certainly not the meaningful unit of information in vision applications – objects are – but algorithmically extracting objects from images remains a difficult problem. In microstructure data, the unit of meaning or actionable information is even more difficult to identify, and is probably noisier than in other machine learning domains. As we proceed through our case studies, proposals will be examined for useful features extracted from microstructure data, but we emphasise that these are just proposals, almost certainly subject to improvement and replacement as the field matures.

REINFORCEMENT LEARNING FOR OPTIMISED TRADE EXECUTION

Our first case study examines the use of machine learning in perhaps the most fundamental microstructure-based algorithmic trading problem, that of optimised execution. In its simplest form, the problem is defined by a particular stock, say AAPL, a share volume V and a time horizon or number of trading steps T.[3] Our goal is to buy[4] exactly V shares of the stock in question within T steps, while minimising our expenditure (share prices) for doing so. We view this problem from a purely agency or brokerage perspective: a client has requested that we buy these shares on their behalf, and stated the time period in which we must do so, and we would like to obtain the best possible prices within these constraints. Any subsequent risk in holding the resulting position of V shares is borne by the client.

Perhaps the first observation to make about this optimised trading problem is that any sensible approach to it will be state-based, that is, will make trading and order placement decisions that are conditioned on some appropriate notion of "state". The most basic representation of state would simply be pairs of numbers (v, t), indicating both the volume $v \leqslant V$ remaining to buy and the number of steps $t \leqslant T$ remaining to do so. To see how such a state representation might be useful in the context of microstructure data and order book reconstruction, if we are in a state where v is small and t is large (thus we have bought most of our target volume, but have most of our time remaining), we might choose to place limit orders deep in the buy book in the hope of obtaining lower prices for our remaining shares. In contrast, if v is large and t is small, we are running out of time and have most of our target volume still to buy, so we should perhaps start crossing the spread and demanding immediate liquidity to meet our target, at the expense of higher expenditures. Intermediate states might dictate intermediate courses of action.

While it seems hard to imagine designing a good algorithm for the problem without making use of this basic (v, t) state information, we shall see that there are many other variables we might profitably add to the state. Furthermore, mere choice of the state space does not specify the details of how we should act or trade in each state, and there are various ways we could go about doing so. One traditional approach would be to design a policy mapping states to trading actions "by hand". For instance, basic VWAP algorithms[5] might compare their current state (v, t) to a schedule of how much volume they "should" have traded by step t according to historical volume profiles for the stock in question, calibrated by the time of day and perhaps other seasonalities. If v is such that we are "behind schedule", we would trade more aggressively, crossing the spread more often, etc; if we are "ahead of schedule", we would trade more passively, sitting deeper in the book and hoping for price improvements. Such comparisons would be made continuously or periodically, thus adjusting our behaviour dynamically according to the historical schedule and currently prevailing trading conditions. In contrast to this hand-designed approach, here we shall focus on an entirely learning-based approach to developing VWAP-style execution algorithms, where we shall learn a state-conditioned trading policy from historical data.

Reinforcement learning (RL), which has its roots in the older field of control theory, is a branch of machine learning designed explicitly for learning such dynamic state-based policies from data (Sutton and Barto 1998). While the technical details are beyond our scope, the primary elements of an RL application are as follows.

- The identification of a state space, whose elements represent the variable conditions under which we shall choose actions. In our case, we shall consider state spaces that include (v, t)

as well as additional components or features capturing order book state.

- The identification of a set of available actions from each state. In our application, the actions will consist of placing a limit order for all of our remaining volume at some varying price. Thus, we shall only have a single outstanding order at any moment, but will reposition that order in response to the current state.

- The identification of a model of the impact or influence our actions have, in the form of execution probabilities under states, learned from historical data.

- The identification of a reward or cost function indicating the expected or average payout (which may be negative) for taking a given action from a given state. In our application, the cost for placing a limit order from a given state will be any eventual expenditures from the (partial) execution of the order.

- Algorithms for learning an optimal policy, ie, a mapping from states to actions, that minimises the empirical cost (expenditures for purchasing the shares) on training data.

- Validation of the learned policy on test data by estimating its out-of-sample performance (expenditures).

Note that a key difference between the RL framework and more traditional predictive learning problems such as regression is that in RL we learn directly how to act in the environment represented by the state space, not simply predict target values.

We applied the RL methodology to the problem of optimised trade execution (using the choices for states, actions, impact and rewards indicated above) to microstructure data for several liquid stocks. Full historical order book reconstruction was performed, with the book simulation used both for computing expenditures in response to order executions, and for computing various order book features that we added to the basic (v, t) state, discussed below.

As a benchmark for evaluating our performance, we compare resulting policies to one-shot submission strategies and demonstrate the benefits of a more dynamic, multi-period, state-based learning approach.[6] One-shot strategies place a single limit order at some price p for the entire target volume V at the beginning of the trading period, and leave it there without modification for all T steps. At the end of the trading period, if there is any remaining volume v, a market order for the remaining shares is placed in order to reach the target of V shares purchased. Thus, if we choose the buying price p to be very low, putting an order deep in the buy book, we are effectively committing ourselves to a market order at the end of the trading period, since none of our order volume will be executed. If we choose p to be very high, we cross the spread immediately and effectively have a market order at the beginning of the trading period. Intermediate choices for p seek a balance between these two extremes, with perhaps some of our order being executed at improved prices and the remaining liquidated as a market order at the end of trading. One-shot strategies can thus encompass a range of passive and aggressive order placements, but, unlike the RL approach, do not condition their behaviour on any notion of state. In the following experiments, we describe the profitability of the policies learned by RL to the optimal (expenditure minimising) one-shot strategy on the training data; we then report the test set performance for both approaches.

The potential promise of the learning approach is demonstrated by Figure 5.1. In this figure, we compare the test set performance of the optimal one-shot strategy with the policies learned by RL. To normalise price differences across stocks, we measure performance by implementation shortfall, namely, how much the average share price paid is greater than the midpoint of the spread at the beginning of the trading period; thus, lower values are better. In the figure, we consider several values of the target volume and the period over which trading takes place, as well as both a coarser and a finer choice for how many discrete values we divide these quantities into in our state-space representation (v, t). In every case we see that the performance of the RL policies is significantly better than the optimal one-shot. We sensibly see that trading costs are higher overall for the higher target volumes and shorter trading periods. We also see that finer-grained discretisation improves RL performance, an indicator that we have enough data to avoid overfitting from fragmenting our data across too large a state space.

Aside from the promising performance of the RL approach, it is instructive to visualise the details of the actual policies learned, and is possible to do so in such a small, two-dimensional state representation. Figure 5.2 shows examples of learned policies, where on the

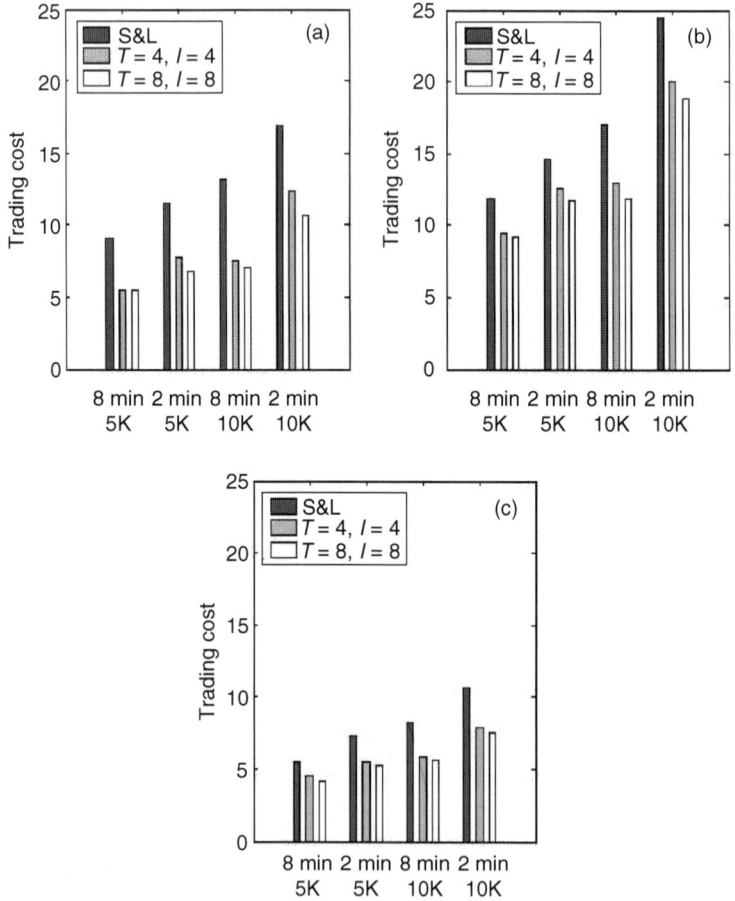

Figure 5.1 Test set performance for optimal one-shot (black bars, leftmost of each triple) and RL policies (grey and white bars, middle and rightmost of each triple) on stocks (a) AMZN, (b) NVDA and (c) QCOM, as measured by implementation shortfall (trading costs)

The x-axis labels indicate the target volume to buy and the trading period, while the legends indicate the resolution of discretisation in the RL state space for v (target volume divided into I levels, from lowest to highest) and t (trading divided into T discrete steps, equally spaced throughout the trading period).

x- and y-axes we indicate the state (v, t) discretised into eight levels each for both the number of trading steps remaining and the inventory (number of shares) left to purchase, and on the z-axis we plot the action learned by RL training relative to the top of the buy book (ask). Thus, action Δ corresponds to positioning our buy order for

Figure 5.2 Sample policies learned by RL

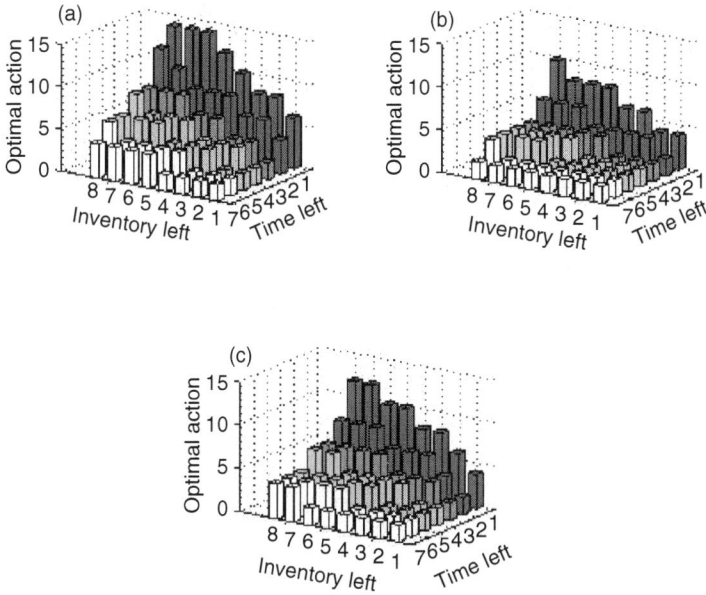

The state (v, t) is indicated on the x- and y-axes as discrete levels of inventory remaining v and number of trading steps or time remaining t. Actions indicate how far into or across the spread to reposition the order for the remaining volume. Smaller x and y indices indicate lower values for the features. (a) AMZN; (b) NVDA; (c) QCOM.

the remaining shares at the bid plus Δ. Negative Δ are orders placed down in the buy book, while positive Δ enters or crosses the spread.

The learned policies are broadly quite sensible in the manner discussed earlier: when inventory is high and time is running out, we cross the spread more aggressively; when inventory is low and most of our time remains, we seek price improvement. But the numerical details of this broad landscape vary from stock to stock, and in our view this is the real value of machine learning in microstructure applications: not in discovering "surprising" strategies per se, but in using large amounts of data to optimise, on a per-stock basis, the fine-grained details of improved performance, in this case for execution. We also note that all of the learned policies choose to enter or cross the spread in all states (positive Δ), but this is likely to be an artefact of the relatively large target volumes and short trading periods we have chosen for such high-liquidity stocks; for smaller

101

volumes, longer periods and lower liquidity, we should expect to see some states in which we place limit orders that sit far down in the order book.

So far we have made minimal use of microstructure information and order book reconstruction, which has been limited to determining execution prices and order book evolution. But the opportunity and challenge of machine learning typically involves the search for improved features or state variables that allow the learned policy to condition on more information and thus improve performance. What are natural order book-based state variables we might add to (v, t) in this quest? While the possibilities are manyfold, here we list some plausible choices for features that might be relevant to the optimised execution problem.

- **Bid–ask spread:** a positive value indicating the current difference between the bid and ask prices in the current order books.

- **Bid–ask volume imbalance:** a signed quantity indicating the number of shares at the bid minus the number of shares at the ask in the current order books.

- **Signed transaction volume:** a signed quantity indicating the number of shares bought in the last 15 seconds minus the number of shares sold in the last 15 seconds.

- **Immediate market order cost:** the cost we would pay for purchasing our remaining shares immediately with a market order.

All of the features above were normalised in a standard fashion by subtracting their means, dividing by their standard deviations and time-averaging over a recent interval. In order to obtain a finite state space, features were discretised into bins in multiples of standard deviation units. Experiments can also be performed using continuous features and a parametric model representation, but are beyond the scope of this chapter.

Along with our original state variables (v, t), the features above provide a rich language for dynamically conditioning our order placement on potentially relevant properties of the order book. For instance, for our problem of minimising our expenditure for purchasing shares, perhaps a small spread combined with a strongly

Table 5.1 Reduction in implementation shortfall obtained by adding features to (v, t)

Feature(s) added	Reduction in trading cost (%)
Bid–ask spread	7.97
Bid–ask volume imbalance	0.13
Signed transaction volume	2.81
Immediate market order revenue	4.26
Spread + signed volume + immediate cost	12.85

negative signed transaction volume would indicate selling pressure (sellers crossing the spread and buyer filling in the resulting gaps with fresh orders). In such a state, depending on our inventory and time remaining, we might wish to be more passive in our order placement, sitting deeper in the buy book in the hopes of price improvements.

We ran a series of similar train-test experiments using the RL methodology on our original state (v, t), augmented with various subsets of the order book features described above. The results are summarised in Table 5.1, which shows, for each of the features described above, the percentage reduction in trading cost (implementation shortfall) obtained by adding that feature to our original (v, t) state space. Three of the four features yield significant improvements, with only bid–ask volume imbalance not seeming especially useful. The final row of the table shows the percentage improvement obtained by adding all three of these informative features, which together improve the (v, t) state by almost 13%.[7]

It is again informative to examine not only performance, but also what has been learned. This is clearly more difficult to visualise and summarise in a five-dimensional state space, but we can get some intuition by projecting the policies learned onto subsets of two features. Like Figure 5.2, Figure 5.3 shows a visualisation plotting a pair of feature values, discretised into a small number of levels, against the action learned for that pair of values, except now we are averaging across the other three features. Despite this projection or averaging, we can still see that sensible, intuitive policies are being learned. For instance, we see that we place more aggressive (spread-crossing) actions whenever the spread is large or the immediate cost of purchasing our remaining shares is low. In the first case, larger

Figure 5.3 Sample policies learned by RL for five-feature state space consisting of (v, t) and three additional order book features, projected onto the features of spread size and immediate cost to purchase remaining shares

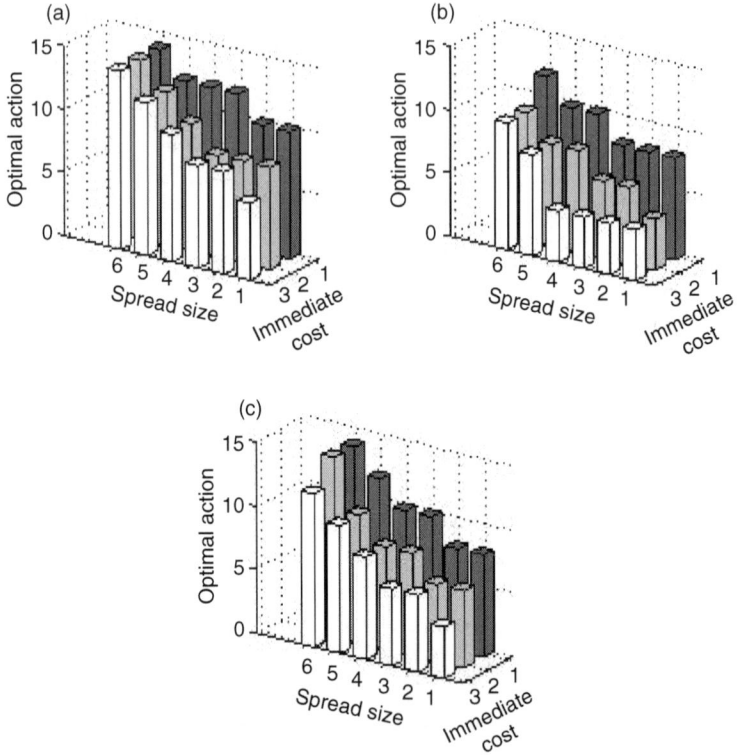

Smaller x and y indices indicate lower values for the features. (a) AMZN; (b) NVDA; (c) QCOM.

spreads simply force us to be more aggressive to initiate executions; in the second, a bargain is available. When both conditions hold simultaneously, we bid most aggressively of all.

PREDICTING PRICE MOVEMENT FROM ORDER BOOK STATE

The case study in the previous section demonstrated the potential of machine learning approaches to problems of pure execution: we considered a highly constrained and stylised problem of reducing trading costs (in this case, as measured by implementation shortfall), and showed that machine learning methodology could provide important tools for such efforts.

It is of course natural to ask whether similar methodology can be fruitfully applied to the problem of generating profitable state-based models for trading using microstructure features. In other words, rather than seeking to reduce costs for executing a given trade, we would like to learn models that themselves profitably decide when to trade (that is, under what conditions in a given state space) and how to trade (that is, in which direction and with what orders), for Alpha generation purposes. Conceptually (only), we can divide this effort into two components.

1. The development of features that permit the reliable prediction of directional price movements from certain states. By "reliable" we do not mean high accuracy, but just enough that our profitable trades outweigh our unprofitable ones.

2. The development of learning algorithms for execution that capture this predictability or Alpha at sufficiently low trading costs.

In other words, in contrast to the previous section, we must first find profitable predictive signals, and then hope they are not erased by trading costs. As we shall see, the former goal is relatively attainable, while the latter is relatively difficult.

It is worth noting that for optimised execution in the previous section, we did not consider many features that directly captured recent directional movements in execution prices; this is because the problem considered there exogenously imposed a trading need, and specified the direction and volume, so momentum signals were less important than those capturing potential trading costs. For Alpha generation, however, directional movement may be considerably more important. We thus conducted experiments employing the following features.

- **Bid–ask spread:** similar to that used in the previous section.
- **Price:** a feature measuring the recent directional movement of executed prices.
- **Smart price:** a variation on mid-price, where the average of the bid and ask prices is weighted according to the inverse of their volume.

- **Trade sign:** a feature measuring whether buyers or sellers crossed the spread more frequently in recent executions.

- **Bid–ask volume imbalance:** similar to that used in the previous section.

- **Signed transaction volume:** similar to that used in the previous section.

We have thus preserved (variants of) most of the features from our optimised execution study, and added features that capture directional movement of both executed prices, buying/selling pressure and bid–ask midpoint movement. As before, all features are normalised in a standard way by subtracting the historical mean value and expressing the value in units of historical standard deviations.

In order to effect the aforementioned separation between predicting directional movement, and capturing such movements in a cost-efficient way, in our first study we make deliberately optimistic execution assumptions that isolate the potential promise of machine learning. More specifically, we consider just two idealised classes of actions available to the learning algorithm: buying one share at the bid–ask midpoint and holding the position for t seconds, at which point we sell the position, again at the midpoint; and the opposite action, where we sell at the midpoint and buy t seconds later. In the first set of experiments, we considered a short period of $t = 10$ seconds. It is important to note that under the assumption of midpoint executions, one of the two actions is always profitable: buying and selling after t seconds if the midpoint increased, and the reverse action if it decreased. This will no longer hold when we consider more realistic execution assumptions.

The methodology can now be summarised as follows.

1. Order book reconstruction on historical data was performed for each of 19 names.[8]

2. At each trading opportunity, the current state (the value of the six microstructure features described above) was computed, and the profit or loss of both actions (buy then sell, sell then buy) was tabulated via order book simulation to compute the midpoint movement.

3. Learning was performed for each name using all of 2008 as the training data. For each state x in the state space, the cumulative

Figure 5.4 Correlations between feature values and learned policies

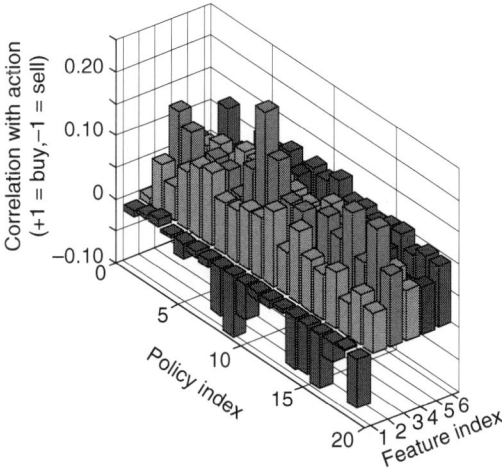

For each of the six features and nineteen policies, we project the policy onto just the single feature compute the correlation between the feature value and action learned (+1 for buying, −1 for selling). Feature indexes are in the order bid–ask spread, price, smart price, trade sign, bid–ask volume imbalance, signed transaction volume.

payout for both actions across all visits to x in the training period was computed. Learning then resulted in a policy, π, mapping states to action, where $\pi(x)$ is defined to be whichever action yielded the greatest training set profitability in state x.

4. Testing of the learned policy for each name was performed using all 2009 data. For each test set visit to state x, we took the action $\pi(x)$ prescribed by the learned policy, and computed the overall 2009 profitability of this policy.

Perhaps the two most important findings of this study are that learning consistently produces policies that are profitable on the test set, and that (as in the optimised execution study), those policies are broadly similar across stocks. Regarding the first finding, for all 19 names the test set profitability of learning was positive. Regarding the second finding, while visualisation of the learned policies over a six-dimensional state space is not feasible, we can project the policies onto each individual feature and ask what the relationship is between the feature and the action learned. In Figure 5.4, for each

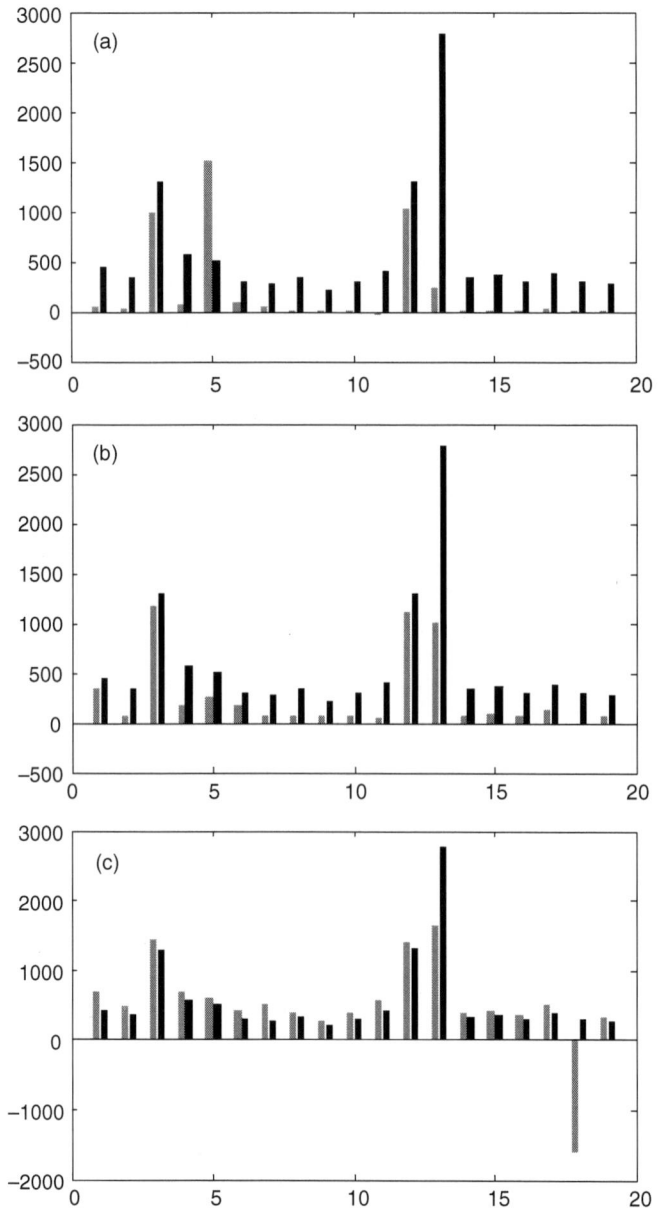

Figure 5.5 Comparison of test set profitability across 19 names for learning with all six features (black bars, identical in each subplot) versus learning with only a single feature (grey bars).

(a) Spread versus all. (b) Price versus all. (c) Smartprice versus all.

Figure 5.5 Continued.

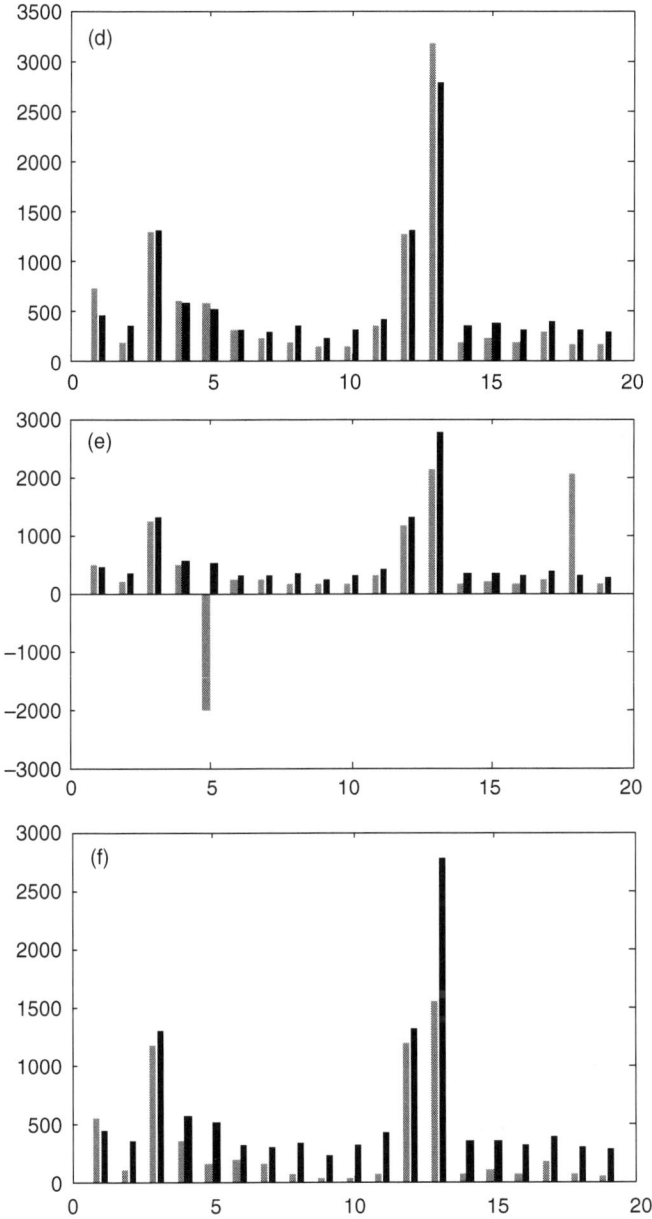

(d) Sign versus all. (e) Imbalance versus all. (f) Volume versus all.

of the 19 policies and each of the six state features, we plot a bar showing the correlation between the value of the feature and the action learned, where by convention we assign a value of $+1$ to buying then selling, and -1 to selling then buying. For virtually every feature, we see that the sign of the correlation is the same across all policies. As in the optimised execution study, however, the numerical values of the correlations vary significantly across names. This again speaks to the strengths of a learning approach: the policies are all "sensible" and qualitatively similar, but the learning performs significant quantitative optimisation on a name-specific basis.

What have these consistent policies learned? Figure 5.4 reveals that, broadly speaking, we have learned momentum-based strategies: for instance, for each of the four features that contain directional information (price, smart price, trade sign, bid–ask volume imbalance and signed transaction volume), higher values of the feature (which all indicate rising execution prices, rising midpoints or buying pressure in the form of spread-crossing) are accompanied by greater frequency of buying in the learned policies. We should emphasise, however, that projecting the policies onto single features does not do justice to the subtleties of learning regarding interactions between the features. As just one simple example, if instead of conditioning on a single directional feature having a high value, we condition on several of them having high values, the correlation with buying becomes considerably stronger than for any isolated feature.

As we did for optimised execution, it is also instructive to examine which features are more or less informative or predictive of profitability. In Figure 5.5 there is a subplot for each of the six features. The black bars are identical in all six subplots, and show the test set profitability of the policies learned for each of the 19 names when all six features are used. The grey bars in each subplot show the test set profitability for each of the 19 names when only the corresponding single feature is used. General observations include the following.

- Profitability is usually better using all six features than any single feature.

- Smart price appears to be the best single feature, and often is slightly better than using all features together, a sign of mild

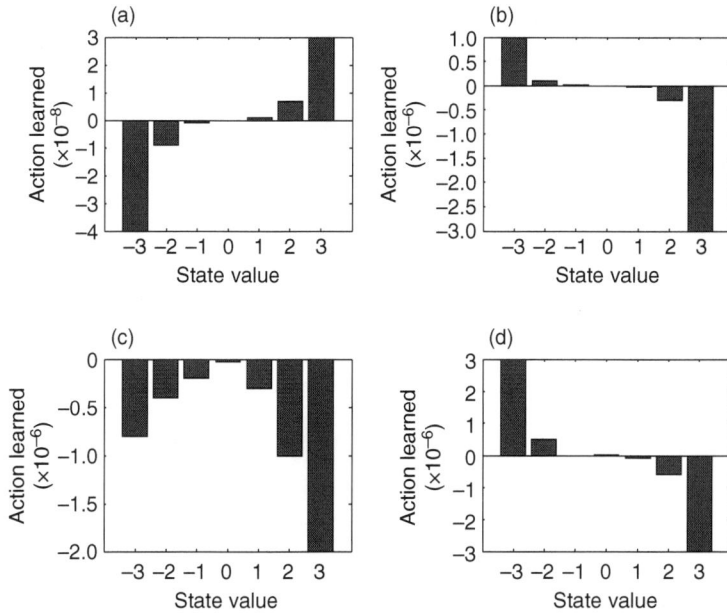

Figure 5.6 Learned policies depend strongly on timescale

For learning with a single feature measuring the recent directional price move, we show the test set profitability of buying in each possible state for varying holding periods. (a) Short term: momentum. (b) Medium term: reversion. (c) Long term: directional drift. (d) Long term, corrected: reversion.

overfitting in training. However, for one stock using all features is considerably better, and for another doing so avoids a significant loss from using smart price only.

- Spread appears to be the less useful single feature, but does enjoy significant solo profitability on a handful of names.

While we see a consistent momentum relationship between features and actions across names, the picture changes when we explore different holding periods. Figure 5.6 illustrates how learning discovers different models depending on the holding period. We have selected a single "well-behaved" stock (DELL)[9] and plot the value of training set profits or losses of a buy order in each possible state of a single-feature state space representing recent price changes.[10] Note that, since executions take place at the midpoints, the values for selling are exactly opposite those shown. We show the values for several different holding periods.

Over very short holding periods (Figure 5.6(a)), we see fairly consistent momentum behaviour: for time periods of milliseconds to seconds, price moves tend to continue. At these time scales, buying is (most) profitable when the recent price movements have been (strongly) upwards, and unprofitable when the price has been falling. This echoes the consistency of learned multi-feature momentum strategies described above, which were all at short holding periods. Features that capture directional moves are positively correlated with future returns: increasing prices, preponderance of buy trades and higher volumes in the buy book all forecast higher returns in the immediate future.

We see a different pattern, however, when examining longer holding periods (dozens of seconds to several minutes). At those horizons (Figure 5.6(b)), our learner discovers reversion strategies: buying is now profitable under recent downward price movements, and selling is profitable after upward price movements. Again, these results are broadly consistent across names and related features.

A desirable property of a "good fit" in statistical learning is to have models with features that partition the variable that they aim to predict into distinct categories. Our short-term momentum and longer-term reversion strategies exhibit such behaviour: in the momentum setting, the highest values of past returns predict the highest future returns, and the most negative past returns imply the most negative subsequent realizations (and vice versa for reversion). Furthermore, this relationship is monotonic, with past returns near zero corresponding to near-zero future returns: in parts (a) and (b) of Figure 5.6 the outermost bars show the largest values. We lose this desirable monotonicity, however, when extending our holding period even further: in the range of 30 minutes to several hours, conditioning on any of our chosen variables no longer separates future positive and negative returns. Instead, we end up just capturing the overall price movement or directional drift; as demonstrated in Figure 5.6(c), the expected value of a buy action has the same (negative) sign across all states, and is distributed more uniformly, being roughly equal to the (negative) price change over the entire training period (divided by the number of training episodes). Thus, since the price went down over the course of the training period, we simply learn to sell in every state, which defeats the purpose of learning a dynamic state-dependent strategy.

The discussion so far highlights the two aspects that must be considered when applying machine learning to high-frequency data: the nature of the underlying price formation process, and the role and limitations of the learning algorithm itself. In the first category, a clean picture of market mechanics emerges: when we look at price evolution over milliseconds to seconds, we are likely to witness large marketable orders interacting with the order book, creating directional pressure. Over several minutes, we see the flip side of this process: when liquidity demanders push prices too far from their equilibrium state, reversion follows. On even longer time scales, our microstructure-based variables are less informative, apparently losing their explanatory power.

On the one hand, it may be tempting to simply conclude that for longer horizons microstructure features are immaterial to the price formation process. On the other hand, longer holding periods are of a particular interest to us. As we have pointed out in our HFT profitability study (Kulesza *et al* 2010), there is a tension between shorter holding periods and the ability to overcome trading costs (specifically, the bid–ask spread). While the direction of price moves is easiest to forecast over the very short intervals, the magnitude of these predictions, and thus the margin that allows trading costs to be covered, grows with holding periods (notice that the scale of the y-axis, which measures profitability, is 100 times larger in Figure 5.6(b) than in Figure 5.6(a)). Ideally, we would like to find some compromise horizon, which is long enough to allow prices to evolve sufficiently in order to beat the spread, but short enough for microstructure features to be informative of directional movements.

In order to reduce the influence of any long-term directional price drift, we can adjust the learning algorithm to account for it. Instead of evaluating the total profit per share or return from a buy action in a given state, we monitor the relative profitability of buying in that state versus buying in every possible state. For example, suppose a buy action in some state x yields 0.03¢ per trade on average; while that number is positive, suppose always buying (that is, in every state) generates 0.07¢ per trade on average (presumably because the price went up over the course of the entire period), therefore making state s relatively less advantageous for buying. We would then assign $-0.04 = 0.03 - 0.07$ as the value of buying in that state. Conversely, there may be a state–action pair that has negative payout associated with it over the training period, but if this action is even more unprofitable when averaged across all states (again, presumably due to a long-term price drift), this state–action pair is be assigned a positive value. Conceptually, such adjustment for average value allows us to filter out the price trend and home in on microstructure aspects, which also makes learned policies perform more robustly out-of-sample. Empirically, resulting learned policies recover the desired symmetry, where if one extremal state learns to buy, the opposite extremal state learns to sell: notice the transformation from Figure 5.6(c) to Figure 5.6(d), where we once again witness mean reversion.

While we clearly see patterns in the short-term price formation process and are demonstratively successful in identifying state variables that help predict future returns, profiting from this predictability is far from trivial. It should be clear from the figures in this section that the magnitude of our predictions is in fractions of a cent, whereas the tightest spread in liquid US stocks is 1¢. So the results should in no way be interpreted as a recipe for profitability: even if all the features we enumerate here are true predictors of future returns, and even if all of them line up just right for maximum profit margins, we still cannot justify trading aggressively and paying the bid–ask spread, since the magnitude of predictability is not sufficient to cover transaction costs.[11]

So what can be done? We see essentially three possibilities. First, as we have suggested earlier, we could hold our positions longer, so that price changes are larger than spreads, giving us higher margins. However, as we have seen, the longer the holding period, the less directly informative market microstructure aspects seem to become, making prediction more difficult. Second, we could trade with limit orders, hoping to avoid paying the spread. This is definitely a fruitful direction, where we can jointly estimate future returns and the probability of getting filled, which then must be weighed against adverse selection (probability of executing only when predictions turn out to be wrong). This is a much harder problem, well outside of the scope of this chapter. And finally, a third option is to find or design better features that will bring about greater predictability, sufficient to overcome transaction costs.

It should be clear by now that the overarching theme of these suggested directions is that the machine learning approach does not offer any easy paths to profitability. Markets are competitive, and finding sources of true profitability is extremely difficult. That being said, what we have covered in this section is a framework for how to look for sources of potential profits in a principled way (by defining state spaces, examining potential features and their interplay, using training-test set methodology, imposing sensible value functions, etc) that should be a part of the arsenal of a quantitative professional, so that we can at least discuss these problems in a common language.

MACHINE LEARNING FOR SMART ORDER ROUTING IN DARK POOLS

The studies we have examined so far apply machine learning to trading problems arising in relatively long-standing exchanges (the open limit order book instantiation of a continuous double auction), where microstructure data has been available for some time. Furthermore, this data is rich, showing the orders and executions for essentially all market participants, comprising multiple order types, etc, and is also extremely voluminous. In this sense these exchanges and data are ideal test beds for machine learning for trading, since (as we have seen) they permit the creation of rich feature spaces for state-based learning approaches.

But machine learning methodology is also applicable to emerging exchanges, with new mechanisms and with data that is considerably less rich and voluminous. For our final case study, we describe the use of a machine learning approach to the problem of smart order routing (SOR) in dark pools. Whereas our first study investigated reinforcement learning for the problem of dividing a specified trade across time, here we examine learning to divide a specified trade across venues, that is, multiple competing dark pools, each offering potentially different liquidity profiles. Before describing this problem in greater detail, we provide some basic background on dark pools and their trade execution mechanism.

Dark pools were originally conceived as a venue for trades in which liquidity is of greater concern than price improvement; for instance, trades whose volume is sufficiently high that executing in the standard lit limit order exchanges (even across time and venues) would result in unacceptably high trading costs and market impact. For such trades, we would be quite satisfied to pay the "current price", say, as measured by the bid–ask midpoint, as long as there were sufficient liquidity to do so. The hope is that dark pools can perhaps match such large-volume counterparties away from the lit exchanges.

In the simplest form of dark pool mechanism, orders simply specify the desired volume for a given name, and the direction of trade (buy or sell); no prices are specified. Orders are queued on their respective side of the market in order of their arrival, with the oldest orders at the front of the queue. Any time there is liquidity on both sides of the market, execution occurs. For instance, suppose at a given instant the buy queue is empty, and the sell queue consists of two orders, for 1,000 and 250 shares. If a new buy order arrives for 1600 shares, it will immediately be executed for 1,250 shares against the outstanding sell orders, after which the buy queue will contain the order for the residual 350 shares and the sell queue will be empty. A subsequent arrival of a buy order for 500 shares, followed by a sell order for 1,000 shares, will result in an empty buy queue and the residual sell order for 150 (= 1,000 − 350 − 500) shares. Thus, at any instant, either one or both of the buy and sell queues will be empty, since incoming orders either are added to the end of the non-empty queue, or cause immediate execution with the other side. In this sense, all orders are "market" orders, in that they express a demand for immediate liquidity.

At what prices do the executions take place, since orders do not specify prices? As per the aforementioned motivation of liquidity over price (improvement), in general dark pool executions take place at the prevailing prices in the corresponding lit (limit order) market for the stock in question, eg, at the midpoint of the bid–ask spread, as measured by the National Best Bid and Offer (NBBO). Thus, while dark pools operate separately and independently of the lit markets, their prices are strongly tied to those lit markets.

From a data and machine learning perspective, there are two crucial differences between dark pools and their lit market counterparts.

(i) Unlike the microstructure data for the lit markets, in dark pools we have access only to our own order and execution data, rather than the entire trading population. Thus, the rich features measuring market activity, buying and selling pressure, liquidity imbalances, etc, that we exploited in earlier sections (see pp. 96ff and 104ff) are no longer available.

(ii) Upon submitting an order to a dark pool, all we learn is whether our order has been (partially) executed, not how much liquidity might have been available had we asked for more. For instance, suppose we submit an order for 10,000 shares. If we learn that 5,000 shares of it have been executed, then we know that only 5,000 shares were present on the other side. However, if all 10,000 shares have been executed, then any number larger than 10,000 might have been available. More formally, if we submit an order for V shares and S shares are available, we learn only the value $\min(V, S)$, not S. In statistics this is known as "censoring". We shall see that the machine learning approach we take to order routing in dark pools explicitly accounts for censored data.

These two differences mean that dark pools provide us with considerably less information not only about the activity of other market participants, but even about the liquidity present for our own trades. Nevertheless, we shall see there is still a sensible and effective machine learning approach.

We are now ready to define the SOR problem more mathematically. We assume that there are n separate dark pools available (at the time of writing $n > 30$ in the US alone), and we assume that these pools may offer different liquidity profiles for a given stock; for instance, one pool may be better at reliably executing small orders quickly, while another may have a higher probability of executing large orders. We model these liquidity profiles by probability distributions over available shares. More precisely, let P_i be a probability distribution over the non-negative integers. We assume that upon submitting an order for V_i shares to pool i, a random value S_i is drawn according to P_i; S_i models the shares available on the other side of the market of our trade (selling if we are buying, buying if we are selling) at the moment of submission. Thus, as per the aforementioned mechanism, $\min(V_i, S_i)$ shares will be executed. The SOR problem can now be formalised as follows: given an overall target volume V we would like to (say) buy, how should we divide V into submissions $V_1, \ldots, V_n$ to the n dark pools such that $\sum_{i=1}^{n} V_i = V$ and we maximise the (expected) number of shares we execute?

As an illustration of how a real distribution of liquidity looks, consider Figure 5.7, which shows submission and execution data for a large brokerage to a US dark pool for the stock DELL. Each

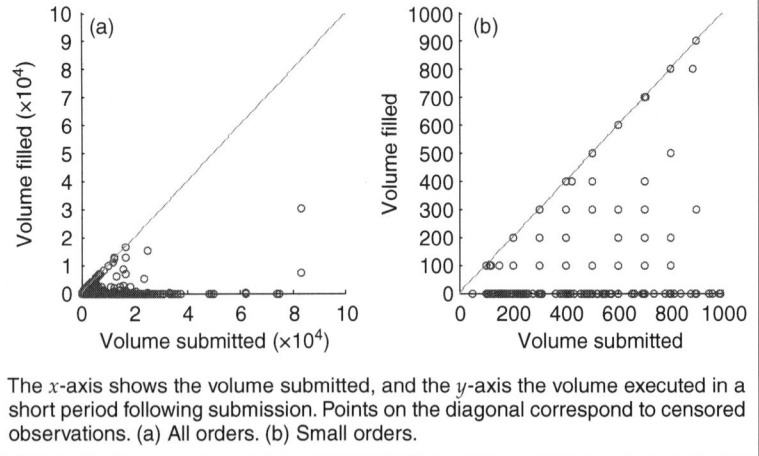

Figure 5.7 Sample submission and execution data for DELL from a large brokerage firm orders to a US dark pool

The x-axis shows the volume submitted, and the y-axis the volume executed in a short period following submission. Points on the diagonal correspond to censored observations. (a) All orders. (b) Small orders.

point in the scatter plot corresponds to a single order submitted. The x value is the volume submitted to the pool, while the y value is the volume executed in the pool in a short period of time (on the order of several seconds). All points lie below the diagonal $y = x$, since we never executed more than we submitted. Part (a) shows all submission data, while part (b) zooms in on only the smaller orders submitted. We see that while the larger orders (say, those exceeding 20,000 shares) rarely result in even partial execution, the smaller orders (part (b), 1,000 shares and smaller) routinely result in partial or full execution. It is empirically the case that such distributions will indeed differ from one dark pool to another, thus suggesting that effective solutions to the SOR problem will divide their orders across pools in an asymmetric fashion.

In our formalisation of the SOR problem, if we have complete knowledge and descriptions of the distributions P_i, it can be shown (Ganchev *et al* 2010) that there is a straightforward algorithmic solution. In order to maximise the fraction of our V shares that are executed, we should determine the allocations V_i in the following fashion. Processing the shares sequentially (strictly for the purposes of the algorithm), we allocate the conceptually "first" share to whichever pool has the highest probability of executing a single share. Then, inductively, if we have already determined a partial allocation of the V shares, we should allocate our "next" share to whichever pool has the highest marginal probability of executing that share, conditioned on the allocation made so far. In this manner we process all V shares and determine the resulting allocation V_i for each pool i. We shall refer to this algorithm for making allocations under known P_i the "greedy" allocation algorithm. It can be shown that the greedy allocation algorithm is an optimal solution to the SOR problem, in that it maximises the expected number of shares executed in a single round of submissions to the n pools. Note that if the submission of our V shares across the pools results in partial executions, leaving us with $V' < V$ shares remaining, we can always repeat the process, resubmitting the V' shares in the allocations given by the greedy algorithm.

The learning problem for SOR arises from the fact that we do not have knowledge of the distributions P_i, and must learn (approximations to) them from only our own, censored order and execution data, ie, data of the form visualised in Figure 5.7. We have developed an overall learning algorithm for the dark pool SOR problem that learns an optimal submission strategy over a sequence of submitted volumes to the n venues. The details of this algorithm are beyond the scope of the chapter, but can be summarised as follows.

1. The algorithm maintains, for each venue i, an approximation $\hat{P}_i$ to the unknown liquidity distribution P_i. This approximation is learned exclusively from the algorithm's own order submission and execution data to that venue. Initially, before any orders have been submitted, all of the approximations $\hat{P}_i$ have some default form.

2. Since the execution data is censored by our own submitted volume, we cannot employ basic statistical methods for estimating distributions from observed frequencies. Instead, we use the Kaplan–Meier estimator (sometimes also known as the product limit estimator), which is the maximum likelihood estimator for censored data (Ganchev et al 2010). Furthermore, since empirically the execution data frequently exhibits instances in which no submitted shares are executed, combined with occasional executions of large volumes (Figure 5.7), we adapt this estimator for a parametric model for the $\hat{P}_i$ that has the form of a power law with a separate parameter for zero shares.

3. For each desired volume V to execute, the algorithm simply behaves as if its current approximate distributions $\hat{P}_i$ are in fact the true liquidity distributions, and chooses the allocations V_i according to the greedy algorithm applied to the $\hat{P}_i$. Each submitted allocation V_i then results in an observed volume executed (which could be anything from zero shares to a censored observation of V_i shares).

4. With this fresh execution data, the estimated distributions $\hat{P}_i$ can be updated, and the process repeated for the next target volume.

In other words, the algorithm can be viewed as a simple repeated loop of optimisation followed by re-estimation: our current distributional estimates are inputs to the greedy optimisation, which determines allocations, which result in executions, which allow us to estimate improved distributions. It is possible, under some simple assumptions, to prove that this algorithm will rapidly converge to the optimal submission strategy for the unknown true distributions P_i. Furthermore, the algorithm is computationally very simple and efficient, and variants of it have been implemented in a number of brokerage firms.

Some experimental validation of the algorithm is provided in Figure 5.8, showing simulations derived using the censored execution data for four US dark pools. Each subplot shows the evolution of our learning algorithm's performance on a series of submitted allocations for a given ticker to the pools. The x-axis measures time or trials for the algorithm, ie, the value of x is the number of rounds of submitted volumes so far. The y-axis measures the total fraction of the submitted volume that was executed across the four pools; higher values are thus better. The grey curves for each name show the performance of our learning algorithm. In each case performance improves rapidly with additional rounds of allocations, as the estimates $\hat{P}_i$ become better approximations to the true P_i.

As always in machine learning, it is important to compare our algorithm's performance to some sensible benchmarks and alternatives. The least challenging comparison is shown by the dashed black line in each figure, which represents the expected fraction of shares executed if we simply divide every volume V equally amongst the pools: there is no learning, and no accounting for the

Figure 5.8 Performance curves for our learning algorithm (grey curve) and a simple adaptive heuristic (black curve), against benchmarks measuring uniform allocations (dashed black line) and ideal allocations (dashed grey line).

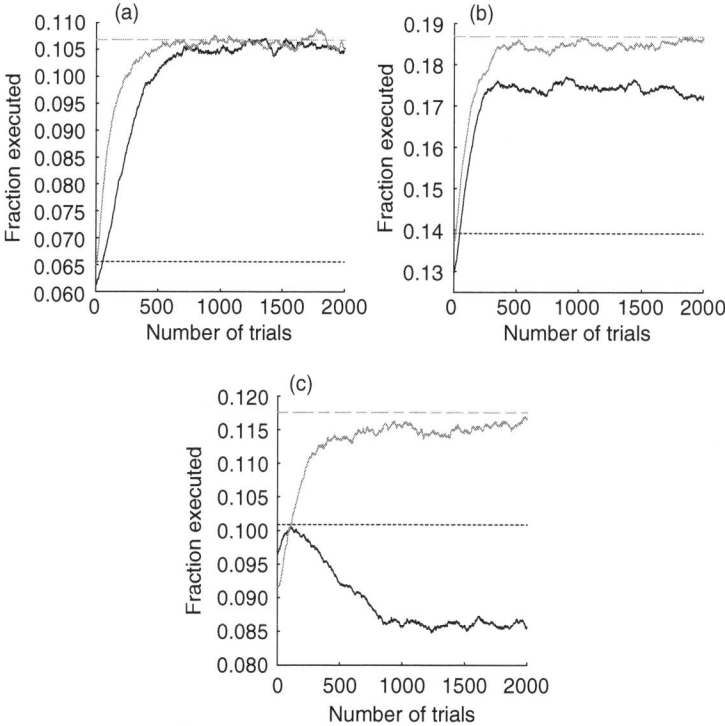

(a) XOM; (b) AIG; (c) NRG.

asymmetries that exist among the venues. Fortunately, we see the learning approach quickly surpasses this sanity-check benchmark.

A more challenging benchmark is the dashed grey line in each subplot, which shows the expected fraction of shares executed when performing allocations using the greedy algorithm applied to the true distributions P_i. This is the best performance we could possibly hope to achieve, and we see that our learning algorithm approaches this ideal quickly for each stock.

Finally, we compare the learning algorithm's performance to a simple adaptive algorithm that is a "poor man's" form of learning. Rather than maintaining estimates of the complete liquidity distribution for each venue i, it simply maintains a single numerical weight

w_i, and allocates V proportional to the w_i. If a submission to venue i results in any shares being executed, w_i is increased; otherwise it is decreased. We see that, while in some cases this algorithm can also approach the true optimal, in other cases it asymptotes at a suboptimal value, and in others it seems to outright diverge from optimality. In each case our learning algorithm outperforms this simple heuristic.

CONCLUSION

We have presented both the opportunities and challenges of a machine learning approach to HFT and market microstructure and considered problems of both pure execution, over both time and venues, and predicting directional movements in search of profitability. These were illustrated via three detailed empirical case studies. In closing, we wish to emphasise a few "lessons learned", common to all of the cases examined.

- Machine learning provides no easy paths to profitability or improved execution, but does provide a powerful and principled framework for trading optimisation via historical data.

- At least for complex trading problems, we are not believers in the use of machine learning as a black box, or in the discovery of "surprising" strategies via its application. In each of the case studies, the result of learning made broad economic and market sense in light of the trading problem considered. However, the numerical optimisation of these qualitative strategies is where the real power lies.

- Throughout, we have emphasised the importance and subtlety of feature design and engineering to the success of the machine learning approach. Learning will never succeed without informative features, and may even fail with them if they are not expressed or optimised properly.

- All kinds of other fine-tuning and engineering are required to obtain the best results, such as the development of learning methods that correct for directional drift (see pages 104ff).

Perhaps the most important overarching implication is that there will always be a "human in the loop" in machine learning applications to HFT (or any other long-term effort to apply machine learning to a challenging, changing domain). But, applied tastefully and with care, the approach can be powerful and scalable, and is arguably necessary in the presence of microstructure data of such enormous volume and complexity as confronts us today.

We thank Alex Kulesza warmly for his collaboration on the research described in the section on "Predicting Price Movement from the Order Book State", and to Frank Corrao for his valuable help on many of our collaborative projects.

1 Various types of hidden, iceberg and other order types can limit the complete reconstruction, but do not alter the fundamental picture we describe here.

2 A fair estimate would be that over 90% of placed orders are cancelled.

3 For simplicity, we shall assume a discrete-time model in which time is divided into a finite number of equally spaced trading opportunities. It is straightforward conceptually to generalise to continuous-time models.

4 The case of selling is symmetric.

5 VWAP denotes volume weighted average price, which refers to both the benchmark of trading shares at the market average per share over a specified time period, and algorithms which attempt to achieve or approximate this benchmark.

6 In principle, we might compare our learning approach to state-of-the-art execution algorithms, such as the aforementioned VWAP algorithms used by major brokerages. But doing so obscures the benefits of a principled learning approach in comparison to the extensive hand-tuning and optimisation in industrial VWAP algorithms, and the latter may also make use of exotic order types, multiple exchanges and other mechanisms outside of our basic learning framework. In practice, a combination of learning and hand-tuning is likely to be most effective.

7 Note that the improvement from combining features is slightly less than the sum of their individual improvements, since there may be redundancy in the information provided by the features.

8 Tickers of names examined are AAPL, ADBE, AMGN, AMZN, BIIB, CELG, COST, CSCO, DELL, EBAY, ESRX, GILD, GOOG, INTC, MSFT, ORCL, QCOM, SCHW and YHOO.

9 The results we describe for DELL, however, do generalise consistently across names.

10 As usual, the feature is normalised by subtracting the mean and binned by standard deviations, so -3 means the recent price change is three standard deviations below its historical mean, and $+3$ means it is three standard deviations above.

11 We have documented this tension empirically at great length in Kulesza *et al* (2010).

REFERENCES

Agarwal, A., P. Bartlett and M. Dama, 2010, "Optimal Allocation Strategies for the Dark Pool Problem", Technical Report, arXiv:1003.2445 [stat.ML].

Bertsimas, D., and A. Lo, 1998, "Optimal Control of Execution Costs", *Journal of Financial Markets* 1(1), pp. 1–50.

Bouchaud, J., M. Mezard and M. Potters, 2002, "Statistical Properties of Stock Order Books: Empirical Results and Models", *Quantitative Finance* 2, pp. 251–6.

Cont, R., and A. Kukanov, 2013, "Optimal Order Placement in Limit Order Markets", Technical Report, arXiv:1210.1625 [q-fin. RTR].

Fama, E., and K. French, 1993, "Common Risk Factors in the Returns on Stocks and Bonds", *Journal of Financial Economics* 33(1), pp. 3–56.

Ganchev, K., M. Kearns, Y. Nevmyvaka and J. Wortman, 2010, "Censored Exploration and the Dark Pool Problem", *Communications of the ACM* 53(5), pp. 99–107.

Guéant, O., C. A. Lehalle and J. F. Tapia, 2012, "Optimal Portfolio Liquidation with Limit Orders", Technical Report, arXiv:1106.3279 [q-fin.TR].

JP Morgan, 2012, "Dark Matters Part 1: Optimal Liquidity Seeker", Report, JP Morgan Electronic Client Solutions, May.

Kharroubi, I., and H. Pham, 2010, "Optimal Portfolio Liquidation with Execution Cost and Risk", *SIAM Journal on Financial Mathematics* 1(1), pp. 897–931.

Kulesza, A., M. Kearns and Y. Nevmyvaka, 2010, "Empirical Limitations on High Frequency Trading Profitability", *Journal of Trading* 5(4), pp. 50–62.

Laruelle, S., C. A. Lehalle and G. Pagès, 2011, "Optimal Split of Orders Across Liquidity Pools: A Stochastic Algorithm Approach", *SIAM Journal on Financial Mathematics* 2(1), pp. 1042–76.

Maglaras, C., C. C. Moallemi and H. Zheng, 2012, "Optimal Order Routing in a Fragmented Market", Working Paper.

Moallemi, C. C., B. Park and B. Van Roy, 2012, "Strategic Execution in the Presence of an Uninformed Arbitrageur", *Journal of Financial Markets* 15(4), pp. 361–91.

Nevmyvaka, Y., Yi Feng and M. Kearns, 2006, "Reinforcement Learning for Optimized Trade Execution", in *Proceedings of the 23rd International Conference on Machine Learning*, pp. 673–80. New York: ACM Press.

Park, B., and B. van Roy, 2012, "Adaptive Execution: Exploration and Learning of Price Impact", Technical Report, arXiv:1207:6423 [q-fin.TR].

Sutton, R. S., and A. G. Barto, 1998, *Reinforcement Learning: An Introduction*. Cambridge, MA: MIT Press.

6

A "Big Data" Study of Microstructural Volatility in Futures Markets

**Kesheng Wu, E. Wes Bethel, Ming Gu,
David Leinweber, Oliver Rübel**
Lawrence Berkeley National Laboratory

Factors such as electronic exchanges, decimalisation of stock prices and automated order slicing created an explosion in the amount of financial data in the first decade of the 21st century, and the number of trades per day has been increasing dramatically. A large portion of the trades happen near opening or closing of the trading day, which creates very high rates of trading activities in short bursts. This high data rate and even higher burst rate make it difficult to understand the market. Many researchers have argued that a better understanding of high-frequency trading, and better regulations, might have prevented events such as the US flash crash of May 6, 2010 (Easley *et al* 2011b; Menkveld and Yueshen 2013). However, academic researchers and government regulators typically lack the computing resources and the software tools to work with large volumes of data from high-frequency markets. We believe that the existing investments in high-performance computing resources for science could effectively analyse financial market data. In this chapter, we use the concrete task of computing a leading indicator of market volatility to demonstrate that a modest machine could analyse over 100 GB of futures contracts quickly.

Scientific research activities such as the Large Hadron Collider[1] and climate modelling[2] produce and analyse petabytes (10^{15} bytes) of data. The data rates from such activities are in fact multiple orders of magnitude higher than those from financial markets. In most cases, scientists are conducting their analysis tasks not with expensive data warehousing systems, but using open-source software tools augmented with specialised data structures and analysis algorithms (Bethel and Childs 2012; Shoshani and Rotem 2010). We view this departure from the reliance on the monolithic database management system as the core feature of the "big data" movement (Lynch 2008; Manyika *et al* 2011). In this chapter, we provide a brief overview of three key pieces of the technology:

1. an efficient file format for organising the market data,
2. a set of techniques to compute the early-warning indicator and the volatility measure, and
3. a strategy to parallelise the computation and take advantage of the many cores available on most computers.

To demonstrate the effectiveness of these techniques, we process a large data set (details are given in the following section) to compute a popular liquidity indicator called volume-synchronised probability of informed trading (VPIN) (Bethel *et al* 2012; Easley *et al* 1996). When the values of VPIN exceed a certain threshold, say two standard deviations larger than the average, we declare a "VPIN event". Within a time window immediately following a VPIN event, we expect the market to be more volatile than usual. To verify this hypothesis, we compute a realised volatility measure called the maximum intermediate return (MIR), which essentially measures the largest range of price fluctuation in a time window (Easley *et al* 2012a; López de Prado 2012). We compare the MIR values following VPIN events against the average MIR value sampled at random time periods. If the MIR following a VPIN event is larger than the average MIR of random time periods, we say the event is a "true positive"; if the MIR following a VPIN event is equal to or less than the average MIR of random time periods, the VPIN event is said to be a "false positive". The functions for computing VPIN and MIR are controlled by six parameters, including the size of the support window for computing VPIN and the time window for computing MIR. With an efficient program, we can explore the parameter space to determine the optimal parameter choices and minimise the false positive rates.

TEST DATA

In our work, we use a comprehensive set of liquid futures trading data to illustrate the techniques to be introduced. More specifically, we use 67 months of tick data of the 94 most liquid futures contracts traded on all asset classes. The data comes to us in the form of 94 comma separated values (CSV) files, one for each futures contract traded. The source of our data is TickWrite, a data vendor that normalises the data into a common structure after acquiring it directly from the relevant exchanges. The total size of all CSV files is about 140 GB. They contain about three billion trades spanning the beginning of January 2007 to the end of July 2012. Five of the most heavily traded futures contracts each have more than 100 million trades during the 67-month period. The most heavily traded futures, E-mini S&P 500 futures (ES), has about 500 million trades, involving a total of about three billion contracts. A complete list of the futures contracts is available in the report by Wu *et al* (2013).

HDF5 FILE FORMAT

To improve the efficiency of data handling, we convert the CSV files into HDF5 files (HDF Group 2011). In a published study on a similar task of computing VPIN values on a month of stock trades, it took 142 seconds using the CSV file, while it only took 0.4 seconds using HDF5 (Bethel *et al* 2012). One reason for this gain in efficiency is that HDF5 stores data in binary form, which requires less storage space. For the data used in this work, the total size of all HDF5 files was about 41 GB, about 29% of the total size of all CSV files. Smaller files take less time to read in to memory.

After reading the content of a CSV file, the program has to convert the ASCII strings into numerical values, which requires additional processing time. In contrast, the values read from a HDF5 file can be used directly by the application code without further interpretation. Furthermore, HDF5 allows for better organisation of the data. For example, in a CSV file, the year, month and day information has to be repeated in each row. Such repetition can be avoided with HDF5, by better organisation of the data records. Better organised data can also make locating certain data records more efficient in some analysis scenarios.

The advantages of using HDF5 to store financial data were noted by Bethel *et al* (2012). Some commercially available software, including StratBox (from PuppetMaster Trading), stores its data as HDF5 files.[3] Additional details on how this work uses HDF5 are given in Wu *et al* (2013).

VOLUME-SYNCHRONISED PROBABILITY OF INFORMED TRADING

VPIN measures the average order flow imbalance in a market (Abad and Yagüe 2012; Easley *et al* 2011b). It takes into account the imbalance of buyer-initiated and seller-initiated orders and, more generally, the imbalance between buying and selling pressure. This difference is important, because not all buying pressure is the result of an excess of buy-initiated orders. Based on a probabilistic model of information imbalance, Easley *et al* (1996, 2011b) have developed a set of elegant formulas for computing VPIN. Here we briefly outline the key computation steps.

Bars

Many standard statistical techniques for data analysis require some uniformity in data. However, the real-world financial trading data arrives at irregular intervals. Common strategies to work around this problem are to take uniform samples or group the data into uniform bins (At-Sahalia *et al* 2005). The VPIN computation generally starts with a set of bins called "bars". There are two commonly used types of bars: time bars and volume bars. Each time bar spans the same duration and each volume bar contains the same volume of trades (Easley *et al* 2011a, 2012a). In this work, we choose the volume bars because they adapt better to temporal bursts in trading (Easley *et al* 2011b).

Each bar is treated as a single trade in the rest of the computation steps. For this purpose, the bar needs to have a nominal price. In the research literature, it is common for the price of the last trade in the bar to be taken as the nominal price of the bar. We refer to this as the closing price. There are other convenient ways of constructing the nominal prices. For example, Wu *et al* (2013) explored the option of using the average price, the median price, the volume weighted average price and the volume weighted median price. The cost of computing the closing prices is minimal. The cost of computing the average prices and the weighted averages is essentially one pass through the data, while the cost of computing the median prices and the weighted median prices is much higher (Wu *et al* 2013, Figure 2).

Volume classification

The computation of VPIN needs to determine directions of trades, as buyer-initiated or seller-initiated, or simply as a "buy" or a "sell"

(Easley *et al* 1996; Lee and Ready 1991). The most popular method used in the market microstructure literature is the tick rule (Lee and Ready 1991). This method relies on the sequential order of trades. However, due to high-frequency trading, there are many trades with the same time stamps. In addition, the time stamps on trades executed by multiple matching engines may not be synchronised to the precision used to record the time stamps. For these reasons, we use the bulk volume classification (BVC) method instead (Chakrabarty *et al* 2012; Easley *et al* 2012a,b).

BVC assigns a fraction of the volume as "buy" and the remainder as "sell", based on the normalised sequential price change (Easley *et al* 2012b). Given a sequence of volume bars with prices, $P_0, P_1, \ldots$, the sequential price changes are $\delta_1 \equiv P_1 - P_0$, $\delta_2 \equiv P_2 - P_1$, and so on. Let v_j^b denote the buy volume for bar j, and v_j be the volume of the bar, we compute v_j^b from v_j as follows (Easley *et al* 2012b)

$$v_j^b = v_j Z\left(\frac{\delta_j}{\varsigma}\right) \tag{6.1}$$

where Z is the cumulative distribution function of either the normal distribution or the Student t-distribution. The parameter ς is the standard deviation of the sequential price changes. The rest of the volume in the bar is considered as sells: $v_j^s = v_j - v_j^b$.

The expression δ_j/ς is a way to normalise the price changes. A common practice is to subtract the average price change before dividing by the standard deviation. However, when working with high-frequency data, the average price change is much smaller than the standard deviation. Following the recommendation from earlier publications (Easley *et al* 2012a,b), our BVC implementation always uses zero as the average. The free parameter we need to choose here is the distribution used for BVC (Table 6.1).

Buckets

After the volume classification, the bars are further aggregated into larger bins known as "buckets". Typically, a fixed number of bars go into a bucket. Within a relatively wide range of choices, the number of bars in a bucket has little influence on the final value of VPIN. Therefore, we follow the recommendation from published literature and fix the number of bars in a bucket at 30 (Easley *et al* 2012a).

To compute VPIN, each bucket needs to record the total volume of trades in all bars in the bucket and the total volume of buys. Let

V_i denote the total volume of the ith bucket, and V_i^b denote the total buys in the same bucket. The VPIN value is given by

$$\text{VPIN} = \frac{\sum \|V_j^b - V_j^s\|}{\sum V_j}$$

The authors of VPIN suggest using the same number of buckets for the same trading instrument. We parametrise the number of buckets as follows.

Let β be the number of buckets per day, and let A be the average daily volume of a futures contract (or an equity). The volume of a bar is $\lceil A/(30\beta) \rceil$, where the operator $\lceil \cdot \rceil$ is the ceiling operator that computes the smallest integer not less than the operand. This ensures each bar has a whole unit of the trading instrument under consideration and prevents us from dividing the trades into tiny pieces when working with infrequently traded instruments. We then aggregate 30 such bars into a bucket. In our tests, we choose β to be between 50 and 1,000 (Table 6.1).

The number of buckets used for computing VPIN is determined by another parameter, called the support for VPIN, σ, which is measured in days. The number of buckets used is $\sigma\beta$. In our tests, σ varies from 0.25 to 2 (Table 6.1).

Cumulative distribution function

The value of VPIN is between 0 and 1. Normally, it would be close to 0. When it is high, we can declare a VPIN event. Generally, the VPIN values span different ranges for different trading instruments. Therefore, it is impossible to define a simple threshold on VPIN values in order to judge whether a particular VPIN value is high or not. Instead, we normalise the VPIN values as follows (Easley *et al* 2011a). Assume the VPIN values follow the normal distribution, and denote their average as μ and their standard deviation as ς. Then its cumulative distribution function (CDF) can be expressed as

$$\text{CDF}(x) = \frac{1}{2}\left[1 + \text{erf}\left(\frac{x - \mu}{\sqrt{2}\varsigma}\right)\right]$$

where erf is the error function. We declare a VPIN event whenever the CDF value is larger than a threshold τ. After this transformation, the same threshold τ could be used on a variety of trading instruments (Easley *et al* 2011b, 2012a). The value τ has a simple interpretation. Assuming all VPIN values follow the normal distribution, if the CDF value is greater than 0.99, then the VPIN value is larger than 99% of all values. In our tests, we assume VPIN follows a truncated lognormal distribution (Wu *et al* 2013).

MAXIMUM INTERMEDIATE RETURN

When the CDF of a VPIN value is above a given threshold τ, we declare a VPIN event, and expect the volatility immediately following the event to be higher than usual. Our next task is to select a measure to quantify the volatility (Shiller 1992), which will enable us to discriminate a true event from a false event. In this work, we assume all events have the same duration throughout the 67-month period, and attempt to determine this event duration through a set of empirical measurements to be discussed later (see pages 133ff). To measure volatility, we use the MIR (Easley *et al* 2012a; López de Prado 2012), defined next.

Many of the well-known volatility measures are based on the realised return over the entire duration of an event (Amihud *et al* 1990; Andersen and Bollerslev 1998; Shiller 1992). However, these measures are not appropriate for events like the US "flash crash" of May 6, 2010, which is generally considered to be a liquidity crisis, where VPIN might be effectively used (Bethel *et al* 2012; Easley *et al* 2011b, 2012a; Kirilenko *et al* 2010). During the flash crash, the return from the official beginning of the crisis (14h32) to the end of the session (16h15) was only −0.5%. However, during the same period, prices had an intermediate collapse of over −6%. The intermediate return is a much better indicator of trouble than the official return of the entire period.

Given prices of N trades, P_i, the intermediate return between trades j and k ($j < k$) is

$$R_{j,k} = \frac{P_k}{P_j} - 1 \qquad (6.2)$$

We call a pair of trades j^* and k^* sentinels if they maximise the intermediate returns

$$(j^*, k^*) = \arg\max_{0 \leqslant j < k < N} \left| \frac{P_k}{P_j} - 1 \right| \qquad (6.3)$$

The maximum intermediate return is the intermediate return of the sentinels

$$\text{MIR} = \frac{P_{k*}}{P_{j*}} - 1 \qquad (6.4)$$

The straightforward approach to computing MIR would use a double nested loop to evaluate Equation 6.3. If we take the event duration to be a day, then for many futures contracts an event duration would include millions of trades. Therefore, the double loop for evaluating Equation 6.3 would need to compute trillions of different pairs of intermediate returns $R_{i,j}$, requiring a very significant amount of computer time. We could significantly reduce the amount of computation by using the prices of buckets or bars instead of individual trades, because there are fewer buckets or bars. However, because the buckets and bars are aggregates of many trades, using them will miss the actual maximum intermediate return in most cases.

To compute the exact MIR quickly, we employ two strategies. The first is to have each volume bar carry the maximum price and the minimum price of trades in the bar along with their positions in the list of trades. The second strategy is to replace the double loop algorithm for computing MIR with a recursive procedure. The details of this procedure are given in Wu *et al* (2013).

PARALLELISATION

The process of computing VPIN and MIR for each futures contract can proceed independently. For example, computing VPIN values on ES does not require any information from any other futures contracts. This allows us to run a number of parallel tasks, one for each contract instruments. This parallelisation strategy is often referred to as the "task parallelism" in high-performance computing literature (Hager and Wellein 2010; Kumar *et al* 1994).

Since different contract instruments have wildly different number of trades (for example, the heaviest traded futures, ES, has 478 million trades, while the lightest traded futures, MW, has only 33 thousand trades), each parallel task may require very different amounts of computer time. To minimise the time spent on the parallel job, we need to ensure the tasks assigned to each parallel process complete in the same amount of time. In our case, the computer time

Table 6.1 Parameters to control the computation of VPIN and MIR

	Description	Choices to consider
π	Nominal price of a bar	Closing, average, weighted average, median, weighted median
β	Buckets per day	50, 100, 200, 500, 1,000
σ	Support window (days)	0.25, 0.5, 1, 2
η	Event duration (days)	0.1, 0.25, 0.5, 1
ν	Parameter for BVC	Normal distribution or Student t-distribution with $\nu = 0.1, 0.25, 1, 10$
τ	Threshold for CDF of VPIN	0.9, 0.93, 0.95, 0.96, 0.97, 0.98, 0.99, 0.999

The six parameter choices form 16,000 different combinations. When any of them are not specified, the following default values are used: π = closing, $\beta = 200$, $\sigma = 1$, $\eta = 1$, normal distribution for BVC, $\tau = 0.99$.

for each task is a linear function of the number of trades for the contract instrument; we choose to assign the instrument with the largest number of trades first.

To show that a modest computer is needed to complete the computational task we have chosen, we decided to use a common workstation with many cores. Our parallel implementation uses POSIX threads to use the different cores (Hager and Wellein 2010; Lewis and Berg 1998). The parallel processes share a common task list, which holds the list of contract instruments. When a process finishes its assigned task, it takes the next available task from this shared list.

EXPERIMENTAL EVALUATION

In this section, we report the time needed to compute VPIN and MIR of the 94 most active futures contracts. Our main goal is to evaluate the efficiency of the new computational procedure described above. Following the timing discussion, we also discuss how to choose the VPIN parameters to minimise the false positive rates.

Table 6.1 lists the six parameters, together with a brief description and the choices to consider. Altogether, there are 16,000 different parameter combinations specified in this table.

We conducted our tests using an IBM DataPlex machine located at the National Energy Research Supercomputing Center (NERSC)[4] The HDF5 files are stored on the global scratch space shared by all NERSC machines. This file system is heavily used and the read

Figure 6.1 A breakdown of time (in seconds) spent in major steps of the C++ program

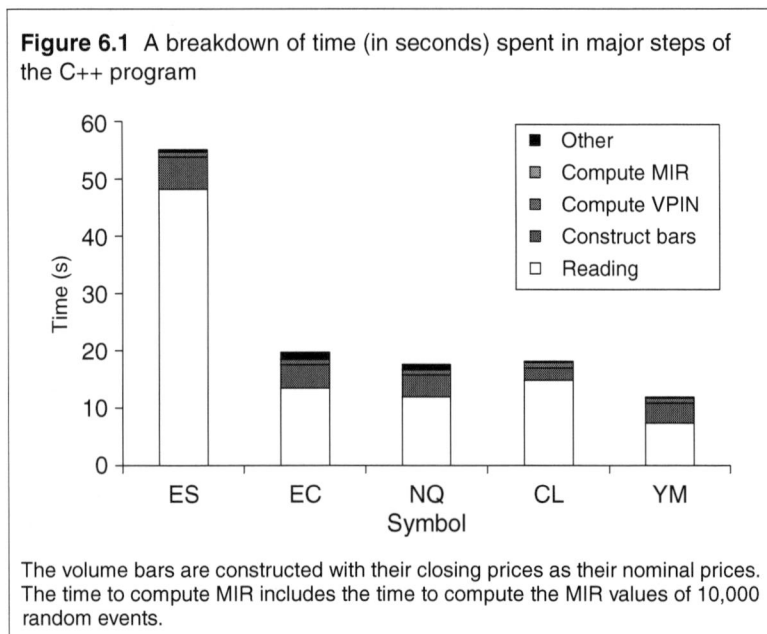

The volume bars are constructed with their closing prices as their nominal prices. The time to compute MIR includes the time to compute the MIR values of 10,000 random events.

speed from a single node is fairly close to what can be expected from a stand-alone workstation. For example, the average read time for ES (about 5.7 GB) is 50.4 s, which gives an average reading speed of about 113 MB/s.

To understand where the computer time is spent in our program, we measure the time used by the key functions. In Figure 6.1, we show four such functions: reading the data from the HDF5 file into memory; constructing the volume bars; computing the VPIN values (including forming the buckets); and computing the MIR values. Overall, the time required to read the data into memory dominates the total execution time.[5] The next largest amount of time is spent on constructing the volume bars. In this case, we are using the closing price as the nominal price of the bar; therefore, the time to form the bars is relatively small. Had we used the median price or the weighted median price, the time to form the volume bars would be longer.

The time needed to compute VPINs and MIRs are about the same in all five cases. Because the data spans the same number of days and trading records from each day is divided into the same number of bars and buckets, there are the same number of buckets and bars for each futures contract. Since the same number of buckets is used to compute the VPIN for each contract, the procedure for computing each VPIN value costs the same. Since there are the same number of buckets for each of these futures contracts in Figure 6.1, the same number of VPIN values are computed. Therefore, the total time for computing VPIN should be the same. The computation of a MIR value operates on the same number of bars; thus, it should cost the same. Since there are different numbers of VPIN events, we compute different numbers of MIR values and might expect the time to compute MIR to be different. Indeed, there are differences. However, the differences are small because the number of random events used as references, 10,000, is much larger than the numbers of VPIN events detected.

The test job that runs over all 16,000 combinations listed in Table 6.1 on all 94 futures contracts took 19 hours 26 minutes and 41 seconds using a 32-core computer node and about 74 GB of memory. In this case, we read the input data into memory once and repeated the different combinations of parameters without reading the data again. This reduces the input/output (I/O) time and makes it much more efficient to try different combinations. The average time to compute VPIN, detect VPIN events and compute the false positive rates is 1.49 seconds on a single CPU core

$$\frac{32 \times (19 \text{ hours} + 26 \text{ minutes} + 41 \text{ seconds})}{16,000 \times 94} = 1.49 \text{ seconds}$$

A PYTHON version of this program that stores bars and buckets in an SQLite database took more than 12 hours to complete one parameter combination on ES, while our program took about 55 seconds on the same machine. Our program is about 785 times faster than the PYTHON program. Note that the 55 seconds used by our program is mostly spent on reading the input file (around 48 seconds). In real-time operations, the computational procedure will directly receive the latest trading records over a high-speed network. In this case, we do not need to spend any time on disk I/O and the in-memory operations can proceed at the same speed as in the larger tests where around 1.5 seconds are enough to process 67 months of data. Thus, we believe it is plausible to compute VPIN and detect VPIN events in real-time during trading.

For each parameter combination in Table 6.1, we compute the false positive rates for each of the 94 futures contracts and then record the unweighted average. Figure 6.2 shows the average false positive

Figure 6.2 The average false positive rates of 94 futures contracts under different VPIN parameter choices

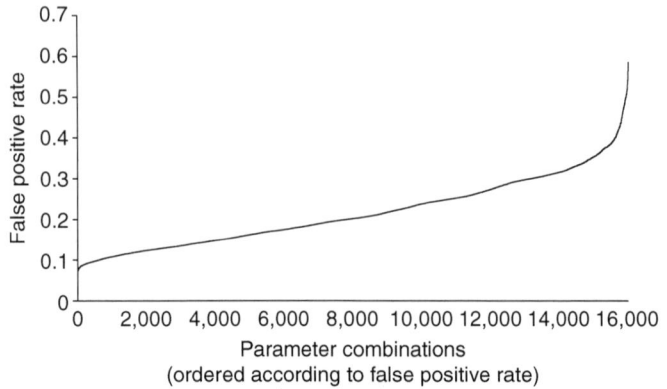

The 16,000 parameter choices are ordered according to their false positive rates.

Table 6.2 The 10 parameter combinations that produced the smallest average false positive rates, α

π	β	σ	μ	ν	τ	α
Median	200	1	0.1	1	0.99	0.071
Weighted median	1,000	0.5	0.1	1	0.99	0.071
Weighted median	200	0.5	0.1	0.25	0.99	0.072
Weighted median	200	0.5	0.1	1	0.99	0.073
Median	200	1	0.1	10	0.99	0.073
Median	500	0.5	0.1	0.1	0.99	0.074
Median	200	1	0.1	Normal	0.99	0.074
Weighted median	200	1	0.1	1	0.99	0.074
Weighted median	200	1	0.25	1	0.99	0.074
Weighted average	200	1	0.1	1	0.99	0.075

rates of 16,000 different parameter combinations. The median value of the false positive rates is about 0.2 (ie, 20%). There are 604 combinations with false positive rates $\alpha < 0.1$, which indicate that there are a large number of parameter choices that could work quite well.

Table 6.2 shows the 10 combinations that produced the lowest average false positive rates. We observe that each of the 10 combinations produces an average false positive rate of around 7%, which is about one-third of the median value (around 20%) of all false positive rates in our test.

Figure 6.3 The average false positive rates of four different classes of futures contracts under the 100 parameter combinations with the lowest overall false positive rates

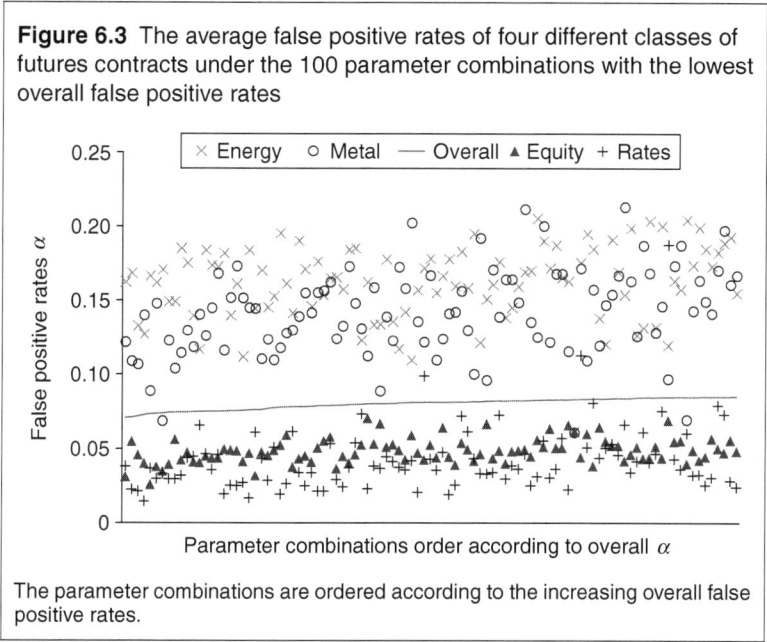

The parameter combinations are ordered according to the increasing overall false positive rates.

Among the ten best parameter combinations in Table 6.2, the threshold τ on CDF is always 0.99, the event duration η is 0.1 days in nine out of ten cases, the number of buckets per day β is 200 in eight cases, the support for computing VPIN σ is one day in six cases, the bulk volume classification parameter v is 1 in six cases, and the weighted median is the preferred pricing method for volume bars in five cases. We generally recommend these choices.

To understand how the parameter choices affect the different classes of futures contracts, we plot in Figure 6.3 the average false positive rates of the four largest classes of futures contracts: equity, interest rates, energy and metal. The names of these futures contracts are listed in Table 6.4. From Figure 6.3, we see that the four classes form two groups. The equity and interest rates form one group with their false positive rates between 3% and 4%, while energy and metal form another group, with their false positive rates between 10 and 20%.

Table 6.3 shows the parameter combinations that minimises the average false positive rates of the four classes of futures contracts shown in Figure 6.3. From this table, we see that it is possible for their average false positive rates to be much lower than 7%. For the

Table 6.3 The best parameter choices for different classes of futures contracts

		π	β	σ	μ	ν	τ	α
Energy	Average	200	0.25	0.1	0.1	0.999	0.037
	Weighted average	100	0.25	0.1	0.1	0.999	0.058
Metal	Weighted median	100	0.25	0.1	0.25	0.999	0.025
	Weighted median	50	0.5	0.1	0.1	0.999	0.042
Equity	Median	200	1	0.1	10	0.99	0.026
	Weighted median	1,000	1	0.5	0.25	0.99	0.027
Interest rates	Closing	500	2	0.1	1	0.98	0.003
	Average	50	1	0.1	0.25	0.99	0.008

Table 6.4 A brief description of four classes of futures contracts: equity, interest rates, metal and energy

	Metal			Energy	
	Description	Volume		Description	Volume
GC	Gold Comex	62,875	CL	Light Crude	165,208
HG	Copper high grade	12,393	CO	Brent Crude ICE	79,182
JA	Platinum	51	GO	Gas oil	15,858
JG	Gold	136	HO	Heating oil #2	22,740
PA	Palladium	1,160	NG	Natural gas	50,847
PL	Platinum	2,086	QG	Natural gas E-mini	2,167
SV	Silver	24,375	QM	Crude oil E-mini	11,436
XG	Gold mini-sized	3,223	WT	WTI Crude	18,164
YS	Silver mini-sized	1,434	XB	RBOB Gasoline	17,575

The volume of trades over a 67-month period is given in thousands. A full list is given in Wu *et al* (2013, Table 7).

Interest rates class, the lowest α is 0.3%. We see that most of the cases in Table 6.3 have $\mu = 0.1$, which agrees with Table 6.2. For the rest of the parameters, we again see two different groups. On the choice of CDF threshold τ, the group including equity and interest rates prefers 0.99, while the group including meta and energy prefers

Table 6.4 Continued.

Equity			Interest rates		
	Description	Volume		Description	Volume
BR	Brazilian Bovespa futures	5,582	AX	Australian 10 yr bond	3,889
CF	CAC 40 index futures	56,521	AY	Australian 3 yr bond	3,159
DA	Dax futures	97,337	BL	Euro-bobl 5 yr	27,228
DJ	DJIA Futures	596	BN	Euro-bund 10 yr	53,292
EN	Nikkei 225 Futures	26,729	BZ	Euro-schatz 2 yr	16,136
ES	S&P 500 E-mini	478,029	CB	Canadian 10 yr	8,276
FT	FTSE 100 index	54,259	ED	Eurodollar	11,864
HI	Hang-Seng index futures	55,812	FV	T-Note 5 yr	59,830
IB	IBEX 35	16,791	GL	Long gilt	16,353
II	FTSE MIB	16,775	JB	Japanese 10 yr bond	5,401
KM	KOSPI 200	46,121	KE	Korean 3 yr	3,707
MD	S&P 400 MidCap	42	ST	Sterling 3 months	1,765
MG	MSCI EAFE Mini	2,022	TS	10-year interest rate swap	41
MI	S&P 400 MidCap E-mini	28,266	TU	T-Note 2 yr	24,912
ND	Nasdaq 100	788	TY	T-Note 10 yr	95,793
NE	Nikkei 225 Futures	8,519	UB	Ultra T-Bond	9,341
NK	Nikkei 225 Futures	6,048	UR	Euribor 3 months	3,747
NQ	Nasdaq 100	173,211	US	T-Bond 30 yr	57,588
NZ	New Zealand Dollar	3,809			
PT	S&P Canada 60	11,374			
RL	Russell 2000	91			
RM	Russell 1000 Mini	418			
SP	S&P 500	6,142			
SW	Swiss Market Index	18,880			
TP	TOPIX	8,416			
TW	MSCI Taiwan	24,533			
VH	STOXX Europe 50	196			
XP	ASX SPI 200	16,716			
XX	EURO STOXX 50	80,299			
YM	Dow Jones E-mini	110,122			

The volume of trades over a 67-month period is given in thousands. A full list is given in Wu *et al* (2013, Table 7).

0.999. On the choice of σ, the value 1 minimises the false positive rates for the first group, while the value 0.25 minimises the false positive rates for the second group. Based on the observations from Figure 6.3, we speculate that there are some fundamental differences between the two groups and plan to study their differences in the future.

CONCLUSION

In this study we set out to apply the HPC experience gathered over decades by the National Laboratories on a set of data analysis tasks on high-frequency market data. While some financial practitioners, such as NANEX, use these techniques routinely, there are still relatively few research publications on handling massive amounts of financial data. By borrowing a few techniques from scientific applications, we are able to produce a program that is orders of magnitude faster than the popular approaches for computing VPIN and MIR. The key techniques used include more efficient data organisation, more efficient data structures for computing VPIN, more efficient algorithms for computing MIR and better use of computer resources through parallelisation. We believe that these techniques are useful to many data analysis challenges posed by today's high-frequency markets.

We implemented a popular liquidity metric known as VPIN on a large investment universe of nearly 100 of the most liquid futures contracts over all asset classes. With our software, we are able to quickly examine 16,000 different parameter combinations for evaluating the effectiveness of VPIN. Our results confirm that VPIN is a strong predictor of liquidity-induced volatility, with false positive rates as low as 7% averaged over all futures contracts. The parameter choices to achieve this performance are: pricing the volume bar with the median prices of the trades, 200 buckets per day, 30 bars per bucket, one-day support window for computing VPIN, an event duration of 0.1 days, a bulk volume classification with Student t-distribution with $\nu = 0.1$ and threshold for CDF of VPIN, equal to 0.99. For different classes of futures contracts, it is possible to choose different parameters to achieve even lower false positive rates. On the class of interest-rates-related futures, we have identified parameters that achieve an average false positive rate of 0.3%.

We thank Dr Marcos López de Prado for valuable discussions on computing VPIN and for insightful information about the financial markets. Without his help, we would not have been able to start or to complete this work. We are grateful to TickData for providing the large data set used in this study. We also thank Professors David Easley and Maureen O'Hara for providing valuable comments on an early draft of this chapter.

This work is supported in part by the generous donations to the Center of Innovative Financial Technologies (CIFT) at Lawrence Berkeley National Laboratory, and by the Director, Office of Laboratory Policy and Infrastructure Management of the US Department of Energy under Contract no. DE-AC02-05CH11231. This work used the resources of the National Energy Research Scientific Computing Center (NERSC).

1   See http://cern.ch/lhc/.

2   See http://cmip-pcmdi.llnl.gov/cmip5/.

3   See the PuppetMaster Trading website, http://www.puppetmastertrading.com/blog/2009/01/04/managing-tick-data-with-hdf5/.

4   Information about NERSC can be found at http://nersc.gov/.

5   Note that using CSV files or storing data into a database system would require even more time to bring the data values into memory.

REFERENCES

Abad, D., and J. Yagüe, 2012, "From PIN to VPIN: An Introduction to Order Flow Toxicity", *The Spanish Review of Financial Economics* 10(2), pp. 74–83.

At-Sahalia, Y., P. A. Mykland and L. Zhang, 2005, "How Often to Sample a Continuous-Time Process in the Presence of Market Microstructure Noise", *Review of Financial Studies* 18(2), pp. 351–416.

Amihud, Y., H. Mendelson and M. Murgia, 1990, "Stock Market Microstructure and Return Volatility: Evidence from Italy", *Journal of Banking and Finance* 14(2), pp. 423–40.

Andersen, T. G., and T. Bollerslev, 1998, "Answering the Skeptics: Yes, Standard Volatility Models Do Provide Accurate Forecasts", *International Economic Review* 39(4), pp. 885–905.

Bethel, E. W., and H. Childs, 2012, *High Performance Visualization: Enabling Extreme-Scale Scientific Insight.* London: Chapman & Hall.

Bethel, E. W., D. Leinweber, O. Rübel and K. Wu, 2012, "Federal Market Information Technology in the Post-Flash Crash Era: Roles for Supercomputing", *The Journal of Trading* 7(2), pp. 9–25.

Chakrabarty, B., R. Pascual and A. Shkilko, "Trade Classification Algorithms: A Horse Race between the Bulk-Based and the Tick-Based Rules", Working Paper, http://ssrn.com/abstract=2182819, December.

Easley, D., N. Kiefer, M. O'Hara and J. Paperman, 1996, "Liquidity, Information, and Infrequently Traded Stocks", *Journal of Finance* 51, pp. 1405–1436.

Easley, D., M. López de Prado and M. O'Hara, 2011a, "The Exchange of Flow Toxicity", *The Journal of Trading* 6(2), pp. 8–13.

Easley, D., M. López de Prado and M. O'Hara, 2011b, "The Microstructure of the 'Flash Crash': Flow Toxicity, Liquidity Crashes and the Probability of Informed Trading", *The Journal of Portfolio Management* 37, pp. 118–28.

Easley, D., M. López de Prado and M. O'Hara, 2012a, "Flow Toxicity and Liquidity in a High Frequency World", *Review of Financial Studies* 25(5), pp. 1457–93.

Easley, D., M. López de Prado and M. O'Hara, 2012b, "The Volume Clock: Insights into the High Frequency Paradigm", Working Paper. URL: http://ssrn.com/abstract=2034858.

Hager, G., and G. Wellein, 2010, *Introduction to High Performance Computing for Scientists And Engineers*. Boca Raton, FL: CRC Press.

HDF Group, 2011, "HDF5 User Guide". URL: http://hdfgroup.org/HDF5/doc/UG/.

Kirilenko, A., A. Kyle, M. Samadi and T. Tuzun, 2010, "The Flash Crash: The Impact of High Frequency Trading on an Electronic Market", Working Paper. URL: http://ssrn.com/abstract=1686004.

Kumar, V., A. Grama, A. Gupta and G. Karypis, 1994, *Introduction to Parallel Computing*. Benjamin/Cummings, Redwood City, CA.

Lee, C., and M. J. Ready, 1991, "Inferring Trade Direction from Intraday Data", *Journal of Finance* 46, pp. 733–46.

Lewis, B., and D. J. Berg, 1998, *Multithreaded Programming with Pthreads*. Englewood Cliffs, NJ: Prentice Hall.

López de Prado, M., 2012, "Advances in High Frequency Strategies", PhD Thesis, Cornell University.

Lynch, C., 2008, "Big Data: How Do Your Data Grow?", *Nature* 455(7209), pp. 28–29.

Manyika, J., M. Chui, B. Brown, J. Bughin, R. Dobbs, C. Roxburgh and A. H. Byers, 2011, "Big Data: The Next Frontier for Innovation, Competition, and Productivity", Report. URL: http://www.mckinsey.com/insights/business_technology/big_data_the_next_frontier_for_innovation.

Menkveld, A. J., and B. Yueshen, 2013, "Anatomy of the Flash Crash", Working Paper. URL: http://ssrn.com/abstract=2243520.

Shiller, R. J., 1992, *Market Volatility*. Cambridge, MA: MIT Press.

Shoshani, A., and D. Rotem, 2010, *Scientific Data Management: Challenges, Technology, and Deployment*, Volume 3. Boca Raton, FL: Chapman and Hall/CRC.

Wu, K., E. W. Bethel, M. Gu, D. Leinweber and O. Ruebel, 2013, "A Big Data Approach to Analyzing Market Volatility", Working Paper, http://ssrn.com/abstract=2274991.

7

Liquidity and Toxicity Contagion

David Easley; Marcos López de Prado; Maureen O'Hara
Cornell University; RCC at Harvard University; Cornell University

Legislative changes in the US (Regulation National Market System (Reg NMS)) of 2005 and Europe (Markets in Financial Instruments Directive (MiFID), in force since November 2007), preceded by substantial technological advances in computation and communication, have revolutionised the financial markets. MiFID fosters greater competition among brokers, with the objective of improving liquidity, cohesion and depth in financial markets. Similarly, Reg NMS encourages competitiveness among exchanges by allowing market fragmentation. Cohesion across markets is recovered through a mechanism for the consolidation of individual orders processed in multiple venues into a single best bid or offer price for the market as a whole (the National Best Bid and Offer (NBBO)). Since the arrival of trading in multiple markets, an "arms race" has developed for the technology and quantitative methods that can squeeze out the last cent of profitability when serving the demands of market participants, hence the advent of high-frequency trading. Easley *et al* (2011a) have argued that these changes are related to a number of new trends in market microstructure.

One area where this competition is particularly intense is in liquidity provision. In this new era of high-frequency trading, liquidity is provided by computers executing adaptive (or machine learning) algorithms. These algorithms operate both within and across markets, reflecting that market making is now often a dynamic process in which bids are placed in one market and asks in another. Indeed, the entire financial market has become a complex network that discovers equilibrium prices by reconciling the actions taken by large numbers

Figure 7.1 Implied pricing relationships of GEH2

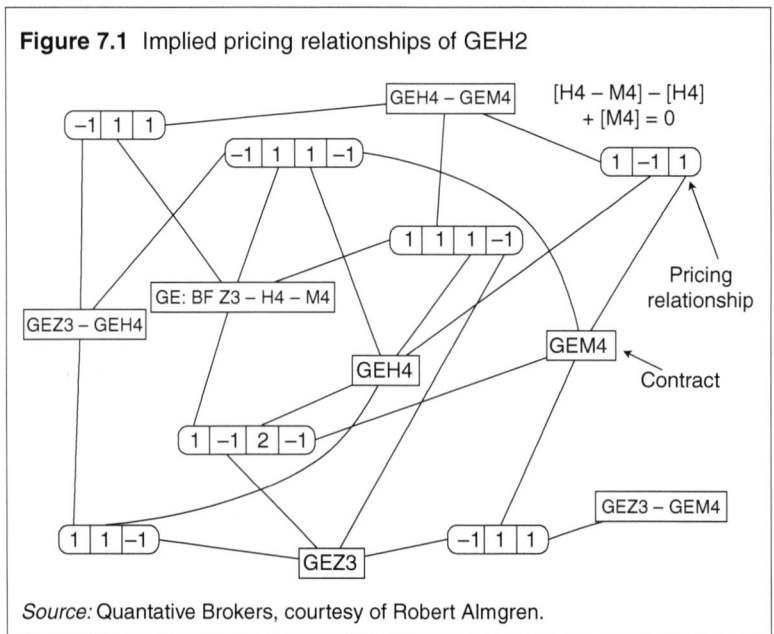

Source: Quantative Brokers, courtesy of Robert Almgren.

of agents interacting with each other. Exchanges operate very much like modems, struggling to route massive numbers of independently and asynchronously generated messages, both to their own order books and to the order books of other venues.

One important implication of this process is that the dynamics of order books are interrelated across multiple products. Figure 7.1 illustrates how, in order to decide the level at which to place a client's order on eurodollar short futures, Quantitative Brokers' algorithms analyse six different relationships in real time, searching for "hidden liquidity" (liquidity that, although it is not displayed in that particular book, may be implied by the liquidity present in the related books). Consequently, in order to operate on the first eight eurodollar contracts, Quantitative Brokers monitors the liquidity conditions for 278 contracts, 539 combos and 1917 edges (see Figure 7.2). This level of sophistication was inconceivable, both technically and mathematically, at the turn of the twenty-first century, but it reflects the new reality of how trading takes place in a high-frequency world.

The technology which interconnects markets allows informed traders to search for liquidity around the globe. Liquidity providers similarly provide liquidity across markets, responding rapidly to changing conditions in one market by revising limit orders in that

Figure 7.2 Complete relationship map

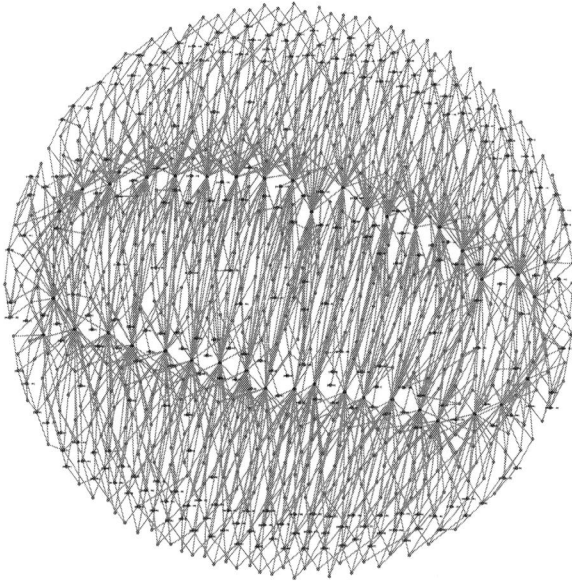

278 contracts (dark dots), 539 combos (light dots) and 1917 edges (grey lines).
Source: Quantative Brokers from CME data, courtesy of Robert Almgren.

market as well as in related markets. As a result, we expect to find order flow from informed traders as well as order flow from liquidity providers, influenced by informed order flow, moving across markets. This order flow is called toxic order flow; it is persistently imbalanced, as it arises from traders who are better informed about future price movements than are the liquidity providers in the market. If traders behave as we conjecture, then we should find evidence that toxic order flow is propagated using the same channels that sophisticated brokers use to place their clients' orders. That is, we should observe contagion in toxic order flow across markets.

The idea that contagion occurs across markets is not new. Brunnermeier and Pedersen (2005) theorised that predatory trading could amplify contagion and price impact in related markets. This amplification would not be driven by a correlation in economic fundamentals or by information spillovers, but rather by the composition of the holdings of large traders who must significantly reduce their positions. Carlin *et al* (2007) developed a model of how predatory trading can lead to episodic liquidity crises and contagion. The approach we take in this chapter is related to these papers, but we begin from a different point of view. We see contagion as the natural consequence of market makers revising their orders in one market in response to changing liquidity conditions in related markets.

In this chapter we build a simple, exploratory model of these contagion effects and we estimate the parameters of the model to quantify the impact of contagion across markets. The next section provides our dynamic model of the toxicity contagion process. Then we give estimates of the parameters of the model to show that toxicity contagion does in fact occur. The final section offers some conclusions.

AN ORDER FLOW TOXICITY CONTAGION MODEL

We define order flow toxicity as the persistent arrival of imbalanced order flow. Contagion occurs when the increase of toxicity in one instrument presages an increase of toxicity in another instrument. One source of contagion is market makers hedging their risk of adverse selection in one instrument by taking liquidity in another, with the hope that over time they will be able to unwind their positions in both instruments at a profit. In this section we study this source of the contagion dynamics of order flow (see López de Prado and Leinweber (2012) for a discussion of advanced hedging methods).

Consider two related financial instruments, such as heating oil and gasoline. These two commodities are the result of the chemical process of cracking crude oil. Because the ratio of their outputs is determined by the efficiency of an industrial process, their relative supply can be modelled quantitatively. So it is only natural that a sudden excess supply (selling pressure) in one contract will eventually result in selling pressure in the other contract. Market makers are aware of that linkage and act accordingly. This intuition suggests that the linkage across markets arises from an order flow imbalance in one market leading to an order flow imbalance in another related market. This linkage will, of course, result in prices being linked across the two markets.[1]

We begin by examining pairs of contracts indexed by $i = \{1, 2\}$. We assume that there is an equilibrium relationship between (absolute) order flow imbalance in one contract at some time and order flow imbalance in the other contract at the same time. This relationship

Figure 7.3 Rolling moving averages (of 750 observations) of order flow imbalances for front-line futures contracts for RBOB Gasoline (XB) and #2 Heating Oil (HO) for the period 2007–12

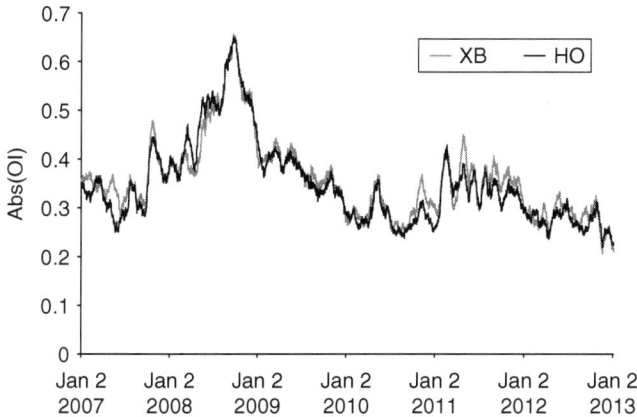

should occur whether we look in calendar time or in trade time. Following the intuition in Easley *et al* (2012c), we focus on trade time, as order flow imbalances are better behaved (statistically) in trade time. The trade time approach provides an estimate of order flow imbalance in a contract for each of the contract's trade buckets; that is, it provides a new estimate of order flow imbalance every time a particular number of trades has occurred.[2] Applying this procedure directly to each contract in any pair of contracts would result in asynchronous updates in order flow imbalance.[3] To synchronise the updates, we estimate order flow imbalance every 30 minutes for each contract, looking back over a fixed number of trades in that contract. This mix of calendar time and trade time results in order flow imbalance estimates that update once every 30 minutes for each contract.

We first consider a simple example of this relationship between order flow imbalances for two contracts. Figure 7.3 provides a graph of rolling moving averages (of 750 observations) of order flow imbalances for front-line futures contracts for RBOB Gasoline (XB) and #2 Heating Oil (HO) for the period 2007–12. These two contracts have mean order flow imbalances of 0.1765 for XB and 0.1715 for HO with standard deviations of 0.1197 and 0.1183, respectively. Both series are positively autocorrelated, with AR1 coefficients of 0.6345 and 0.6312, respectively. Figure 7.3 suggests that the two series are also

Figure 7.4 Moving average simple correlations, using a window of one-month, between the order imbalances for RBOB Gasoline (XB) and #2 Heating Oil (HO) for the period 2007–12

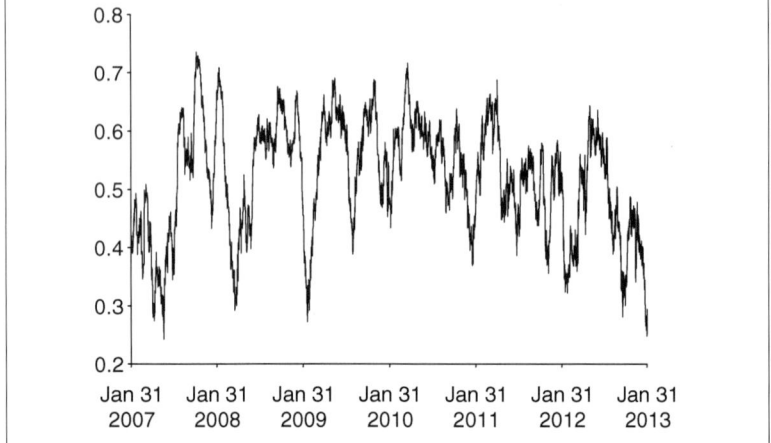

positively correlated. As a first step towards understanding these co-movements we compute moving average simple correlations, using a window of one month, between the order imbalances for these two contracts. Figure 7.4 provides a graph of these moving average simple correlations for our two example contracts. It is apparent from Figure 7.4 that these correlations are not constant. So, looking at an average of these correlations over our sample period would be misleading. In fact, Figure 7.4 suggests that there is a deeper, dynamic structure here than can be revealed by simple correlations.

To capture this underlying relationship between order flow imbalances we need a model of the dynamic relationship between them. We begin by building a simple illustrative model of the dynamics, which we then apply to various pairs of contracts.

Let $OI_{i,\tau}$ denote order flow imbalance in contract i at time τ, where τ indexes the sequential observations of order imbalance. For the technological reasons stated earlier, we shall posit that there is a proportional, long-run relationship between the order imbalances of two related instruments, such as heating oil and gasoline

$$OI_{i,\tau} = K\,OI_{2,\tau} \tag{7.1}$$

where K is the constant of proportionality. In logarithmic form we have $oi_{1,\tau} = k + oi_{2,\tau}$, where the lower case indicates the natural logarithm of the upper case variables.

Even though there is a long-run relationship between these order imbalances, they are subject to shocks and thus do not need to move in lockstep. However, we expect that deviations from the equilibrium condition expressed in Equation 7.1 will be corrected over time, and we analyse this correction process with a simple error-correction model. Error-correction models are closely related to the concept of cointegration (Almgren applied this latter concept in Chapter 3) although they are not in general identical.[4]

When a shock occurs to the order flow imbalance in one contract we do not expect order flow imbalance in the other contract to immediately adjust to its long-run equilibrium level. Instead, we expect it to adjust over trade time. As a simple model of a form that the dynamics might take, we assume that the short-run, out-of-equilibrium relationship between $OI_{1,\tau}$ and $OI_{2,\tau}$ can be represented as

$$oi_{1,\tau} = \beta_0 + \beta_1 \, oi_{2,\tau} + \beta_2 \, oi_{2,\tau-1} + \alpha_1 \, oi_{1,\tau-1} + \varepsilon_\tau \qquad (7.2)$$

where ε_τ is an independent and identically distributed, mean-zero shock. We also assume that this dynamical system has an equilibrium and that in the absence of shocks it converges to this equilibrium. For the dynamical system represented by Equation 7.2 at an equilibrium (OI_1^*, OI_2^*), it must be that

$$oi_1^* = \beta_0 + \beta_1 \, oi_2^* + \beta_2 \, oi_2^* + \alpha_1 \, oi_1^* \qquad (7.3)$$

which implies

$$oi_1^* = \frac{\beta_0}{1 - \alpha_1} + \frac{\beta_1 + \beta_2}{1 - \alpha_1} \, oi_2^*$$

This determines the relationship between the parameters of our dynamical system and those of the long-run relationship between our two variables as

$$\left. \begin{array}{l} k = \dfrac{\beta_0}{1 - \alpha_1} \\[2mm] \beta_1 + \beta_2 = 1 - \alpha_1 \end{array} \right\} \qquad (7.4)$$

To simplify the notation we define $y \equiv \beta_1 + \beta_2$. The equilibrium condition then implies that $\beta_2 = y - \beta_1$ and $\alpha_1 = 1 - y$. Thus, our dynamic equation can be rewritten as the following equation in differences

$$\Delta \, oi_{1,\tau} = \beta_0 + \beta_1 \Delta \, oi_{2,\tau} + y(oi_{2,\tau-1} - oi_{1,\tau-1}) + \varepsilon_\tau \qquad (7.5)$$

where $y(oi_{2,\tau-1} - oi_{1,\tau-1})$ is the "error-correction" term that, over time, corrects cumulative hedging errors and ensures the convergence of the order imbalances to a long-run equilibrium.

Before proceeding with the analysis it may be useful to note what our system does or does not determine. We have a discrete-time, dynamic system in two variables (the two order imbalances). The dynamic system, Equation 7.2, provides only one equation for these two variables. So we do not specify a full system determining the two order imbalances. More precisely, if we know the values of the two variables at time $\tau - 1$ and the shock in Equation 7.2, we have a relationship between the two variables at time τ, but not their actual values. One way to interpret this is that there may be some process driving one of the variables, say $OI_{2,\tau}$, and, given that process, we know the other one, $OI_{1,\tau}$, evolves. Our assumption that there is a long-run relationship between our two variables and that the error-correction process converges to it imposes conditions on the driving equation, which we do not need to specify for our analysis of the relation between the two variables.

Note that stability of the system described by Equation 7.5 (ie, in the absence of disturbances ($\Delta oi_{2,\tau}, \varepsilon_\tau$), oi_1 converging to its equilibrium level) requires $y > 0$. To see this, suppose that $\Delta oi_{2,\tau} = 0$, $\varepsilon_\tau = 0$. Then

$$\Delta oi_{1,\tau} = \beta_0 + y(oi_{2,\tau-1} - oi_{1,\tau-1})$$

Applying the equilibrium conditions leaves us with

$$\Delta oi_{1,\tau} = y(k + oi_{2,\tau-1} - oi_{1,\tau-1})$$

where $k + oi_{2,\tau-1}$ is the equilibrium value of oi_1 for observation $\tau - 1$. If

$$k + oi_{2,\tau-1} - oi_{1,\tau-1} > 0$$

then oi_1 is less than its equilibrium level at $\tau - 1$, in which case the error correction must compensate for the difference to ensure convergence (ie, y must be positive). This has the important consequence that, given our maintained stability hypothesis, a test of significance on y should be one-tailed, with $H_0: y \leqslant 0$.

Table 7.1 Front-contract energy commodity futures

Symbol	Description	Roll	Exchange	Buffer size
CL	Light CrudeNYMEX	*19	NYMEX	2296
HO	Heating Oil #2	*27	NYMEX	321
NG	Natural Gas	0	NYMEX	739
QG	Natural Gas E-mini	0	NYMEX	28
QM	Crude Oil E-mini	*19	NYMEX	152
XB	RBOB Gasoline	*27	NYMEX	251

The six futures contracts under consideration are all traded on the New York Mercantile Exchange (NYMEX). For each contract the buffer size is one-fiftieth of the average daily activity in that contract for the period January 1, 2007, to February 4, 2013. An asterisk followed by an integer value indicates that the roll was applied that number of days before expiration, unless the volume shifted to the next serial contract before that day. A zero value in the roll column indicates that the roll date was purely determined by the transfer of volume from one contract to the next.

EMPIRICAL ANALYSIS

Our theoretical model provides a structure for the linkage between markets through the adjustment of order flow imbalances. In this section we fit the model to data to determine if the order flow adjustment process is in fact consistent with our approach.

We studied the six front-line futures contracts listed in Table 7.1, for the period January 1, 2007, to February 4, 2013. These are actively traded products all trading on the same exchange (NYMEX). We focused on a single US exchange so as to avoid the possibility of introducing artificial lead–lag relationships resulting from the clocks of different exchanges possibly not being well synchronised.

We used level 1 tick (trade-by-trade) data as provided by Globex. First, we loaded the data into a database and generated a properly rolled series for each instrument. Second, we computed the average number of trades per session (ADT). Third, every 30 minutes we generated a bucket containing the previous ADT/50 trades, ie, a bucket equivalent to one-fiftieth of the average number of trades in a session. Fourth, for each bucket we estimated the order imbalance, using the bulk volume method introduced by Easley *et al* (2012a). This method assigns a fraction of the trades in each bucket as buys or sells, based on the price change from beginning to end of the bucket relative to the distribution of price changes in the sample. Intuitively, if there is no price change over the bucket, then the trade is assumed to be balanced, ie, half of the trades are buys and half are sells. If prices increase, then the fraction assumed to be buys is greater than one-half; how much greater depends on the magnitude of the price increase relative to the distribution of price changes. Details for this procedure and an evaluation of its accuracy are provided in Easley *et al* (2012b).

The result of this procedure is that we create estimates of (absolute) order imbalance, chronologically synchronised for each product, timed at half and whole hours. Each order imbalance is based on transactional buffers of comparable size (one-fiftieth of the respective average daily activity). If the order imbalance is zero for a half-hour period in one contract in a pair, that data point must be dropped, as we shall examine logs of order imbalances. This procedure generates 15 pairs of order imbalance series. Summary statistics about these pairs of order imbalances are provided in Table 7.2.

We estimated Equation 7.5 for each of the pairs of instruments in Table 7.2, which yielded the results listed in Table 7.3. The estimated residuals from a simple regression based on Equation 7.5 are not serially uncorrelated and homoscedastic. So we compute the Newey–West heteroscedasticity- and autocorrelation consistent (HAC) estimates of the regressors in order to determine their statistical significance. Following Newey and West (1994), we apply a Bartlett kernel on a number of lags equal to $\text{Int}[4(n/100)^{2/9}]$, where n is the total number of observations.

The number of contemporaneous observations in our regressions ranges between 49,144 and 66,187, depending on how much of the daily activity between two products overlaps. The adjusted R-squared value ranges between 0.1155 and 0.3065. All of the regressions are statistically significant, as evidenced by the high values the F-statistic of model significance. We also report the estimates of $\hat{\beta}_0$, $\hat{\beta}_1$ and $\hat{\gamma}$, which are statistically different from zero to any reasonable critical level. In particular, $\hat{\gamma} \gg 0$, with values between 0.2308 and 0.5693.

The fact that $\hat{\gamma}$ is statistically significant and positive is the evidence we needed to conclude the existence of contagion. More formally, our results indicate that order flow imbalances in our pairs of contracts can be viewed as following an error-correction process. Most importantly, order flow imbalances are related across

Table 7.2 Summary statistics for order imbalances for our pairs of contracts, January 1, 2007 to February 4, 2013

Instr1	Instr2	Mean1	Mean2	SD1	SD2	Skew1	Skew2	Kurt2	Kurt1	AR1$_1$	AR1$_2$
QG	QM	0.1796	0.2068	0.1194	0.1172	0.3990	0.0822	2.1735	2.5735	0.4463	0.3289
QG	XB	0.1805	0.1752	0.1192	0.1195	0.3747	0.5405	2.5349	2.5664	0.4168	0.6038
QG	HO	0.1808	0.1710	0.1194	0.1182	0.3717	0.6187	2.7203	2.5548	0.4224	0.6084
QG	NG	0.1796	0.1396	0.1193	0.1168	0.3962	1.0291	3.4511	2.5785	0.4415	0.7497
QG	CL	0.1799	0.1917	0.1195	0.1164	0.3957	0.3120	2.3531	2.5638	0.4473	0.4512
QM	XB	0.2061	0.1772	0.1172	0.1198	0.0929	0.5142	2.4893	2.1799	0.3502	0.6442
QM	HO	0.2060	0.1728	0.1172	0.1185	0.0933	0.5934	2.6714	2.1806	0.3595	0.6515
QM	NG	0.2062	0.1430	0.1172	0.1180	0.0928	0.9820	3.2929	2.1817	0.3731	0.7756
QM	CL	0.2061	0.1914	0.1173	0.1166	0.0934	0.3245	2.3654	2.1814	0.3880	0.5177
XB	HO	0.1765	0.1715	0.1197	0.1183	0.5215	0.6119	2.7070	2.5003	0.6345	0.6312
XB	NG	0.1765	0.1415	0.1196	0.1169	0.5240	1.0017	3.3811	2.5105	0.6341	0.7485
XB	CL	0.1780	0.1911	0.1199	0.1163	0.5023	0.3237	2.3679	2.4683	0.6418	0.4711
HO	NG	0.1729	0.1408	0.1185	0.1170	0.5919	1.0123	3.3981	2.6670	0.6408	0.7599
HO	CL	0.1733	0.1913	0.1186	0.1163	0.5876	0.3239	2.3662	2.6588	0.6503	0.4840
NG	CL	0.1443	0.1913	0.1183	0.1163	0.9596	0.3235	2.3720	3.2365	0.7733	0.4985

Columns show mean, standard deviation, skewness, kurtosis and the AR1 coefficient. The data is presented in pairs, because if the order imbalance is zero for a half-hour period in one contract in a pair, that data point is dropped for the pair. This procedure generates fifteen pairs of order imbalance series.

Table 7.3 Results of Fitting the error correction model

Instr1	Instr2	Obs	Adj R^2	F-value	F-prob	Beta0	Beta1	Gamma	Beta0 prob	Beta1 prob	Gamma prob
QG	QM	51151	0.1847	5795.1677	0.0000	-0.0115	0.1916	0.3683	0.0000	0.0000	0.0000
QG	XB	49144	0.1155	3208.1384	0.0000	0.0790	0.1182	0.2308	0.0000	0.0000	0.0000
QG	HO	50451	0.1189	3405.4949	0.0000	0.0867	0.1222	0.2346	0.0000	0.0000	0.0000
QG	NG	51312	0.1431	4284.9100	0.0000	0.1461	0.2098	0.2549	0.0000	0.0000	0.0000
QG	CL	51702	0.1554	4758.6063	0.0000	0.0454	0.1542	0.3056	0.0000	0.0000	0.0000
QM	XB	60924	0.1822	6786.4844	0.0000	0.1222	0.2353	0.3585	0.0000	0.0000	0.0000
QM	HO	62831	0.1861	7182.6699	0.0000	0.1325	0.2512	0.3601	0.0000	0.0000	0.0000
QM	NG	63330	0.1358	4975.7936	0.0000	0.1679	0.1419	0.2747	0.0000	0.0000	0.0000
QM	CL	66187	0.2969	13977.2348	0.0000	0.0853	0.4045	0.5016	0.0000	0.0000	0.0000
XB	HO	61408	0.3010	13224.0926	0.0000	0.0180	0.3928	0.5591	0.0000	0.0000	0.0000
XB	NG	60057	0.2058	7781.7165	0.0000	0.1103	0.2217	0.4125	0.0000	0.0000	0.0000
XB	CL	61700	0.2934	12807.8561	0.0000	-0.0874	0.3577	0.5549	0.0000	0.0000	0.0000
HO	NG	61865	0.2095	8200.1635	0.0000	0.1063	0.2298	0.4178	0.0000	0.0000	0.0000
HO	CL	63627	0.3065	14059.2175	0.0000	-0.1069	0.3991	0.5693	0.0000	0.0000	0.0000
NG	CL	64186	0.1789	6991.2849	0.0000	-0.1485	0.1887	0.3565	0.0000	0.0000	0.0000

Obs denotes the number of observations used in the error correction model that combines instruments 1 and 2. Adj R^2 is the adjusted R-squared value, F-value is the statistic of the F-test, and F-prob is the associated probability. Beta0, Beta1 and Gamma are the regression coefficients. The probabilities that Beta0 and Beta1 are statistically different from zero are reported in the columns Beta0 prob and Beta1 prob. The probability that Gamma is statistically greater than zero is reported by Gamma prob. These probabilities are consistent with Newey–West HAC estimates.

pairs of the contracts in our sample. The autoregressive coefficients reported in Table 7.2 are well within the unit circle, providing evidence that the series of the logarithms of order imbalances are stationary. Thus, although these series are not cointegrated, there is an error-correction term that regulates the convergence to a long-run equilibrium between the logarithms of the order imbalances.

We began our discussion arguing that market makers hedge their risk of adverse selection. They do so by hedging their accumulated inventories with offsetting positions in related instruments, such as heating oil versus gasoline (XB–HO). A long inventory of XB may be acquired by providing liquidity, but hedging a short position in HO requires the taking of liquidity. This is the microstructural mechanism that spreads toxicity across related products, which we have called toxicity contagion. For this particular pair, $\hat{y} \approx 0.56$. This is consistent with the presence of a long-run equilibrium between the order imbalances of both products, only perturbed by short-lived disturbances. It is precisely this error-correction mechanism, empirically shown by $\hat{y} > 0$, that is responsible for the contagion of order flow toxicity.

Our results are not surprising, as market interconnectivity provides a venue for brokers as well as predators to search for hidden liquidity globally. A consequence of these connections is that market makers' ability to diversify the risk of being adversely selected by providing liquidity to a wide number of order books is limited. Effective hedging against flow toxicity may thus require alternative solutions, such as the one discussed in Easley *et al* (2011b).

CONCLUSION

Our analysis of toxicity contagion focused on energy commodities because of the physical arbitrage nature of the relationship between them. But our approach could be applied to other asset classes with interrelated products and we would expect to find similar conclusions. Toxicity contagion should occur across any related products because of the actions of market makers and other market participants who trade across markets. In our analysis we focused on pairs of products, but the analysis could also be extended to larger groups of products.

The toxicity contagion results in our study provide a caution for researchers analysing order flow imbalance on a product-by-product basis. We showed that there is an error-correction relationship between order flow imbalances across related products. One important consequence of this relationship is that there is information in the order flow imbalance in one product about order flow imbalance, and thus price changes, across related products.

This relationship between order flow imbalances across markets has intriguing implications for both traders and regulators. Traders seeking to minimise the cost of implementing any desired transaction can better predict the impact of their orders on quotes if they take into account order flow imbalance not only for the contract they want to trade, but also for any related contracts. This is because, as we have shown, there is feedback between related markets. Similarly, regulators who are interested in predicting liquidity events in one market can improve their predictions by taking into account not only order flow imbalance in their own market, but also order flow imbalances for any related contracts in other markets. Our particular model of the relationship between order flow imbalances across contracts is only meant to be an exploratory model of this potentially complex relationship. Applications to trading or regulation would need more a complete analysis, but, as our results indicate, this is a fruitful area for future research.

We thank Robert Almgren for allowing us to reproduce materials owned by Quantitative Brokers.

1   We could examine linkages in order flow, in price or in price changes across markets. We study order flows because they cause the price changes. Thus, studying order flows give us an ability to understand a cause of price volatility.

2   As an example, we could compute the order imbalance after every 40,000 contracts are traded. The 40,000 would be the "bucket size" and the imbalance we seek to estimate is the percentage of those contracts initiated by buyers as opposed to those initiated by sellers. If the number of buyer-initiated contracts where the same as the seller-initiated contracts, then there would be zero imbalance.

3   This is because, while time is constant across all contracts, the volume traded is not. If we calculate order imbalance every 40,000 contracts traded, then it is likely that one market will be ahead of the other.

4   If there is a stationary linear combination of nonstationary random variables $oi_{1,\tau}$ and $oi_{2,\tau}$, then the variables are said to be cointegrated (Granger 1981). Engle and Granger's representation theorem (Engle and Granger 1987) states that cointegrated random variables accept an error-correction representation, and error-correcting, integrated series accept a cointegration representation. For more on the relationship between cointegration and error-correction models, see Alogoskoufis and Smith (1991). De Boef and Keele (2008) provide a discussion of the use of error-correction models for stationary time series.

REFERENCES

Alogoskoufis, G., and R. Smith, 1991, "On Error Correction Models: Specification, Interpretation, Estimation", *Journal of Economic Surveys* 5(1), pp. 97–128.

Brunnermeier, M., and L. H. Pedersen, 2005, "Predatory Trading", *Journal of Finance* 40(4), pp. 1825–63.

Carlin, B., M. Sousa Lobo and S. Viswanathan, 2007, "Episodic Liquidity Crises: Cooperative and Predatory Trading", *Journal of Finance* 42(5), pp. 2235–74.

De Boef, S. and L. Keele, 2008, "Taking Time Seriously", *American Journal of Political Science* 52(1), pp. 184–200.

Easley, D., M. López de Prado and M. O'Hara, 2011a, "The Microstructure of the Flash Crash: Flow Toxicity, Liquidity Crashes and the Probability of Informed Trading", *Journal of Portfolio Management* 37(2), pp. 118–28.

Easley, D., M. López de Prado and M. O'Hara, 2011b, "The Exchange of Flow Toxicity", *The Journal of Trading* 6(2), pp. 8–13.

Easley, D., M. López de Prado and M. O'Hara, 2012a, "Flow Toxicity and Liquidity in a High Frequency World", *Review of Financial Studies* 25(5), pp. 1457–93.

Easley, D., M. López de Prado and M. O'Hara, 2012b, "Bulk Volume Classification", Working Paper. URL: http://ssrn.com/abstract=1989555.

Easley, D., M. López de Prado and M. O'Hara, 2012c, "The Volume Clock: Insights into the High Frequency Paradigm", *Journal of Portfolio Management* 39(1), pp. 19–29.

Engle, R., and C. Granger, 1987, "Co-integration and Error Correction: Representation, Estimation and Testing", *Econometrica* 55(2), pp. 251–75.

Granger, C., 1981, "Some Properties of Time Series Data and Their Use in Econometric Model Specification", *Journal of Econometrics* 16, pp. 121–30.

López de Prado, M., and D. Leinweber, 2012, "Advances in Cointegration and Subset Correlation Hedging Methods", *The Journal of Investment Strategies* 1(2), pp. 67–115.

Newey, W. K., and West, K. D., 1994, "Automatic Tag Selection in Covariance Matrix Estimation", *Review of Economic Studies* 61(4), pp. 631–54.

8

Do Algorithmic Executions Leak Information?

George Sofianos, JuanJuan Xiang

Goldman Sachs Equity Execution Strats

Asset managers are concerned that the algorithms they use to execute their orders may leak information to predators. Predators are traders who use this information to trade in the same direction as the asset managers, increasing the asset managers' trading costs. Asset managers are particularly concerned about leaking information to high-frequency trading (HFT) predators.

In this chapter, we develop and empirically test a framework for evaluating whether algorithmic ("algo") executions leak information. Based on the Goldman Sachs Electronic Trading (GSET) algo executions we tested, our main finding is that these algo executions do not leak information that predators, including HFT predators, can profitably exploit. The algos we tested, by slicing up large high-Alpha orders into smaller orders and executing them over time, make it expensive for predators to identify and profitably trade along these orders.

In the next section, we define information leakage and distinguish between good and bad information leakage. We next show how bad information leakage increases execution shortfall and introduce the BadMax approach for testing whether algos leak information to predators. In the BadMax approach, we pretend to be BadMax, a fictitious predator. As BadMax, we use historical data to back-test whether BadMax can construct profitable predatory strategies. We next describe the historical data we use in our back-tests and estimate the BadMax gross and net Alpha for several BadMax predatory strategies. In our back-tests we assume that BadMax can somehow

Figure 8.1 Good and bad information leakage (hypothetical example)

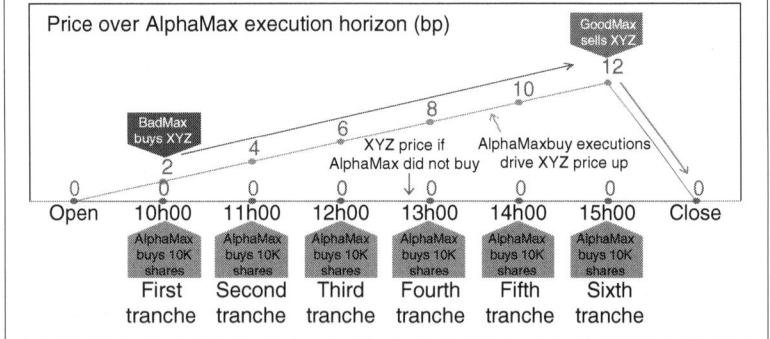

identify GSET buy and sell algo executions. In practice, BadMax will have a very hard time identifying GSET buy and sell algo executions from the real-time publicly disseminated trade prices ("the Tape"). We summarise our findings in the final section.

DEFINING INFORMATION LEAKAGE

Using AlphaMax, a fictitious trader, we define information leakage as follows: if other traders can reliably generate Alpha signals from AlphaMax's order executions, AlphaMax's executions leak information.[1] AlphaMax executions leak information if they cause the signal generated by other traders. This causality from AlphaMax executions to the signal generated by other traders is the defining feature of information leakage: if AlphaMax did not trade, other traders would not generate this signal. In our empirical tests, we use this causality to identify executions that may leak information. But first we must distinguish between good and bad information leakage.

In Figure 8.1, AlphaMax buys 60,000 shares XYZ in six tranches, from 10h00 to 15h00. The AlphaMax "buy" executions increase the price by 12 basis points (bp) and then the price reverts. Good information leakage occurs when AlphaMax "buy" executions prompt another trader, GoodMax, to sell. In Figure 8.1 at 15h00, GoodMax expects the price will fall and immediately sells XYZ. GoodMax sells while AlphaMax is buying. GoodMax, therefore, provides liquidity to AlphaMax and reduces AlphaMax's trading costs.[2]

Bad information leakage occurs when AlphaMax "buy" executions prompt another trader, BadMax, to buy. In Figure 8.1 at 10h00,

BadMax expects the price will continue to increase and immediately buys XYZ along with AlphaMax, increasing AlphaMax's
trading costs. BadMax is a predator, using the Alpha signal created by AlphaMax's executions to capture Alpha at the expense of
AlphaMax.[3]

Figure 8.1 also illustrates the important causality that defines
information leakage. If AlphaMax did not try to buy 60,000 shares,
the XYZ price would have been flat from open to close and BadMax
would not have generated the signal to buy XYZ.

Our examination of information leakage focuses on BadMax and
bad information leakage. AlphaMax may leak information to Bad-
Max at any point in the order life cycle. Figure 8.2 traces the life
cycle of an algo order beginning with the AlphaMax portfolio manager (PM) creating a parent order for 500,000 shares and ending with
executions of 100 shares reported to the Tape.

PMs, buy-side traders, algos, smart routers, execution venues
and the Tape may all leak information. PMs may leak information
through headcount turnover. An AlphaMax PM, for example, moves
to BadMax and replicates the AlphaMax investment strategy. Buy-
side traders may leak information when they shop orders with several brokers. Algos may leak information by slicing large orders into
predictable patterns. Smart routers may leak information by repeatedly executing on the same venue. Exchanges may leak information
when they display limit orders.

In Figure 8.3, we use a sample of GSET algo orders to show that
the Alpha signal diminishes as orders move down the algo order
life cycle.[4] We first look at the beginning of the algo order life cycle,
at algo parent orders. Our sample includes 15,000 large algo parent
orders (more than 50,000 shares). On these large orders, the average
Alpha from arrival to same-day close is 29bp.[5] This 29bp Alpha is
the signal AlphaMax wants to protect and the signal BadMax wants
to identify.

We next look at the end of the algo order life cycle, at the executions reported to the Tape. Our sample has 15 million algo executions
and the average execution size is 153 shares. The average Alpha from
execution to same-day close is −3bp.[6] These 15 million executions
include the executions from the 15,000 large high-Alpha algo parent
orders. But they also include executions from many small low-Alpha
algo parent orders. Algos, by slicing large high-Alpha parent orders

Figure 8.2 Order life cycle

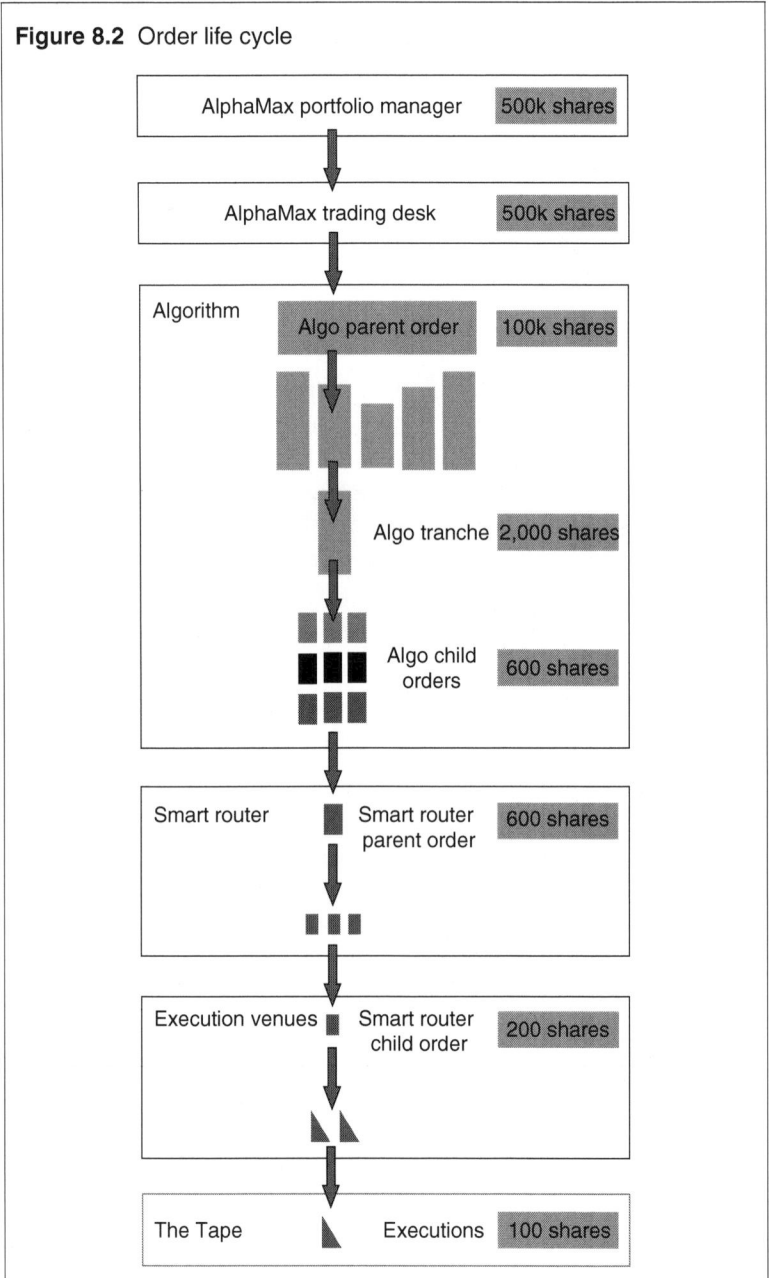

AlphaMax portfolio manager	500k shares

AlphaMax trading desk	500k shares

Algorithm

Algo parent order	100k shares

Algo tranche | 2,000 shares

Algo child orders | 600 shares

Smart router

Smart router parent order | 600 shares

Execution venues

Smart router child order | 200 shares

The Tape

Executions | 100 shares

into small child orders and mixing them with small low-Alpha parent orders, eliminate the Alpha signal at the end of the order life cycle.

Figure 8.3 The Alpha signal of algo orders

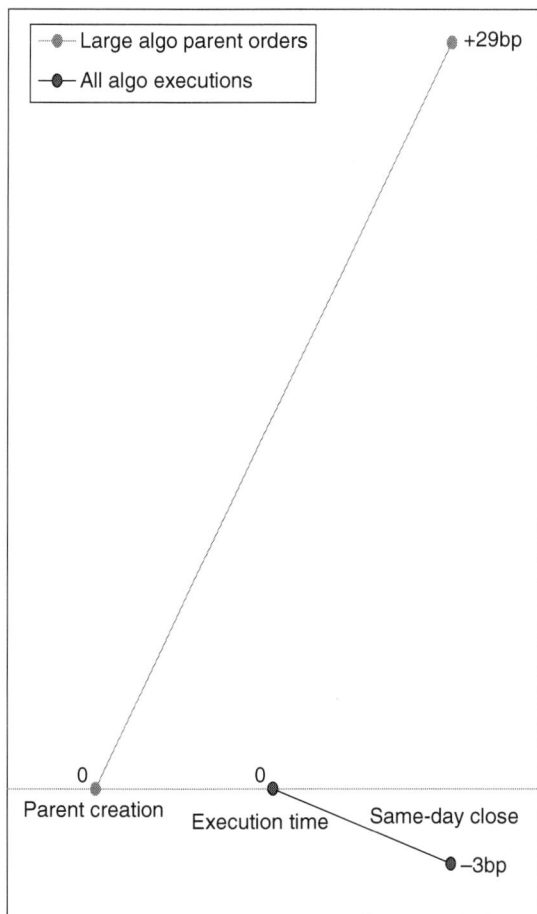

GSET algo orders and executions, October 3–28, 2011; re-stitched parent orders including both filled and non-filled shares.

One of the questions we try to answer in this chapter is whether BadMax can identify large high-Alpha parent orders from clusters of small child order executions at the end of the order life cycle.

AlphaMax may leak information to predators in three ways.

1. AlphaMax executions may leak information to predators through the Tape. AlphaMax, for example, may leak information by executing buy orders above the mid-quote (and sell orders below the mid). By analysing the Tape, BadMax

will observe that above-mid executions are usually followed by a price increase. AlphaMax's above-mid buy executions, therefore, may trigger BadMax buy orders.[7] AlphaMax may also leak information through the Tape by slicing large orders into small orders and executing them in a predictable pattern (eg, 150 shares every 15 seconds). By analysing the Tape, BadMax may identify the pattern, anticipate AlphaMax large-order executions and trade along. In both these examples, it is the AlphaMax executions, and not the AlphaMax orders, that leak information.[8]

2. AlphaMax orders may leak information to predators who ping. BadMax, for example, may use small peg mid instant or cancel (IOC) orders to ping a dark pool. Several successful BadMax "sell" pings in rapid succession may indicate the presence of a large AlphaMax non-displayed buy order and trigger BadMax buy orders.

3. AlphaMax may leak information to predators with an inside view. BadMax, for example, may have an inside view of a dark pool's book, seeing non-displayed orders as they arrive. Or BadMax may have an inside view of an algo provider's blotter, seeing the client algo parent orders as they arrive. Either a Badmax inside view is unauthorised or the venue providing BadMax with an inside view of non-displayed orders is violating its obligation not to display. In both cases, an inside view is most probably illegal and the penalty likely to be severe.

We next discuss how bad information leakage increases AlphaMax execution shortfall.

BAD INFORMATION LEAKAGE AND EXECUTION SHORTFALL

Figure 8.4 shows two scenarios of how bad information leakage increases AlphaMax execution shortfall. For buy orders, execution shortfall is the execution price minus mid at order arrival as a percentage of the mid at order arrival. In both scenarios, AlphaMax buys 60,000 shares from 10h00 to 15h00 in six tranches. In scenario A the AlphaMax order has high Alpha (29bp Alpha-to-close) and in scenario B the AlphaMax order has no Alpha (zero Alpha-to-close).

In scenario A, without bad information leakage (grey line), AlphaMax shortfall is 2bp on the first tranche, 15bp on the last tranche and

Figure 8.4 Bad information leakage and execution shortfall (hypothetical example)

A: AlphaMax flow has high Alpha

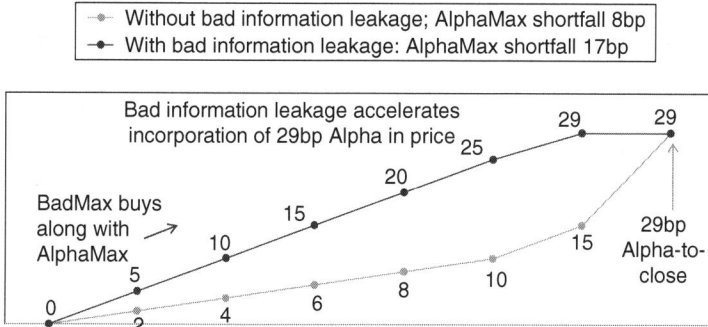

Without bad information leakage; AlphaMax shortfall 8bp
With bad information leakage: AlphaMax shortfall 17bp

Bad information leakage accelerates incorporation of 29bp Alpha in price

BadMax buys along with AlphaMax

29bp Alpha-to-close

B: AlphaMax flow has zero Alpha.

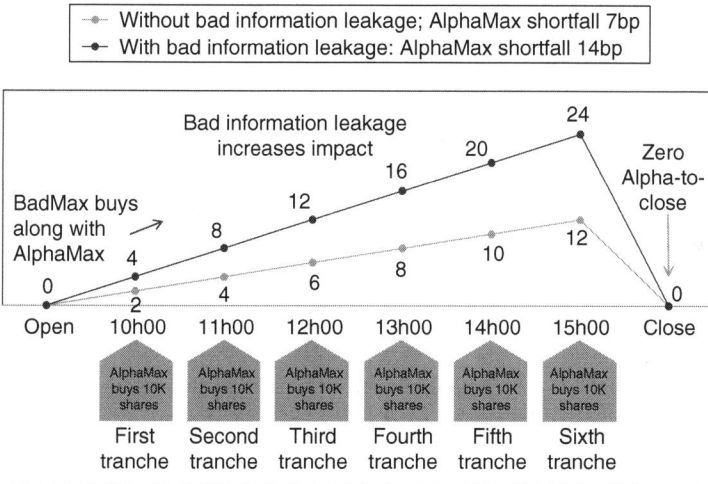

Without bad information leakage; AlphaMax shortfall 7bp
With bad information leakage: AlphaMax shortfall 14bp

Bad information leakage increases impact

BadMax buys along with AlphaMax

Zero Alpha-to-close

Open 10h00 11h00 12h00 13h00 14h00 15h00 Close

AlphaMax buys 10K shares (×6)

First tranche Second tranche Third tranche Fourth tranche Fifth tranche Sixth tranche

8bp overall, and AlphaMax captures 21bp Alpha. With bad information leakage, BadMax realises AlphaMax is executing a large high-Alpha buy order and buys along. The AlphaMax shortfall is now 5bp on the first tranche, 29bp on the last tranche and 17bp overall, and AlphaMax captures only 12bp Alpha. Bad information leakage accelerated the incorporation of the 29bp Alpha-to-close into the price and reduced AlphaMax Alpha capture.[9]

In scenario A, BadMax tries to capture some of AlphaMax's high Alpha. In scenario B AlphaMax has zero Alpha, but the AlphaMax execution has market impact and temporarily drives the price up. In this scenario, BadMax tries to capture some of this temporary price increase. Without bad information leakage, the AlphaMax shortfall is 2bp on the first tranche, 12bp on the last tranche and 7bp overall. With bad information leakage, BadMax realises AlphaMax is driving the price up and buys along. AlphaMax shortfall is now 4bp on the first tranche, 24bp on the last tranche and 14bp overall. Bad information leakage aggravated the temporary price impact and increased AlphaMax shortfall.[10]

Figure 8.4 shows that the execution shortfall measure captures the cost of bad information leakage. In scenario A, bad information leakage increased AlphaMax shortfall from 8bp to 17bp, and in scenario B, from 7bp to 14bp. All else being equal, therefore, the algo with more bad information leakage will have a higher shortfall.

In practice, however, it is impossible to ensure all else is equal over an order's life cycle; many other factors may cause the higher price path in Figure 8.4. Other portfolio managers, for example, may use the same stock selection model as AlphaMax, generate the same trading idea at the same time and buy along with AlphaMax. Or a careless algo may increase liquidity impact without bad information leakage, by "walking up the book" (aggressively executing at progressively worse prices). In practice, therefore, it is futile to try to test whether an algo leaks information by comparing algo performance. We developed, instead, the BadMax approach.

THE BADMAX APPROACH AND DATA SAMPLE

In order to test whether algo executions leak information, we pretend to be a fictitious predator, BadMax. As BadMax, we use historical data on GSET algo executions to back-test the profitability of different information leakage scenarios. In one test, for example, we assume that BadMax can identify marketable GSET algo buy executions and test whether BadMax can use this information to generate profitable buy signals.

Our tests assume BadMax has more information on GSET algo executions than any real-world predator is ever likely to have. A real-world predator, for example, will find it extremely difficult to identify GSET algo executions from publicly available data. Our tests, therefore, provide upper-bound estimates of BadMax net Alpha.

Table 8.1 GSET algo executions: symbol A

	Time	Symbol	Type	Side	Size
	9:30:00				
1	9:38:42	A	Marketable	Buy	100
2	9:38:42	A	Marketable	Buy	47
3	9:38:43	A	Marketable	Buy	100
4	11:25:11	A	Non-marketable	Sell	60
5	11:25:11	A	Non-marketable	Sell	40
6	11:25:18	A	Non-marketable	Sell	1
7	11:25:32	A	Non-marketable	Sell	47
8	11:25:32	A	Non-marketable	Sell	53
9	11:25:32	A	Marketable	Sell	99
10	11:26:42	A	Marketable	Sell	125
11	13:14:55	A	Peg mid	Sell	100
12	15:28:22	A	Peg mid	Sell	100
13	15:28:22	A	Peg mid	Sell	100
14	15:28:22	A	Peg mid	Sell	100
15	15:28:24	A	Peg mid	Sell	100
	16:00:00				

We next assume that BadMax can identify GSET algo executions and use a sample of 15 million GSET algo executions to back-test whether BadMax can use this information to construct profitable predatory trading strategies.[11] In a predatory trading strategy, Bad-Max trades along with GSET algos, buying when the algo is buying or selling when the algo is selling. A predatory strategy is profitable if BadMax net Alpha is positive and statistically significant.

We classify the 15 million executions into three types.

1. Non-marketable: buy at bid or sell at ask on public exchanges.[12]
2. Peg mid: buy or sell at mid-quote mostly on dark pools.[13]
3. Marketable: buy at ask or sell at bid on public exchanges.[14]

In our sample, 47% of executions are non-marketable, 23% are peg mid and 30% marketable. The average execution size is 153 shares, execution price is US$32 and half spread at execution is 4bp.

In our tests, we assume BadMax can observe each GSET algo execution as it occurs and can identify the symbol, side and order type. Table 8.1, for example, shows all 15 GSET algo executions in symbol A on one day. BadMax observes the first execution as it occurs at

Table 8.2 BadMax gross Alpha when trading along with GSET algo executions

| Trade triggers | BadMax holding periods | | | | | | |
| | HFT holding periods | | | Longer holding periods | | | |
	+1 s	+5 s	+15 s	+30 s	+60 s	+5 min	Close
Non-marketable	(2.8)	(3.7)	(4.1)	(4.3)	(4.3)	(3.8)	(3.6)
GSET algo executions	*0.00*	*0.00*	*0.00*	*0.01*	*0.01*	*0.02*	*0.08*
Peg mid	(1.2)	(1.2)	(1.0)	(0.7)	(0.3)	0.7	(2.3)
GSET algo executions	*0.00*	*0.00*	*0.01*	*0.01*	*0.01*	*0.02*	*0.13*
Marketable	0.7	1.3	1.8	2.2	2.8	4.1	(2.2)
GSET algo executions	*0.00*	*0.00*	*0.01*	*0.01*	*0.01*	*0.02*	*0.12*

The sample is 14,822,997 GSET algo executions, October 3–28, 2011. Standard errors are shown in italics.

9:38:42 and correctly identifies it as a marketable GSET algo buy execution in symbol A. In the same way, BadMax observes the second execution, and so on for all 15 executions.

BADMAX GROSS AND NET ALPHA

We first look at BadMax gross Alpha.[15] BadMax predatory strategies with negative gross Alpha are not profitable even before taking into account the round-trip cost and we drop them from consideration. Table 8.2 shows BadMax gross Alpha for seven holding periods (going across the table) and three trade triggers (going down the table). To address concerns over predatory high-frequency trading, three of the seven holding periods we tested (one second to fifteen seconds) may be considered high frequency.

The first row in Table 8.2 shows the BadMax gross Alpha when BadMax trades along with non-marketable algo executions. BadMax gross Alpha is negative for all holding periods. The second row shows the BadMax gross Alpha when BadMax trades along with peg mid algo executions. BadMax gross Alpha is again negative for all holding periods, except five minutes. The five-minute gross Alpha is positive, but only 0.7bp and easily swamped by the round-trip cost.[16] The third row shows the BadMax gross Alpha when BadMax

Table 8.3 BadMax net Alpha when trading along with marketable GSET algo executions

	BadMax holding periods					
	+1 s	+5 s	+15 s	+30 s	+60 s	+5 min
BadMax gross Alpha (bp)	0.7	1.3	1.8	2.2	2.8	4.1
Half-spread roundtrip cost (bp)	4.7	4.8	4.8	4.8	4.8	4.8
BadMax net Alpha (bp)	(4.0)	(3.5)	(3.0)	(2.6)	(2.0)	(0.7)
	0.00	*0.00*	*0.01*	*0.01*	*0.01*	*0.02*

The sample is 4,370,360 marketable GSET algo executions, October 3–28, 2011. Standard errors are shown in italics.

trades along with marketable algo executions. BadMax gross Alpha is now positive for all holding periods, except to the close.

Figure 8.3, therefore, indicates that trading along with non-marketable or peg mid GSET algo executions is not a viable predatory strategy. 70% of GSET algo executions are non-marketable or peg mid. Most GSET algo executions, therefore, are not vulnerable to predators. Only the 30% of GSET algo executions that are marketable are potentially vulnerable to predators.

We next focus on the potentially vulnerable marketable GSET algo executions and on the six holding periods with positive gross Alpha and calculate BadMax net Alpha. To calculate net Alpha, we must specify the round-trip cost of the BadMax strategy. Since gross Alpha is only 4.1bp at five minutes and much lower for HFT holding periods, BadMax must keep the round-trip cost as low as possible by establishing small positions and by using peg mid orders at trade-in.[17] For the five-minute holding period, for example, the BadMax round-trip strategy is:

- BadMax observes a marketable GSET algo buy execution in symbol XYZ;

- BadMax immediately sends a 200-share peg mid IOC order to buy XYZ; the expected fill rate is only 20% but BadMax buys at mid and does not pay the half-spread at trade-in;[18]

- BadMax trades out five minutes later selling at bid and paying the half-spread.

The BadMax round-trip cost, therefore, is the half spread at trade-out.[19] Table 8.3 shows the BadMax net Alpha for the six holding periods with positive gross Alpha. BadMax net Alpha is negative for all six holding periods. For the five-minute holding period, for example, BadMax gross Alpha is 4.1bp, the half-spread at trade-out is 4.8bp and the BadMax net Alpha is −0.7bp. Even with superior information, therefore, BadMax cannot generate positive net Alpha by trading along with marketable GSET algo executions. BadMax must try harder. In the next section, BadMax tries to generate positive net Alpha from clusters of marketable GSET algo executions.

CLUSTERING ANALYSIS AND THE HIGH ALPHA OF LARGE CLUSTERS

Figure 8.3 shows that large GSET algo parent orders have high Alpha. Tables 8.2 and 8.3 suggest that when GSET algos slice up these large parent orders into small child orders, mix them with small low-Alpha orders and execute them over time the high Alpha disappears. But can BadMax identify the large high-Alpha algo parent orders from clusters of small algo executions? To answer this question we examine sequences of GSET algo executions, identify clusters and measure their Alpha signal.

We tested many clustering definitions. We present the results for the following definition: executions form a cluster if they are less than 60 seconds apart, have the same symbol, the same side and originate from marketable GSET algo child orders.[20] Using this definition, the first three executions in Table 8.1 form a three-execution cluster of marketable GSET algo buy executions in symbol A. The ninth execution in Table 8.1 stands alone with no same symbol and no same-side marketable GSET algo execution within 60 seconds and so forms a one-execution non-cluster.[21]

Using our clustering definition, we constructed 703,765 clusters of marketable GSET algo executions. The average cluster has six executions with five seconds between executions. In Table 8.4, we arrange the 703,765 clusters into 10 groups: one-execution non-clusters, two-execution clusters, etc, all the way to extreme clusters with more than 100 executions. The one-execution non-clusters account for 44% of all clusters but include only 7% of all executions; the extreme clusters account for only 1% of all clusters but include 26% of all

Table 8.4 Clusters of marketable GSET algo executions

Cluster group	A	B	C	D	E	F
1	1	311,130	311,130	44	7	NA
2	2	127,004	254,008	18	6	9
3	3	368,066	204,198	10	5	9
4	4–5	67,322	296,317	10	7	9
5	6–10	61,469	461,707	9	11	8
6	11–15	22,486	285,176	3	7	8
7	16–25	18,921	372,819	3	9	7
8	26–50	14,745	520,084	2	12	5
9	51–100	7,508	520,926	1	12	4
10	>100	5,114	1,143,995	1	26	3
All	All	703,765	4,370,360	100	100	5

The sample is 4,370,360 marketable GSET algo executions, October 3–28, 2011. A, Executions in cluster; B, number of clusters; C, number of executions; D, percentage of clusters; E, percentage of executions; F, execution gap (in seconds).

executions. The average time between executions is nine seconds on two-execution clusters and only three seconds on extreme clusters.[22]

Part (a) of Figure 8.5 shows the five-minute net Alpha of different size clusters. To calculate this net Alpha we first calculate the gross Alpha for each cluster group. To calculate the five-minute gross Alpha of three-execution clusters, for example, we focus on the three-execution clusters in our sample and calculate the mid-quote move from first execution in each three-execution cluster to five minutes later.[23] To calculate the five-minute net Alpha we subtract the half-spread at trade-out from gross Alpha. The graph shows that the five-minute net Alpha increases with cluster size. The five-minute net Alpha, which averaged −0.7bp across all marketable GSET algo executions (Table 8.3), is −3.3bp for two-execution clusters, increases to 2.7bp for clusters with 16–25 executions and is a spectacular 13.1bp on extreme clusters.

BadMax wants to identify the large clusters and capture their high Alpha. To capture this high Alpha BadMax must identify large clusters and trade in at the first clustered execution. GSET algos, however, generate many small clusters and few large clusters. Our sample contains 506,000 clusters with less than four executions (gross

Figure 8.5 The Alpha signal from clusters of marketable GSET algo executions

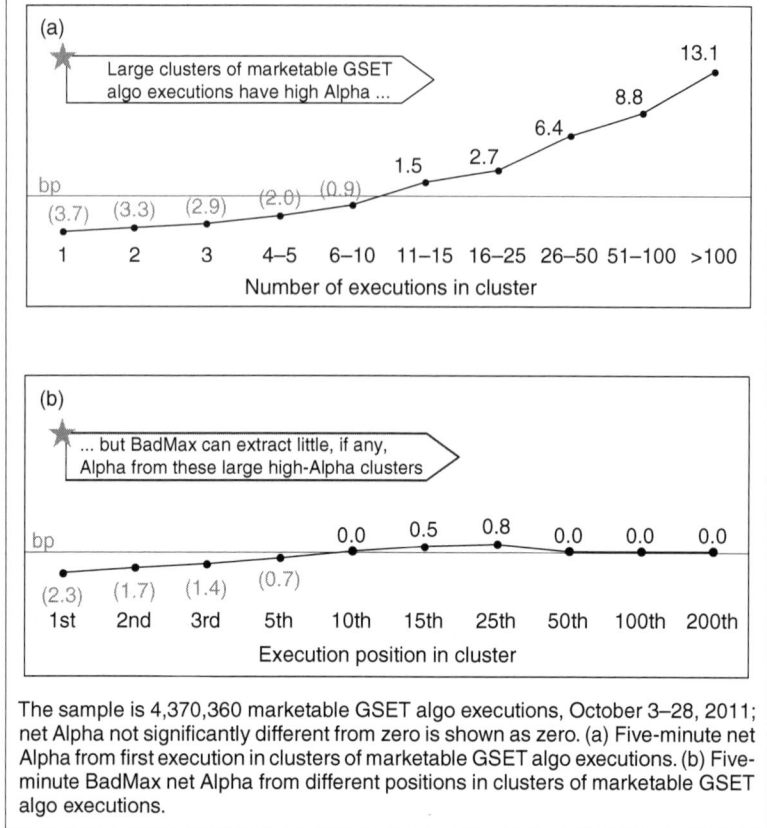

(a)

Large clusters of marketable GSET
algo executions have high Alpha ...

13.1

8.8

6.4

1.5   2.7

bp
(3.7) (3.3) (2.9) (2.0) (0.9)

1   2   3   4–5   6–10   11–15 16–25 26–50 51–100 >100

Number of executions in cluster

(b)

... but BadMax can extract little, if any,
Alpha from these large high-Alpha clusters

0.0   0.5   0.8   0.0   0.0   0.0

bp
(2.3) (1.7) (1.4) (0.7)

1st   2nd   3rd   5th   10th   15th   25th   50th   100th 200th

Execution position in cluster

The sample is 4,370,360 marketable GSET algo executions, October 3–28, 2011;
net Alpha not significantly different from zero is shown as zero. (a) Five-minute net
Alpha from first execution in clusters of marketable GSET algo executions. (b) Five-
minute BadMax net Alpha from different positions in clusters of marketable GSET
algo executions.

Alpha less than 2.3bp) but only 27,000 clusters with more than 25 executions (gross Alpha more than 11.2bp). Because BadMax observes
executions as they occur over time, at the first clustered execution
BadMax cannot distinguish between the many small low-Alpha
clusters and the few large high-Alpha clusters.

To identify large high-Alpha clusters, BadMax must count clustered executions sequentially as they occur over time. On observing
a second clustered execution, for example, BadMax filters out all
one-execution low-Alpha non-clusters. On observing a third clustered execution, BadMax also filters out all two-execution low-Alpha
clusters, and so on. As BadMax waits for each successive clustered
execution, however, BadMax loses Alpha. BadMax, therefore, faces

a trade-off:

- as BadMax waits longer to observe more clustered executions, it filters out more of the small low-Alpha clusters and buys into the larger higher-Alpha clusters;
- but as BadMax waits longer, BadMax loses more Alpha.

To quantify this trade-off and choose the wait time that maximises BadMax net Alpha, we calculate BadMax net Alpha from each successive execution in a sequence of clustered executions. At the second clustered execution we calculate BadMax net Alpha relative to mid at second execution.[24] At the third clustered execution we calculate BadMax net Alpha relative to mid at third execution, and so on.

Part (b) of Figure 8.5 shows the five-minute BadMax net Alpha at ten different positions in a sequence of clustered executions. BadMax net Alpha at the second clustered execution, for example, is −1.7bp, at the tenth clustered execution is zero and peaks at a mere 0.8bp at the twenty-fifth clustered execution.[25] The BadMax optimal strategy, therefore, is to wait for the twenty-fifth clustered execution.

Comparing the graphs in Figure 8.5, we see that the high Alpha of large clusters in part (a) disappears when BadMax tries to identify the large clusters and capture their high Alpha (part (b)). Figure 8.5, therefore, highlights our most striking finding: large clusters of marketable GSET algo executions have high Alpha, but BadMax can extract little if any Alpha from these large high-Alpha clusters.

We next focus on clusters with 26–50 executions and show why even though these clusters have high-Alpha BadMax cannot capture it. In Figure 8.5 the five-minute net Alpha from the first execution in clusters with 26–50 executions is 6.4bp, but when BadMax optimally trades in at the twenty-fifth clustered execution the net Alpha is only 0.8bp. Figure 8.6 plots the intra-cluster Alpha for clusters with 26–50 executions and shows that BadMax loses 9.9bp Alpha waiting for the twenty-fifth clustered execution.[26]

BadMax also loses Alpha by trading-out after the Alpha peaked. Figure 8.6 shows that large clusters of GSET algo executions are associated with high impact and reversal (from 12.6bp at last execution to 9.0bp to the close). With a five-minute holding period, BadMax will trade out well after the Alpha peaked. At the twenty-fifth clustered execution, BadMax buys into many 25-execution clusters where the price is about to revert and buys into few 100-execution clusters where the price will continue rising.

Figure 8.6 Intra-cluster Alpha and reversal for clusters with 26–50 executions

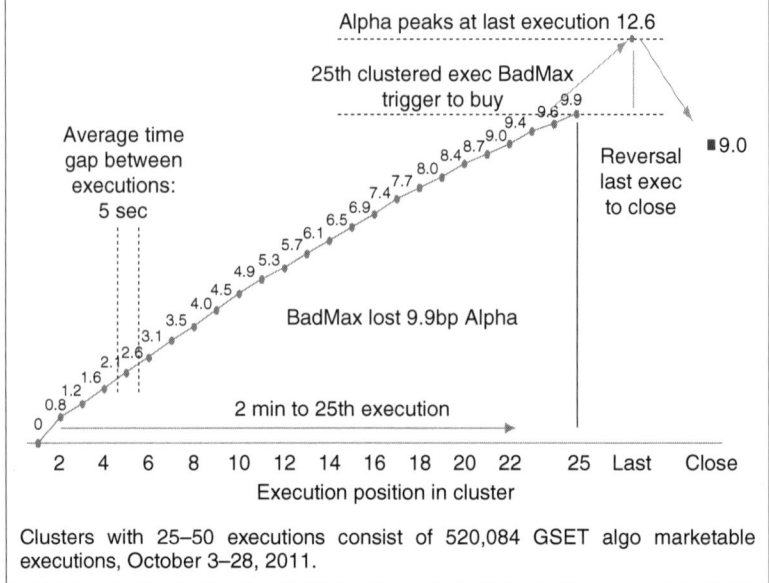

Alpha peaks at last execution 12.6

25th clustered exec BadMax trigger to buy 9.6 9.9

9.4

9.0

Average time gap between executions: 5 sec

Reversal last exec to close

■9.0

8.7
8.4
8.0
7.7
7.4
6.9
6.5
6.1
5.7
5.3
4.9
4.5
4.0
3.5
3.1
2.6
2.1
1.6
1.2
0.8
0

BadMax lost 9.9bp Alpha

2 min to 25th execution

2   4   6   8   10 12 14 16 18 20 22   25   Last   Close

Execution position in cluster

Clusters with 25–50 executions consist of 520,084 GSET algo marketable executions, October 3–28, 2011.

Figure 8.7 Tape footprint of marketable GSET algo execution

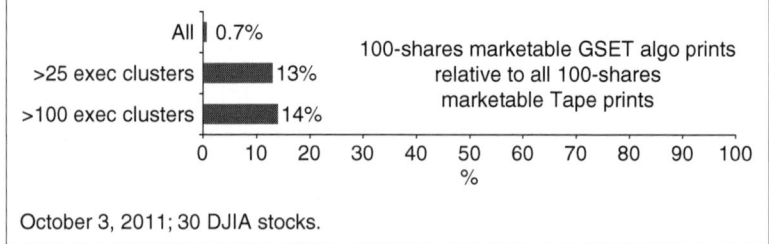

All ┃ 0.7%

>25 exec clusters ▮ 13%

>100 exec clusters ▮ 14%

100-shares marketable GSET algo prints relative to all 100-shares marketable Tape prints

0   10 20 30 40 50 60 70 80 90 100
%

October 3, 2011; 30 DJIA stocks.

IDENTIFYING GSET ALGO EXECUTIONS FROM THE TAPE

So far we have assumed that BadMax had superior information and could identify marketable GSET algo executions. In this section, we make the more realistic assumption that BadMax gets execution information from the Tape, and we examine whether BadMax can identify marketable GSET algo executions in this way. BadMax can easily identify marketable executions from the Tape by comparing execution price to mid-quote: above-mid execution prices indicate marketable buy executions and below-mid prices indicate marketable sell executions.[27] But how can BadMax distinguish the marketable GSET algo executions from all other marketable execution on the Tape? Our data shows that 71% of marketable GSET algo executions are for 100 shares. So the typical Tape footprint of marketable GSET algo buy executions is above-mid 100-shares prints. On a typical day, 62% of all above-mid Tape prints are for 100 shares and GSET algos account for only 0.7% of these prints (Figure 8.7).[28]

Can BadMax easily identify large clusters of marketable GSET algo executions from the Tape? To answer this question, we focused on clusters with more than 25 marketable GSET algo executions. For each cluster, we then counted all same-symbol same-side marketable 100-shares Tape prints over the cluster's duration; GSET algo prints account for only 13% of these prints. We repeated the calculation for extreme clusters with more than 100 marketable GSET algo executions; in this case, GSET algo prints account for only 14% of all Tape prints. Even large clusters of marketable GSET algo executions, therefore, leave almost no footprint on the Tape. BadMax cannot extract GSET algo Alpha by analysing the Tape.

CONCLUSION

Based on the predatory strategies we have back-tested so far, GSET algo executions do not leak information that predators can profitably exploit by trading along. Our back-tests show the following.

- Non-marketable and peg mid algo executions are associated with negative Alpha and therefore do not leak information that predators can exploit.

- Marketable algo executions are associated with low positive Alpha but this Alpha does not cover the predators' round-trip cost; marketable executions, therefore, also do not leak information that predators can exploit.

- Large clusters of marketable algo executions are associated with high positive Alpha, but, because these clusters are expensive to identify, predators can capture little if any Alpha.

GSET algo users that are still concerned that their marketable executions may leak information should be reassured by the relatively low usage GSET algos make of marketable executions: only 30% of GSET algo executions are marketable and vulnerable to predators.

Table 8.5 Alpha from first execution in clusters of marketable GSET algo executions

Exec. in cluster	Cluster no.	Exec. no.	Exec. size (shares)	Half spread (bp)	Exec. gap (s)	Exec. price (US$)	Gross Alpha (bp) from mid at first execution to mid at:						
							1s	5s	15s	30s	60s	5m	Close
1	311,130	311,130	120 *0.71*	5.6 *0.01*		33 *0.04*	0.3 *0.01*	0.5 *0.01*	0.7 *0.02*	0.8 *0.02*	0.9 *0.03*	1.9 *0.06*	6.2 *0.37*
2	127,004	254,008	124 *0.51*	5.2 *0.02*	9 *0.05*	32 *0.06*	0.5 *0.01*	0.8 *0.02*	0.9 *0.02*	1.0 *0.03*	1.0 *0.04*	1.8 *0.10*	4.6 *0.57*
3	68,066	204,198	129 *1.11*	5.2 *0.03*	9 *0.04*	31 *0.09*	0.6 *0.01*	1.0 *0.02*	1.4 *0.04*	1.5 *0.05*	1.5 *0.06*	2.3 *0.13*	4.0 *0.78*
4–5	67,322	296,317	133 *0.72*	5.3 *0.03*	9 *0.03*	30 *0.09*	0.7 *0.02*	1.2 *0.03*	1.8 *0.04*	2.1 *0.05*	2.4 *0.07*	3.4 *0.14*	5.8 *0.82*
6–10	61,469	461,707	141 *1.35*	5.2 *0.03*	8 *0.02*	30 *0.09*	0.6 *0.02*	1.3 *0.03*	2.1 *0.04*	2.7 *0.06*	3.6 *0.08*	4.5 *0.16*	4.2 *0.88*
11–15	22,486	285,176	153 *2.09*	4.8 *0.05*	8 *0.03*	31 *0.15*	0.6 *0.02*	1.3 *0.05*	2.3 *0.08*	3.2 *0.10*	4.9 *0.14*	6.7 *0.28*	4.8 *1.51*
16–25	18,921	372,819	157 *4.60*	4.5 *0.04*	7 *0.02*	31 *0.16*	0.5 *0.03*	1.4 *0.05*	2.5 *0.09*	3.4 *0.12*	5.1 *0.15*	8.1 *0.31*	7.0 *1.66*
26–50	14,745	520,084	166 *3.41*	4.2 *0.04*	5 *0.02*	31 *0.18*	0.5 *0.03*	1.6 *0.07*	3.0 *0.11*	4.2 *0.14*	6.2 *0.19*	11.2 *0.40*	9.0 *1.99*
51–100	7,508	520,926	185 *8.00*	4.1 *0.06*	4 *0.01*	31 *0.26*	0.6 *0.05*	1.6 *0.09*	3.1 *0.17*	4.5 *0.23*	6.4 *0.31*	12.8 *0.62*	6.1 *2.93*
>100	5,114	1,143,995	192 *6.22*	3.9 *0.07*	3 *0.01*	29 *0.27*	0.7 *0.07*	1.9 *0.14*	3.6 *0.21*	4.6 *0.28*	7.0 *0.41*	16.4 *1.01*	10.3 *3.80*

Table 8.5 *Continued*

Exec. in cluster	Half spread (bp)							Net Alpha (bp) from mid at first execution to bid at						
	1s	5s	15s	30s	60s	5m	Close	1s	5s	15s	30s	60s	5m	Close
1	5.8	5.9	5.9	5.9	5.9	5.8	0.0	(5.3)	(5.2)	(5.0)	(4.9)	(4.7)	(3.7)	**6.2**
	0.01	*0.01*	*0.01*	*0.01*	*0.01*	*0.01*		*0.02*	*0.02*	*0.02*	*0.03*	*0.03*	*0.06*	*0.4*
2	5.4	5.5	5.5	5.5	5.5	5.4	0.0	(4.7)	(4.5)	(4.4)	(4.3)	(4.2)	(3.3)	**4.6**
	0.02	*0.02*	*0.02*	*0.02*	*0.02*	*0.02*		*0.02*	*0.02*	*0.03*	*0.04*	*0.05*	*0.10*	*0.6*
3	5.4	5.5	5.6	5.5	5.5	5.5	0.0	(4.6)	(4.4)	(4.0)	(3.9)	(3.8)	(2.9)	**4.0**
	0.03	*0.03*	*0.03*	*0.03*	*0.02*	*0.02*		*0.03*	*0.04*	*0.04*	*0.05*	*0.07*	*0.14*	*0.8*
4–5	5.5	5.6	5.7	5.6	5.6	5.5	0.0	(4.6)	(4.3)	(3.8)	(3.5)	(3.1)	(2.0)	**5.8**
	0.03	*0.03*	*0.03*	*0.03*	*0.03*	*0.03*		*0.03*	*0.04*	*0.05*	*0.06*	*0.07*	*0.14*	*0.8*
6–10	15.4	5.5	5.5	5.5	5.5	5.5	0.0	(4.6)	(4.2)	(3.4)	(2.8)	(1.9)	(0.9)	**4.2**
	0.03	*0.03*	*0.03*	*0.03*	*0.03*	*0.03*		*0.03*	*0.04*	*0.05*	*0.06*	*0.08*	*0.16*	*0.9*
11–15	4.9	5.0	5.0	5.0	5.1	5.0	0.0	(4.2)	(3.6)	(2.6)	(1.7)	(0.2)	**1.5**	**4.8**
	0.05	*0.05*	*0.04*	*0.04*	*0.05*	*0.04*		*0.05*	*0.06*	*0.08*	*0.11*	*0.14*	*0.3*	*1.5*
16–25	4.6	4.7	4.7	4.8	4.7	4.8	0.0	(3.9)	(3.2)	(2.2)	(1.3)	0.3	**2.7**	**7.0**
	0.04	*0.04*	*0.04*	*0.04*	*0.04*	*0.05*		*0.05*	*0.07*	*0.09*	*0.12*	*0.3*	*0.3*	*1.7*
26–50	4.3	4.4	4.5	4.5	4.4	4.4	0.0	(3.6)	(2.8)	(1.5)	(0.3)	**1.5**	**6.4**	**9.0**
	0.04	*0.04*	*0.04*	*0.04*	*0.04*	*0.04*		*0.05*	*0.08*	*0.12*	*0.15*	*0.2*	*0.4*	*2.0*
51–100	4.2	4.3	4.3	4.3	4.3	4.3	0.0	(3.4)	(2.5)	(1.2)	0.0	**2.0**	**8.8**	**6.1**
	0.06	*0.06*	*0.06*	*0.06*	*0.06*	*0.10*		*0.08*	*0.12*	*0.20*	*0.26*	*0.3*	*0.7*	*2.9*
>100	3.9	4.0	4.0	4.0	4.0	4.1	0.0	(3.0)	(1.9)	(0.2)	**0.8**	**3.4**	**13.1**	**10.3**
	0.07	*0.07*	*0.07*	*0.07*	*0.07*	*0.08*		*0.12*	*0.18*	*0.26*	*0.3*	*0.5*	*1.2*	*3.8*

Sample consists of 4,370,360 GSET algo marketable executions, October 3–28, 2011; standard errors are shown in italics.

Table 8.6 The BadMax profitability grid: BadMax net Alpha is shown by execution position in the cluster

Pos. in cluster	Exec. no.	Exec. size (shares)	Half spread (bp)	Exec. price (US$)	Gross Alpha (bp) from mid at first execution to mid at:						
					1s	5s	15s	30s	60s	5m	Close
1	703,765	127	5.3	32	0.5	0.8	1.2	1.5	1.8	3.0	5.6
					0.00	*0.01*	*0.01*	*0.02*	*0.02*	*0.04*	*0.25*
2	392,635	133	5.1	31	0.6	1.1	1.5	1.8	2.2	3.4	4.5
					0.01	*0.01*	*0.02*	*0.02*	*0.03*	*0.06*	*0.34*
3	265,631	137	5.1	30	0.7	1.2	1.7	2.0	2.4	3.8	4.0
					0.01	*0.01*	*0.02*	*0.03*	*0.04*	*0.08*	*0.42*
5	157,272	143	5.0	30	0.8	1.4	2.0	2.4	2.9	4.4	3.5
					0.01	*0.02*	*0.03*	*0.04*	*0.05*	*0.11*	*0.57*
10	75,966	149	4.6	31	0.8	1.5	2.1	2.6	3.2	4.7	2.5
					0.01	*0.03*	*0.04*	*0.06*	*0.08*	*0.17*	*0.85*
15	49,447	156	4.3	31	0.8	1.6	2.3	2.8	3.3	5.0	1.8
					0.02	*0.04*	*0.06*	*0.07*	*0.11*	*0.22*	*1.09*
25	28,589	159	4.1	30	0.9	1.7	2.4	2.9	3.6	4.9	0.1
					0.03	*0.05*	*0.08*	*0.11*	*0.15*	*0.31*	*1.46*
50	12,951	172	4.0	30	0.9	1.6	2.0	2.4	3.1	4.0	(4.2)
					0.05	*0.09*	*0.13*	*0.18*	*0.25*	*0.48*	*2.26*
100	5,183	183	3.8	29	0.8	1.6	1.9	2.4	2.9	4.3	(7.0)
					0.07	*0.14*	*0.22*	*0.33*	*0.44*	*0.84*	*3.71*
200	1,819	173	3.8	27	0.7	1.2	1.0	1.7	3.1	6.4	(17.8)
					0.12	*0.21*	*0.39*	*0.54*	*0.83*	*1.41*	*6.35*

Sample consists of 4,370,360 GSET algo marketable executions, October 3–28, 2011; standard errors are shown in italics.

Table 8.6 Continued.

Exec. in cluster	Half spread (bp)							Net Alpha (bp) from mid at first execution to bid at						
	1s	5s	15s	30s	60s	5m	Close	1s	5s	15s	30s	60s	5m	Close
1	5.5	5.6	5.6	5.6	5.6	5.5	0.0	(4.8)	(4.6)	(4.2)	(4.0)	(3.6)	(2.3)	5.6
	0.01	*0.01*	*0.01*	*0.01*	*0.01*	*0.01*		*0.01*	*0.01*	*0.01*	*0.02*	*0.02*	*0.05*	*0.3*
2	5.3	5.4	5.4	5.4	5.4	5.3	0.0	(4.5)	(4.2)	(3.8)	(3.5)	(3.1)	(1.7)	4.5
	0.01	*0.01*	*0.01*	*0.01*	*0.01*	*0.01*		*0.01*	*0.01*	*0.02*	*0.02*	*0.03*	*0.06*	*0.3*
3	5.3	5.4	5.4	5.4	5.3	5.3	0.0	(4.4)	(4.1)	(3.6)	(3.2)	(2.7)	(1.4)	4.0
	0.01	*0.01*	*0.01*	*0.01*	*0.01*	*0.01*		*0.02*	*0.02*	*0.02*	*0.03*	*0.03*	*0.06*	*0.4*
5	5.1	5.2	5.2	5.2	5.2	5.1	0.0	(4.2)	(3.8)	(3.2)	(2.8)	(2.2)	(0.7)	3.5
	0.02	*0.02*	*0.02*	*0.02*	*0.02*	*0.02*		*0.02*	*0.02*	*0.03*	*0.04*	*0.05*	*0.1*	*0.6*
10	4.7	4.8	4.8	4.8	4.8	4.7	0.0	(3.7)	(3.2)	(2.6)	(2.1)	(1.4)	(0.0)	2.5
	0.02	*0.02*	*0.02*	*0.02*	*0.02*	*0.02*		*0.03*	*0.04*	*0.05*	*0.06*	*0.08*	*0.2*	*0.9*
15	4.5	4.6	4.6	4.6	4.6	4.5	0.0	(3.5)	(2.8)	(2.2)	(1.7)	(1.2)	0.5	1.8
	0.03	*0.03*	*0.03*	*0.03*	*0.03*	*0.03*		*0.03*	*0.05*	*0.06*	*0.08*	*0.1*	*0.2*	*1.1*
25	4.3	4.3	4.4	4.4	4.4	4.3	0.0	(3.2)	(2.5)	(1.8)	(1.3)	(0.5)	0.8	0.1
	0.03	*0.03*	*0.03*	*0.03*	*0.04*	*0.04*		*0.04*	*0.06*	*0.09*	*0.1*	*0.2*	*0.3*	*1.5*
50	4.1	4.2	4.2	4.2	4.2	4.2	0.0	(3.0)	(2.3)	(1.9)	(1.4)	(0.5)	(0.1)	(4.2)
	0.05	*0.05*	*0.05*	*0.07*	*0.07*	*0.07*		*0.07*	*0.1*	*0.2*	*0.2*	*0.3*	*0.5*	*2.3*
100	3.9	4.0	4.0	4.0	4.0	4.0	0.0	(2.9)	(2.4)	(2.0)	(1.5)	(0.6)	0.3	(7.0)
	0.07	*0.07*	*0.07*	*0.07*	*0.07*	*0.08*		*0.1*	*0.2*	*0.3*	*0.4*	*0.5*	*1.0*	*3.7*
200	3.9	4.0	4.0	4.1	4.1	4.0	0.0	(2.7)	(2.5)	(2.6)	(1.9)	(0.2)	1.7	(17.8)
	0.13	*0.13*	*0.13*	*0.13*	*0.14*	*0.14*		*0.2*	*0.3*	*0.5*	*0.7*	*0.9*	*1.4*	*6.4*

Sample consists of 4,370,360 GSET algo marketable executions, October 3–28, 2011; standard errors are shown in italics.

Concerned algo users can further reduce their marketable algo executions by choosing more passive algo settings, but must be careful not to end up being too passive.[29] Concerned algo users can also further reduce the Tape footprint of marketable algo executions by pinging the mid-quote before reaching across the market and executing at the quote.

APPENDIX: THE BADMAX PROFITABILITY GRID

In this appendix we describe in more detail some of the BadMax back-tests we ran on clusters of marketable GSET algo executions. Table 8.5 shows the gross and net Alpha of ten different cluster groups for seven different holding periods.

In Table 8.5, we calculate the Alpha of a cluster from first execution. To calculate the five-minute gross Alpha of three-execution buy clusters, for example, we focus on the three-execution buy clusters and calculate Alpha as the mid-quote five minutes after first execution minus the mid at first execution as a percentage of the mid at first execution in basis points. Net Alpha equals gross Alpha minus the half spread at trade-out. The five-minute net Alpha, for example, equals the five-minute gross Alpha minus the half spread five minutes after first execution. For holding to close, we use the closing price to calculate gross Alpha and assume that the round-trip cost is zero. For all holding periods except to the close, gross and net Alpha increase with cluster size. Figures in bold show the holding periods and cluster sizes where the BadMax strategy would have been profitable if BadMax could have identified the cluster size at first execution and established the position at first execution. A strategy is profitable if net Alpha is positive and statistically significant (the t-statistic is greater than 2).

But this is not a realistic strategy. In practice, BadMax will identify large clusters by counting clustered executions as they occur in sequence over time. Table 8.6 shows the BadMax gross and net Alpha for this more realistic strategy. We call Table 8.6 the BadMax profitability grid. The grid shows BadMax gross and net Alpha from ten different positions in a sequence of clustered executions and for the same seven holding periods as in Table 8.5. The five-minute gross Alpha from the third clustered buy execution, for example, equals the mid five minutes after the third clustered execution minus the mid at the third clustered execution as a percentage of the mid at the third clustered execution, in basis points. Net Alpha again equals gross Alpha minus the half spread at trade-out. The figures in bold show the holding periods and cluster sizes where the BadMax strategy is profitable.

Table 8.6 shows that HFT BadMax strategies (holding periods from one second to one minute) are not profitable. In general, ignoring holding to close, only two strategies are profitable, and in both cases the net Alpha is small. Because the round-trip cost of holding to close is zero, five of the ten holding-to-close strategies are profitable. The most profitable holding-to-close strategy is when BadMax trades in at the first non-clustered execution (net Alpha 5.6bp). In this strategy, by only establishing positions at the first non-clustered execution, BadMax avoids all subsequent clustered executions where the price has already moved away. All the holding-to-close strategies, however, are associated with high risk and low Sharpe ratios.

This chapter is based on two Goldman Sachs reports by the authors ("Information Leakage", Street Smart no. 45, and "Do algo executions leak information?" (with Mark Gurliacci), Street Smart no. 46, both dated February 2, 2012). This material was prepared by the Goldman Sachs Execution Strategies Group and is not the product of Goldman Sachs Global Investment Research. It is not a research report and is not intended as such.

The information in this chapter has been taken from trade data and other sources deemed reliable, but we do not state that such information is accurate or complete and it should not be relied upon as such. This information is indicative, based on among other things, market conditions at the time of writing and is subject to change without notice. Goldman Sachs' algorithmic models derive pricing and trading estimates based on historical volume patterns, real-time market data and parameters selected by the user. The ability of Goldman Sachs' algorithmic models to achieve the performance described in this chapter may be affected by changes in market conditions, systems or communications failures, etc. Finally, factors such as order quantity, liquidity and the parameters selected by the user may affect the performance results. The opinions expressed in this chapter are the authors' and do not necessarily represent the views of Goldman, Sachs & Co. These opinions represent the authors' judgement at this date and are subject to change. Goldman, Sachs & Co. is not soliciting any action based on this chapter. It is for general information and does not constitute a personal recommendation or take into account the particular investment objectives, financial situations or needs of individual users. Before acting on any advice or recommendation herein, users should consider whether it is suitable for their particular circumstances. Copyright 2013 by Goldman, Sachs & Co.

1   "Other traders" may include competing agency algos. In this chapter, we use three fictitious traders to facilitate the exposition: AlphaMax is a fictitious buy-side trader, BadMax is a fictitious predator buying along with AlphaMax and GoodMax is a fictitious trader selling when AlphaMax is buying.

2   Statistical arbitrage and pairs trading strategies are examples of good information leakage.

3   Figure 8.1 raises the intriguing possibility that BadMax may also be GoodMax: BadMax may at some point buy along with AlphaMax and at another point sell to AlphaMax.

4   The sample period is October 3 to October 28, 2011.

5   For buy orders, we measure Alpha as same-day closing price minus mid at order arrival as a percentage of the mid at order arrival.

6   For buy executions, we measure Alpha as same-day closing price minus mid at execution time as a percentage of the mid at execution time.

7   Below-mid executions are usually followed by a price drop, and below-mid AlphaMax sell executions may trigger BadMax sell orders.

8   AlphaMax orders may also leak information through the Tape. This happens when AlphaMax chooses to display limit orders. Most of the time this is good information leakage intended to attract counterparties. But displaying orders may also result in bad information leakage. Significantly more displayed depth at bid than at ask, for example, is usually associated with a subsequent drop in price. If AlphaMax displays a large sell limit at the bid, therefore, AlphaMax may trigger BadMax sell orders.

9   This scenario also shows that bad information leakage does not always lead to post-trade reversal.

10 In this scenario, AlphaMax's impact is BadMax's Alpha signal. For the strategy to be profitable, BadMax must unwind the position before the price reverts.

11 The sample period is October 3 to 28, October 2011. We focus on NYSE and Nasdaq-listed common stock and drop stocks less than US$1 or more than US$150. We also drop executions before 09h35 or after 15h55 and filter out outliers.

12 We classify executions as non-marketable if they were generated by non-marketable algo child orders.

13 We classify executions as peg mid if they were generated by marketable peg mid algo child orders; a small fraction of peg mid orders execute at better than the mid (price improvement).

14 We classify executions as marketable if they were generated by marketable algo child orders; a small fraction of marketable orders execute inside the spread (price improvement).

15 For BadMax buy orders, gross Alpha equals mid at trade-out (end of holding period) minus mid at trade-in as a percentage of the mid at trade-in, in basis points (see also the appendix).

16 See the next section for more details on the BadMax round-trip cost.

17 The assumption of small positions is also important for the validity of our back-tests.

18 We get the 20% fill rate estimate from a May 2011 (internal, unpublished) analysis of small peg mid IOC orders sequentially routed to five dark pools and exchanges (27% fill rate, average size 159 shares).

19 We ignore broker and venue fees.

20 Why 60 seconds? Thinking like BadMax, we tested several time gaps and chose 60 seconds because it provided the strongest Alpha signal. The clustering definition can also be algo specific (eg, clusters of VWAP algo executions) or venue specific (eg, clusters of SIGMA X executions). We tested many different clustering definitions.

21 The tenth execution in Table 8.1 also forms a one-execution marketable sell non-cluster.

22 The average number of executions in the extreme clusters is 224.

23 More precisely, for buy clusters, we calculate the five-minute Alpha as the mid five minutes after the first execution in the cluster minus the mid at first execution as a percentage of the mid at the first execution, in basis points.

24 More precisely, for buy clusters, we calculate the five-minute gross Alpha at second clustered execution as the mid five minutes after the second clustered execution minus the mid at second clustered execution as a percentage of the mid at second clustered execution, in basis points.

25 In Figure 8.5, we focus on the five-minute holding period because it gives the strongest Alpha signal; in the Appendix, we present results for all of the seven holding periods we tested.

26 Intra-cluster Alpha is the price (mid-quote) move from first execution to subsequent executions in the cluster.

27 This rule (known as the Lee–Ready rule) correctly identifies as marketable 88% of the marketable GSET algo executions in our sample; the remaining 12% get price improvement executing at mid or better and the Lee–Ready rule cannot correctly identify them.

28 Our sample consists of tick data on the 30 DJIA stocks for October 3, 2011.

29 While passive (non-marketable) orders are not vulnerable to information leakage, they are vulnerable to adverse selection.

9

Implementation Shortfall with Transitory Price Effects

Terrence Hendershott; Charles M. Jones; Albert J. Menkveld

University of California, Berkeley; Columbia Business School; VU University Amsterdam

At the time of writing, regulators and some large investors have raised concerns about temporary or transitory volatility in highly automated financial markets.[1] It is far from clear that high-frequency trading, fragmentation and automation are contributing to transitory volatility, but some institutions have complained that their execution costs are increasing. In this chapter, we introduce a methodology for decomposing the price process of a financial instrument into its permanent and transitory components, and we explore the insights from applying this methodology to execution cost measurement. Our methodology allows an institutional investor to accurately measure the contributions of transitory price movements to its overall trading costs. The methodology is particularly applicable to an investor that splits a large order into small pieces and executes it gradually over time.

The importance of transitory price impact has been well known in the academic literature since the early work on block trading (see, for example, Kraus and Stoll 1972).[2] While it is fairly straightforward to measure the transitory price impact of a block trade, it is a much greater challenge to measure the transitory price impact when a large institutional parent order is executed in perhaps hundreds of smaller child order executions. The key innovation of our approach is that we estimate the temporary component at each point in time and, in particular, whenever a child order is executed. By summing over all child orders, we can thus measure the effect of the temporary component on overall trading costs.

To be more precise, we extend the classic Perold (1988) "implementation shortfall" approach to decompose *ex post* transaction costs into various components, one of which accounts for the trading costs associated with transitory pricing errors. Because trading cost analysis is often performed on an institution's daily trading, we first illustrate our transaction cost measurement approach at a daily frequency. However, our methods are much more precise when more disaggregated trading data are available. Using detailed information on the intra-day child order executions from a larger institutional parent order, we show how the transitory price component evolves with trading on a minute-by-minute basis, and we show how this transitory price component contributes to overall implementation shortfall.

In some ways, our work is most closely related to Almgren *et al* (2005), who assume a particular functional form for both permanent and transitory price impacts, with limited persistence in the latter. They then apply their model to a large set of institutional orders to characterise permanent and transitory components of transaction costs as a function of various stock and order characteristics.[3] In contrast, we allow the data to determine the persistence of the temporary component.

IMPLEMENTATION SHORTFALL

Even for those who are intimately familiar with trading cost analysis, Perold (1988) is worth rereading. For example, he frames the discussion on p. 4:

> After selecting which stocks to buy and which to sell, "all" you have to do is implement your decisions. If you had the luxury of transacting on paper, your job would already be done. On paper, transactions occur by [a] mere stroke of the pen. You can transact at all times in unlimited quantities with no price impact and free of all commissions. There are no doubts as to whether and at what price your order will be filled. If you could transact on paper, you would always be invested in your ideal portfolio.
>
> There are crucial differences between transacting on paper and transacting in real markets. You do not know the prices at which you will be able to execute, when you will be able to execute, or even whether you will ever be able to execute. You do not know

whether you will be front-run by others. And you do not know whether having your limit order filled is a blessing or a curse – a blessing if you have just extracted a premium for supplying liquidity, a curse if you have just been bagged by someone who knows more than you do. Because you are so much in the dark, you proceed carefully, and strategically.

These comments are just as apt in 2013 as they were in 1988, except that in 2013 the concern about front-running is mainly a worry about being sniffed out by algorithmic traders. Some algorithms use sophisticated forecasting and pattern recognition techniques to pre-dict future order flow and thus future price changes. To the extent that the slicing and dicing of large institutional orders into many smaller trades leaves a footprint in the data, algorithms may attempt to identify and trade ahead of these large institutional orders. Any such order anticipation could increase the transitory impact of a large order and thereby increase its overall cost.

With a few notational changes we follow the methodology of Per-old (1988, Appendix B) for measurement and analysis of implemen-tation shortfall. At the beginning of a measurement period, the paper portfolio is assumed to be worth the same amount as the real port-folio. At the end of the period, any differences in value capture the implementation shortfall. In general, the length of the measurement period is not important. For many institutions, the preferred period length is one day, but it can be longer or shorter. The key constraint is that if implementation shortfall is to be measured for an order that is executed gradually over time, the measurement period must span the time over which the order is executed.

Assume there are N securities with one being cash. Let n_i denote the number of shares of security i in the paper portfolio, w_i^b be the number of shares of security i in the real portfolio at the beginning of the period, and w_i^e be the number of shares held at the end of the period. w_i^e differs from w_i^b by the shares traded in security i.

Denote the times of trades by $j = 1, \ldots, K$. Denote the number of shares traded in security i at time j by t_{ij}; t_{ij} is positive for buys, negative for sales and zero when there is no trade. Therefore, the ending shareholding in security i is

$$w_i^e = w_i^b + \sum_{j=1}^{K} t_{ij} \qquad (9.1)$$

Denote the prices at which transactions take place by p_{ij}; p_{ij} are net of incremental costs such as commissions and transfer taxes. Let the price of security i be p_i^b at the beginning of the period and p_i^e at the end. While the p_{ij} must be transaction prices, the two benchmark prices can be either trade prices or quote midpoints.

Assuming there are no net cashflows into or out of the real portfolio, all transactions are financed with proceeds of other transactions. That is, at each time j, $\sum t_{ij}p_{ij}$ is zero when summed over $i = 1$ to N.

Let the value of the paper and real portfolios at the beginning of the period be

$$V_b = \sum n_i p_i^b \tag{9.2}$$

Let the end-of-period values of the paper and real portfolios be V_p and V_r, respectively

$$V_p = \sum n_i p_i^e \quad \text{and} \quad V_r = \sum w_i^e p_i^e \tag{9.3}$$

The performance of the paper portfolio is $V_p - V_b$, and the performance of the real portfolio is $V_r - V_b$. The implementation shortfall is the difference between the two.

The performance of the real portfolio can be expanded as

$$\sum (w_i^e p_i^e - w_i^b p_i^b) = \sum w_i^e (p_i^e - p_i^b) - \sum p_i^b (w_i^e - w_i^b)$$
$$= \sum w_i^e (p_i^e - p_i^b) - \sum \sum (p_{ij} - p_i^b) t_{ij} \tag{9.4}$$

The performance of the paper portfolio can be expanded as

$$\sum n_i (p_i^e - p_i^b) \tag{9.5}$$

Subtracting the real portfolio performance from paper portfolio performance completes the calculation

implementation shortfall

$$= \underbrace{\sum \sum (p_{ij} - p_i^b) t_{ij}}_{\text{execution cost}} + \underbrace{\sum \sum (p_i^e - p_i^b)(n_i - w_i^e)}_{\text{opportunity cost}} \tag{9.6}$$

The term $(p_{ij} - p_i^b)$ is the per-share cost of transacting at p_{ij} instead of at p_i^b, and this cost is applied to t_{ij} traded shares. The weighted sum is the total execution cost relative to the pre-trade benchmark. The term $(p_i^e - p_i^b)$ is the paper return on security i over the period. The opportunity cost is the sum of these returns weighted by the size of the unexecuted orders. While opportunity costs are a real concern for institutional investors, our methodology does not offer much insight into them, and in the rest of the chapter we focus only on the execution cost component.

OBSERVED PRICES, EFFICIENT PRICES AND PRICING ERRORS

The implementation shortfall incorporates the total price impact of a large order. However, to better understand the sources of the shortfall, it may be useful to decompose the price impact into its permanent and transitory components. To do this we must define and measure the efficient price and any deviations from it at each moment in time. We take the standard approach of assuming the efficient price is unpredictable, ie, it follows a random walk.

Minus trading frictions, the efficient price at the daily or intra-day frequency can be characterised as a martingale process. Let m_j be this latent price

$$m_j = m_{j-1} + w_t \qquad (9.7)$$

Sometimes the quote midpoint is assumed to represent this latent price. However, quote midpoints are not generally martingales with respect to all available order flow, in which case Hasbrouck (1995, p. 1179) proposes to view the random-walk component of a Stock and Watson (1988) decomposition as the "implicit efficient price". Hasbrouck (2007, Chapters 4 and 8) constructs an efficient price more generally as the projection of m_t onto all available conditioning variables, ie, the so-called filtered state estimate

$$\tilde{m}_{ij} = E^*[m_j \mid p_{ij}, p_{i,j-1}, \dots] \qquad (9.8)$$

where $E^*[\cdot]$ is the linear projection of m_{ij} on a set of lagged prices.[4] A standard approach to implementing such a projection is through autoregressive integrated moving average (ARIMA) time series econometrics (Hasbrouck 2007, Chapter 4). The filtered estimate can be enriched by expanding the set of conditioning variables with trade-based variables (eg, signed order flow), news-based variables (eg, the Reuters sentiment score of press releases), etc.[5]

A more general approach constructs the "efficient price" based on a state-space model. This nests the ARIMA approach but has the following advantages. First, it allows for using both past and future information to estimate the efficient state. This is particularly relevant in decomposing a price change into a permanent price change (ie, the efficient price change) and a (transitory) pricing error. For a particular in-sample price change, we do in fact want to "peek into the future" to establish whether it was largely permanent or transitory. A state-space model produces, in addition to a filtered price estimate, a so-called smoothed price estimate that also takes future price information into account, ie

$$\hat{m}_{ij} = E^*[m_j \mid \ldots, p_{i,j+1}, p_{ij}, p_{i,j-1}, \ldots] \tag{9.9}$$

Second, the state-space approach extends naturally to multi-market trading, where there are potentially multiple price quotes for the same security at any instant of time. It also accounts optimally for missing observations that arise, for example, when various markets do not perfectly overlap. Third, structural models often generate a system of equations in state-space form. This system can then be taken to the data without further (potentially imperfect) transformations. A further discussion of the approach and the implementation details are given in Menkveld *et al* (2007).

The efficient price estimate enables an observed price to be decomposed into a (smoothed) efficient price and a pricing error

$$p_{ij} = \hat{m}_{ij} + s_{ij} \tag{9.10}$$

Hereafter, the focus is mainly on the smoothed price estimate (as opposed to the filtered estimate), as implementation shortfall is about *ex post* evaluation and therefore "future" price information is available and relevant.[6]

Let us reconsider part of the quote of Perold (1988):

> And you do not know whether having your limit order filled is a blessing or a curse – a blessing if you have just extracted a premium for supplying liquidity, a curse if you have just been bagged by someone who knows more than you do.

The efficient price estimate enables the standard implementation shortfall calculation of Equation 9.6 to be further refined by recognising the size of these two components. The execution cost component of the implementation shortfall can be rewritten as

$$\text{execution cost} = \underbrace{\sum\sum(p_{ij} - \hat{m}_{ij})t_{ij}}_{\text{liquidity cost}} + \underbrace{\sum\sum(\hat{m}_{ij} - \hat{m}_i^b)t_{ij}}_{\text{informational cost}}$$

$$+ \underbrace{\sum\sum(\hat{m}_i^b - p_i^b)t_{ij}}_{\text{timing cost}} \quad\quad (9.11)$$

The first component captures liquidity cost relative to the efficient price. If we buy at a price above the efficient price, we effectively pay a liquidity premium, and if we buy at a lower price, we earn the premium. The liquidity costs incorporate both the bid–ask spread and any transitory price effects. For example, if a sequence of trades causes the current quoted price to differ from the efficient price, this temporary price impact is captured in the liquidity cost component.

This differs from the standard approach to measuring temporary price impact, which compares the price immediately after execution with a price some time later. In the standard approach, the temporary impact reflects the correlation between the direction of the order and subsequent price movements. For example, there is temporary impact if prices fall after the completion of a large buy order. The state-space approach captures this general idea, as it incorporates future price movements to estimate the permanent and temporary price decomposition. However, the main advantage of the state-space approach is that it calculates efficient prices throughout the execution period. The temporary component can be measured and incorporated into the liquidity cost component for each of the N executions. In contrast, the standard approach can only measure the temporary price impact at the end of the execution period based on its dissipation thereafter.

The second component of the implementation shortfall captures the informational cost, as it measures the covariation between executed signed order flow and the efficient price change. This is sometimes referred to as the permanent price impact of the trades. If for some reason signed flow does not correlate with efficient price changes, then the informational cost is zero. In most financial markets, however, the order flow is potentially informationally motivated, so this component is positive on average. For example, in a classic market-making model a liquidity supplier cannot distinguish informed from uninformed flow and therefore charges all incoming flow the same price impact (see, for example, Glosten and Milgrom 1985). In reality, a small informational cost component could reflect the skill of a trader or algorithm in camouflaging the order and having it perceived as uninformed. This component can also reflect variation in the information environment over time. For example, informational costs may be greater just before scheduled earnings announcements.

The third component measures whether the timing of the trade is correlated with the temporary component. If the parent order is a buy, for example, then starting it when the quote midpoint is above the efficient price increases the overall cost of the trade, all else being equal. Conversely, starting a buy order when the price is below the efficient price should improve its overall execution. We capture this by assigning a negative timing cost when a trade begins in these favourable conditions.

ILLUSTRATION OF OUR APPROACH

Decomposing the price process into its permanent and transitory components is fundamental to our approach. Hasbrouck (2007, Chapter 8) provides a detailed discussion of the challenges in identifying the two components. Here we follow an approach developed for analysing cyclical macroeconomic time series. This approach puts enough structure on the persistence of the transitory price component to identify the two components. Morley *et al* (2003, p. 240) show that the most parsimonious allowable specification for the temporary component is an AR(2):

> the order condition for identification of the unrestricted UC-ARMA(p, q) model, in the sense of having at least as many moment equations as parameters, is $p > 0, p > q + 2$, and it is just satisfied with $p = 2, q = 0$.

In the state-space representation, the observation equation is

$$p_t = \begin{bmatrix} 1 & 1 & 0 \end{bmatrix} \begin{bmatrix} m_t \\ s_t \\ s_{t-1} \end{bmatrix} \tag{9.12}$$

The state equation is

$$\begin{bmatrix} m_t \\ s_t \\ s_{t-1} \end{bmatrix} = \begin{bmatrix} 1 & 0 & 0 \\ 0 & \varphi_1 & \varphi_2 \\ 0 & 1 & 0 \end{bmatrix} \begin{bmatrix} m_{t-1} \\ s_{t-1} \\ s_{t-2} \end{bmatrix} + \begin{bmatrix} 1 & 0 \\ 0 & 1 \\ 0 & 0 \end{bmatrix} \begin{bmatrix} w_t \\ \varepsilon_t \end{bmatrix} \tag{9.13}$$

where the variance–covariance matrix of state innovations is

$$\Omega = \begin{bmatrix} \sigma_w^2 & \rho\sigma_w\sigma_\varepsilon & 0 \\ \rho\sigma_w\sigma_\varepsilon & \sigma_\varepsilon^2 & 0 \\ 0 & 0 & 0 \end{bmatrix} \qquad (9.14)$$

The unknown parameters in the state-space model are

$$(\sigma_w, \sigma_\varepsilon, \rho, \varphi_1, \varphi_2)$$

The observed price can be net of any market or industry sector movements. This is appropriate and efficient if trading occurs only in individual securities. Controlling for market and other factor movements is more complicated if the trading is part of a larger portfolio transaction that could possibly affect market or factor prices.

As discussed above, additional information can be used in decomposing the price process into its permanent and transitory components. The most common approach is to add additional state variables reflecting publicly available order flow information, such as buy and sell liquidity demand or the imbalance between the two. Brogaard *et al* (2012) extend this approach in the state-space context by using non-public information from Nasdaq on whether or not the liquidity demander in each trade is a high-frequency proprietary trading firm. Hendershott and Menkveld (2011) use NYSE market-maker inventory data, and Menkveld (2011) uses data from a high-frequency trading firm's inventory positions. The amount of data that can potentially be incorporated into the estimation is enormous. For example, all orders, trades and news in every related market and security could be utilised. For parsimony in our examples we only use past prices, in one case adjusted for an industry factor.

Implementation shortfall calculations

To illustrate our approach, we use two different examples with trading data observed at different frequencies: one example with daily trading data, and one example of a parent order where we observe the size, time and price of the individual child order executions during the trading day. In the daily example, we have two months' worth of trades by the same fund in the same stock, aggregated at the daily level, and we estimate the efficient and transitory price components at a daily frequency. This approach is most relevant to investors that make each day's trading decisions overnight while the market is closed, because in that trading environment the implementation shortfall is naturally calculated relative to the previous closing price.

It is worth noting that the decomposition in Equation 9.11 requires the efficient price estimate at the time of each transaction, $\hat{m}_{ij}$. In the daily example, however, we only calculate end-of-day efficient price estimates because we do not know when the trades actually take place during the day. This timing mismatch reduces the precision of the implementation shortfall decomposition and may also introduce bias. The main issue is the allocation of the shortfall between the first two terms of Equation 9.11: the liquidity and information costs. These two components can be thought of as corresponding to temporary and permanent price impacts, respectively. If there is positive correlation between the direction of trading and the movement in the efficient price, then using an estimate of the efficient price prior to transaction j will overestimate the liquidity cost and underestimate the information cost. Conversely, using an estimate of the efficient price after transaction j will underestimate the liquidity cost and overestimate the information cost. If only coarse execution data is available and temporary components are sufficiently persistent, however, the decomposition may still prove useful.

For the intra-day example, we obtain an efficient price estimate for each minute of the trading day. We use these efficient price estimates to evaluate the execution of a single parent order that is gradually executed over the course of about 30 minutes. The intra-day horizon allows for an evaluation of the high-frequency price dynamics during order execution.

To calculate our implementation shortfall decomposition we use Equation 9.11 with the prices at time j modified as follows:

- the subscript i is dropped as there is only one security;
- p_j is the average price at which the institution's trades execute at time j;
- p^b is the quote midpoint prior to beginning execution;
- $\hat{m}_j$ is the estimate of the efficient price at time j;
- $\hat{m}^b$ is the estimate of the efficient price prior to beginning execution.

Using these prices, the per-share execution costs can be represented as

$$\frac{1}{\sum |t_j|} \left(\underbrace{\sum (p_j - \hat{m}_j)\text{sign}(t_j)\,|t_j|}_{\text{liquidity cost } j} + \underbrace{\sum (\hat{m}_j - \hat{m}^b)\text{sign}(t_j)\,|t_j|}_{\text{informational cost } j} \right.$$

$$\left. + \underbrace{\sum (\hat{m}^b - p^b)\text{sign}(t_j)\,|t_j|}_{\text{timing cost } j} \right) \quad (9.15)$$

Daily estimation

For our first example, the execution data are from a long–short equity hedge fund with approximately US$150 million in assets under management and an average holding period of about one month. For each stock traded by this fund, we know the total number of shares bought and sold each day along with the weighted average execution price. In this case, we do not have information on individual intra-day trade executions. This is the standard granularity for institutional trading cost analysis, because this information along with a pre-trade benchmark price (such as the previous closing price, the opening price on the day of execution or the price at the time the order is released) is sufficient to measure implementation shortfall.

The chosen example is for AEC, which is the ticker symbol for Associated Estates Realty Corporation, a real estate investment trust (REIT) listed on the New York Stock Exchange with a market cap of around US$650 million during the sample period. We examine the fund's trading in AEC during November and December 2010. The fund traded a total of 559,356 shares of AEC during this time period on 20 separate trading days. The stock has an average daily volume of roughly 460,000 shares over these two months, so the analysed trades constitute about 2.8% of the total trading volume in AEC during this interval.

The implementation shortfall decomposition is illustrated based on daily data and one investor's trades in a single security. The index j runs over days and the price snapshot is taken at the end-of-day (closing) price, ie, the bid–ask midpoint at the end of the trading day.

The state-space model characterised in Equations 9.12–9.14 is estimated on daily data from January 4, 2010, to September 28, 2012. We use daily closing stock prices to calculate excess returns over the MSCI US REIT index, which is commonly referred to by its ticker symbol, RMZ. To be precise, the observed p_t is the log closing price

Table 9.1 Parameter estimates

Parameter	Estimate	Description
σ_w	91bp	Standard deviation efficient price innovation
σ_ε	44bp	Standard deviation pricing error residual
ρ	0.38	corr(w, ε)
φ_1	0.65	AR1 coefficient pricing error
φ_2	−0.05	AR2 coefficient pricing error

Figure 9.1 The end-of-day mid-quote, the efficient price estimate and the average execution price of the investor's (parent) orders for each day in the sample

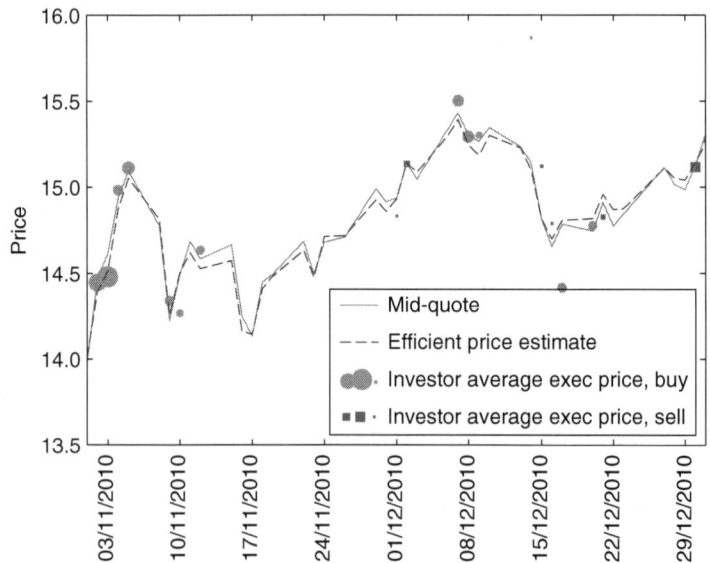

The efficient price estimate is based on a state-space model that was estimated for the entire sample: January 4, 2010, to September 28, 2012. The price estimate is based on the entire sample to obtain maximum efficiency. Dot size denotes order size.

of AEC adjusted for dividends minus the log RMZ index level. The parameter estimates are given in Table 9.1.

Figure 9.1 illustrates the estimates by plotting the observed end-of-day (closing) mid-quote, the efficient price estimate, and the investor's trades each day for the trading period November 2, 2010, to December 31, 2010. Because the pricing error follows a somewhat

Table 9.2 Total implementation shortfall

Cost	Basis points
Average liquidity cost	7.0
Average information cost	65.1
Average timing cost	−20.5
Average total cost	51.6

persistent AR(2) process, the daily pricing error innovation of 44 basis points (bp) scales up to a 71bp standard deviation for the pricing error itself. This means that the typical temporary component is estimated to account for 11¢ on this US$15 stock. This is roughly five times the typical bid–ask spread for this stock over our sample period. The temporary component is of the same order of magnitude as the standard deviation of daily innovations on the efficient price (91bp).

Based on the resulting estimates of efficient prices, the total implementation shortfall of 51.6bp can be decomposed as in Table 9.2.

The negative timing cost component of −20.5bp measures the contribution to fund performance from following a mean-reversion trading strategy that takes advantage of temporary pricing errors. The other notable quantity is the liquidity cost component, which is a modest 7.0bp. Recall that, when the model is implemented at the daily horizon, the liquidity cost component measures the average difference between execution prices and the post-trade efficient price at the close. The gap between trade time and measurement of the efficient price argues against making direct use of the numbers as estimates of the cost of temporary price moves when the price decomposition is performed at the daily horizon. Instead, we advocate using this component on a relative basis to compare executions across brokers, across stocks and over time.

To illustrate the breakdown of execution costs across days, Figure 9.2 plots the size of the total costs and each of its components for each day's trading. As in Figure 9.1, the size of the dot is proportional to the amount traded ($|t_j|$).[7]

As is often the case with execution cost measurement, there is substantial variation in the costs. Daily implementation shortfalls in this case are between −2.5% and 3.3%. The total costs are highest in the beginning of the sample, especially for the first few large orders,

Figure 9.2 Plots of the various components of the implementation shortfall on investor trades each day

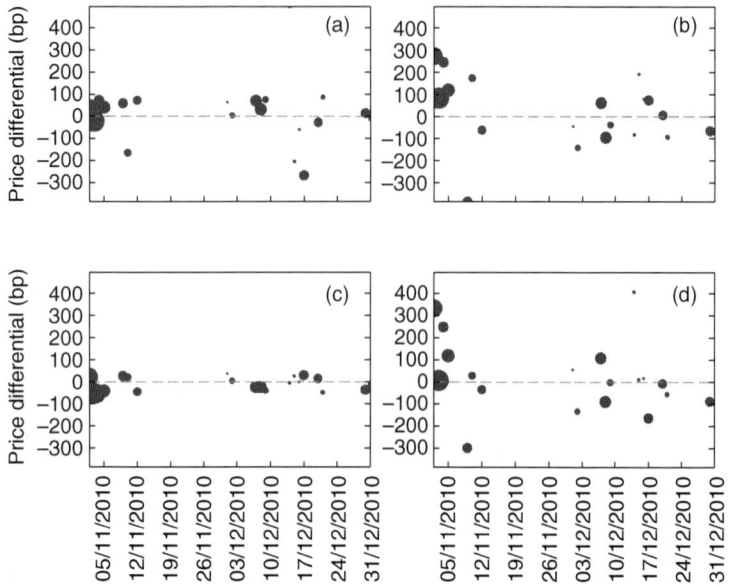

Graphs are based on efficient price estimates obtained from a state-space model and based on the entire sample: January 4, 2010, to September 28, 2012. The components are defined in Equation 9.15. (a) Liquidity cost component; (b) informational cost component; (c) timing cost component; (d) total cost.

suggesting that the fund quickly became aware of its price impact and subsequently traded in smaller sizes. For these first few large orders, the timing costs are negative, indicating that these orders began when prices were relatively attractive, but the large informational costs quickly swamped the timing benefit. Because we are using an end-of-day post-trade efficient price estimate to split the price impact into liquidity (temporary) and informational (temporary) components, we do not want to overinterpret this part of the decomposition. However, because it is a post-trade price, our liquidity component bears a strong resemblance to the traditional measure of the temporary component discussed earlier. In fact, some traders regularly measure trading costs against a post-trade price. Our innovation is to gain additional insight by using a post-trade efficient price from the state-space model rather than use a closing quote or closing auction price.

Table 9.3 Values for filtered estimates

Cost	Basis points
Average liquidity cost	10.4
Average information cost	69.4
Average timing cost	−28.2
Average total cost	51.6

Recalculation based on filtered estimates

It is also possible to decompose the implementation shortfall using filtered estimates of the efficient price instead of smoothed estimates by substituting $\tilde{m}_j$ for $\hat{m}_j$ in Equation 9.15. The filtered estimates yield the values in Table 9.3.

Of course, the total implementation shortfall is calculated using observed prices, so it remains unchanged. The timing cost component using filtered estimates is of particular interest, because it has a natural interpretation as the gross short-term alpha conditional on the subset of information included in the model available at the designated pre-trade time (the previous close in this case). Using filtered estimates, the timing cost component for this example is more negative at −28.2bp, indicating that an important source of overall return for this investor (or equivalently, an important source of trading cost minimisation) is trading against temporary pricing errors.

Intra-day estimation

Our second example uses data from a well-known firm that provides equity transactions cost analysis to institutional clients. We know the size and release time of the parent order, and the size, price and time of each child order execution. To illustrate the method, we choose one such parent order arbitrarily from a set of recent large orders in less active mid-cap stocks. We also require the order to be executed in one day. The chosen example is a December 13, 2012, sell order in HMST, which is the symbol for Homestreet, Inc, a Nasdaq-listed community bank on the west coast of the US with a market cap of around US$360 million. The sell order was for 6,365 shares, and the stock had an average daily volume of 119,000 shares during December 2012.

The order was released around 11h00, and it was fully completed in 50 child order executions over the space of about 30 minutes.

Table 9.4 Parameter estimates from the one-minute state-space model

Parameter	Estimate	Description
σ_w	11bp	Standard deviation efficient price innovation
σ_ε	6bp	Standard deviation pricing error residual
ρ	0.15	corr(w, ε)
φ_1	0.76	AR1 coefficient pricing error
φ_2	0.19	AR2 coefficient pricing error

Table 9.5 Implementation shortfall using smoothed estimates

Cost	Basis points
Average liquidity cost	48
Average information cost	219
Average timing cost	−5
Average total cost	262

During the half hour from 11h00 to 11h30, total trading volume in this symbol was 34,192 shares, so this client ended up trading 18.6% of the total volume during this interval.[8]

We estimated the state-space model using national best bid and offer (NBBO) midpoints at each minute during regular trading hours for 15 trading days from December 1, 2012, to December 21, 2012.[9] We discarded quote midpoints for the first five minutes, from 09h30 to 09h35, as we found that prices right around the open exhibited a different pattern of persistence and were much more volatile. Thus, the state-space model is designed to model share price behaviour after the beginning of the trading day and, at least in this case, the resulting implementation shortfall decomposition is best applied to trading that avoids the opening five-minute period.

The parameter estimates from the one-minute state-space model are given in Table 9.4.

As noted in the earlier example, the average size of the temporary component is much bigger than the standard deviation of the innovation due to the substantial persistence implied by the AR(2) specification. In this case, the standard deviation of the temporary component innovation is 5.9bp, and the temporary component itself has a standard deviation of 51bp, or about 12.5¢ on this US$25 stock.

The autoregressive (AR) coefficients imply a slow decay of the temporary component, with an estimated half-life of 14 minutes. As in the earlier example, the correlation between innovations to the two unobserved components continues to be positive, though it is somewhat smaller here. The standard deviation of the random walk component is 11bp over the one-minute interval, which scales up as the square root of t to 216bp per trading day.

Combining the smoothed estimates of the efficient price with the child order executions, we obtain the decomposition of the implementation shortfall given in Table 9.5.

The overall implementation shortfall is 262bp, and the large information cost component reflects the fact that this order is selling as the estimated efficient price is falling. The negative timing cost component of −5bp simply reflects the fact that the sell parent order was released at a time when the observed midpoint was slightly above the estimated efficient price.

Perhaps the most interesting component of our decomposition is the liquidity cost, and it is particularly useful to compare our implementation shortfall decomposition to a more traditional one. Recall that the liquidity cost component measures the average difference between execution prices and the estimated efficient price in effect at the time. While the child orders here execute an average of 48bp below the estimated efficient price, the liquidity cost would only be 9bp if we compare trades to quote midpoints in effect at the time of the child order execution. This is a substantial difference and highlights that the temporary component in prices clearly contributes to the overall trading costs for this order.

Figure 9.3 illustrates the estimates by plotting the observed end-of-minute NBBO mid-quote, the efficient price estimate and the investor's trades each minute. An initial burst of selling coincides with a sharp price decline. We cannot make causal statements, but it is certainly possible that the selling pressure from this parent order caused the price decline. Much of the decline appears to be temporary. The share price bounces back by noon, once this order is completed and the selling pressure abates. This armchair empiricism is confirmed by the efficient price estimate, which never moves down as far as the observed quote midpoint and is as much as 14¢ above the mid-quote during this order execution. The deviation between the observed mid-quote and efficient price begins to

Figure 9.3 The end-of-minute mid-quote, the efficient price estimate and the average execution price of the investor's trades for each minute in the sample

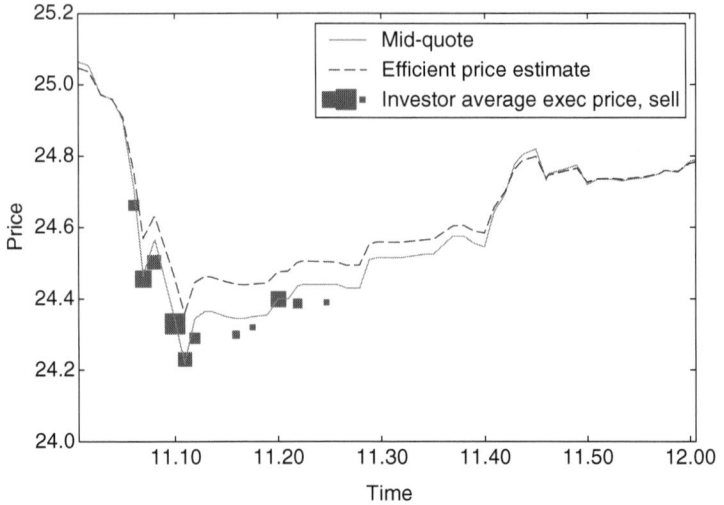

The efficient price estimate is obtained from a state-space model using NBBO midpoints at each minute during regular trading hours for 15 trading days from December 1, 2012, to December 21, 2012, discarding quote midpoints for the first five minutes of trading (09h30 to 09h35).

appear as child orders begin to be executed. After selling 4,365 shares in the space of five minutes from 11.05 to 11.09 (or 23% of the 19,096 HMST shares that trade in this interval), the transitory component reaches its maximum deviation. Thereafter, execution slows and the transitory component gradually shrinks.

To illustrate the minute-by-minute breakdown of execution costs, Figure 9.4 plots the size of the total costs and each of its components for trades in each minute. As in Figure 9.3, the size of the dot is proportional to the number of shares filled in each minute. As noted earlier, the efficient price moves down sharply as the first few minutes of selling unfold. This is reflected in the initial upwards trend in the informational cost component. The liquidity component increases rapidly from 39bp for executions at 11h05 to 64bp for the 11h11 fills. Thereafter, the liquidity component generally declines, although the scaling of the graph makes this difficult to see. The timing component is constant at -5bp, as this illustration is for a single parent order. Because the informational costs are by far the

Figure 9.4 The various components of the implementation shortfall for trades aggregated within each minute

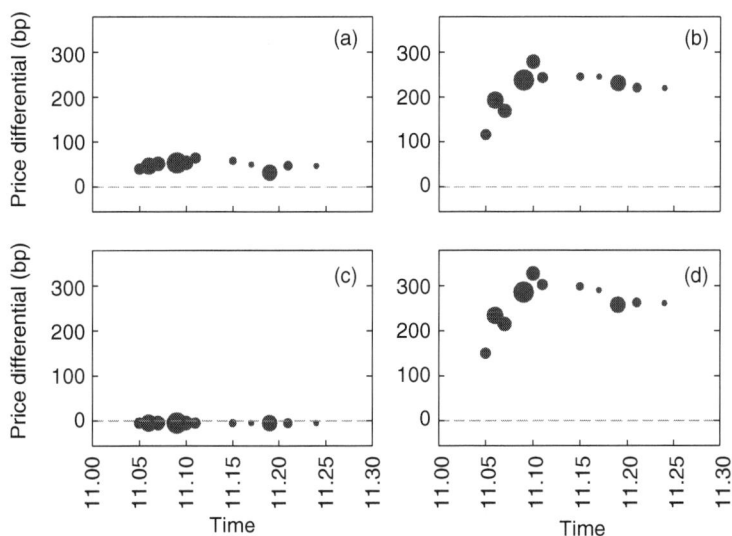

The graphs are based on efficient price estimates obtained from a state-space model using NBBO midpoints at each minute during regular trading hours for 15 trading days from December 1, 2012, to December 21, 2012, discarding quote midpoints for the first five minutes of trading (09h30 to 09h35). The components are defined in Equation 9.15. (a) Liquidity cost component; (b) informational cost component; (c) timing cost component; (d) total cost.

largest component of the implementation shortfall, the pattern for total costs closely tracks the informational cost component.

CONCLUSION

In this chapter, we decompose a sequence of observed asset prices into a permanent component and a temporary component. We use this price process decomposition to provide a novel and useful decomposition of the standard implementation shortfall transaction cost measure.

Investors often think in terms of earning the spread, evaluating individual executions relative to the prevailing quote midpoint. Our methodology provides an alternative benchmark. Individual executions should be evaluated against the estimated efficient price, which can be far from the current quote midpoint (a root-mean-squared average of 51bp in the case of HMST, our intra-day example).

Our methodology also captures the fact that a sequence of trades in the same direction can generate or contribute to a temporary component, and it allows an institutional investor to measure how much its own trading has done so. This seems particularly important in an automated equity market structure, where transitory price impact may be due to some traders following order anticipation strategies. An institutional investor or algorithm provider can use these empirical techniques to discern whether its algorithms or trading practices minimise these temporary price moves. The empirical examples indicate that the temporary component could be an important contributor to overall trading costs: 48bp out of a total of 262bp for the intra-day example that we study.

We have provided two simple applications of the methodology here. While we only use past prices, we want to reiterate that additional variables can and probably should be added to the filtration. Signed order flow, information on short sales and position data can all be valuable in determining the latent efficient price.

Finally, our decomposition may be useful in implementing the optimal trading strategy in Gârleanu and Pedersen (2013). They derive an elegant and insightful closed-form solution for optimal dynamic execution in the presence of quadratic costs and decaying sources of alpha. Their model draws a distinction between temporary and permanent price impacts, and our estimates of the permanent and temporary components of transaction costs can be used to operationalise their results.

APPENDIX: IMPLEMENTATION DETAILS

A useful general reference on state-space models (SSMs) is Durbin and Koopman (2001). One standard way to the estimate parameters of a state-space model is maximum likelihood. The Kalman filter is used to calculate the likelihood given a particular set of parameters.

One standard approach to implement maximum likelihood is to use the expectation-maximisation (EM) algorithm.[10] Its appeal over Newton–Raphson-type approaches is that it avoids a numerically expensive calculation of the inverse of the matrix of second-order partials, and with each step the likelihood is guaranteed to increase. Its relative disadvantage is that convergence is relatively slow in the latter stages. Both approaches, however, could converge to a local maximum. One way to avoid local maximums is to search over a parameter grid.

We use two different estimation methods for the two examples presented in our illustration (see pp. 192ff). The intra-day example employs the state-space estimation commands in STATA. To investigate robustness, we experimented with different hill-climbing algorithms, starting values and convergence tolerances. In every case, we ended up with the same estimates, suggesting that the likelihood function is well behaved.

The likelihood optimisation for the daily example is implemented in PYTHON and uses the PYKALMAN package.[11] The EM algorithm is combined with a parameter grid search for the AR parameters of the pricing error process: φ_1 and φ_2. The choice for a grid on this subset of model parameters is informed by studying convergence based on random sets of starting values. It turns out that the parameters at the optimum are particularly sensitive to starting values of φ_1 and φ_2. The grid search involved a grid over $[-0.8, -0.6, -0.4, -0.2, 0, 0.2, 0.4, 0.6, 0.8]^2$ and finer grids with step sizes down to 0.05 around the optimum.

1   See, for example, the US Securities and Exchange Commission's 2010 concept release on equity market structure (Release No. 34-61358).

2   See Duffie (2010) for an extensive discussion of temporary price impacts from large informationless demands for liquidity.

3   Engle and Ferstenberg (2007) also estimate implementation shortfall costs on a sample of institutional orders, focusing on the variance of the execution costs as well as their mean.

4   The observed p_{ij} in this section can be either trade prices or quote midpoints. In this chapter we always use mid-quotes.

5   Non-public information can also be incorporated into the estimation. See Hendershott and Menkveld (2011) for an application using NYSE market-maker inventory data, Menkveld (2011) using data from a high-frequency trading firm's inventory positions and Brogaard et al (2012) using data on the aggregate trading of 26 high-frequency trading firms.

6   Filtered price estimates are more natural in the case of real-time trade decisions, which necessarily only have historical information available.

7   On most days the fund traded in only one direction. However, on three days the fund bought and sold shares. On those days, only the net trade enters the analysis, along with the average price across all trades that day. For example, if the fund bought 35,000 shares at US$15 and sold 5,000 shares at US$16, then the net trade that day was a buy of 30,000 shares at a price of $(35{,}000 \times \$15 - 5{,}000 \times \$16)/30{,}000 = \$14.83$.

8   There was no news released on HMST that day, and during the 11–11h30 period, the S&P 500 fell by 0.2%, compared with a share price drop of about 2% over the same interval in HMST. Thus, it appears that most of the price moves documented here are idiosyncratic.

9   We also experimented with estimating the state-space model trade-by-trade rather than in calendar time. We found relatively little persistence in the temporary component when the model is estimated in trade time, most likely because the specification imposes an exponential decay on the temporary component that does not seem to fit the trade-by-trade time series.

In addition, the results were very sensitive to how we aggregated trades that are within a few milliseconds of each other but are not exactly simultaneous.

10 See Dempster *et al* (1977) for EM and Shumway and Stoffer (1982) for EM and SSMs.

11 Package documentation is at http://pykalman.github.com/.

REFERENCES

Almgren, R., C. Thum, E. Hauptmann and H. Li, 2005, "Equity Market Impact", *Journal of Risk* July, pp. 57–62.

Brogaard, J., T. Hendershott and R. Riordan, 2012, "High Frequency Trading and Price Discovery", Manuscript, University of California, Berkeley.

Dempster, A. P., N. M. Laird and D. B. Rubin, 1977, "Maximum Likelihood from Incomplete Data via the EM Algorithm", *Journal of the Royal Statistical Society* 39, pp. 1–38.

Duffie, D., 2010, "Presidential Address: Asset Price Dynamics with Slow-Moving Capital", *Journal of Finance* 65, pp. 1237–67.

Durbin, J., and S. J. Koopman, 2001, *Time Series Analysis by State Space Models.* Oxford University Press.

Engle, R. F., and R. Ferstenberg, 2007, "Execution Risk", *Journal of Portfolio Management* 33(2), pp. 34–44.

Gârleanu, N., and L. H. Pedersen, 2013, "Dynamic Trading with Predictable Returns and Transaction Costs", *Journal of Finance*, forthcoming.

Glosten, L., and P. Milgrom, 1985, "Bid, Ask, and Transaction Prices in a Specialist Market with Heterogeneously Informed Agents", *Journal of Financial Economics* 14, pp. 71–100.

Hasbrouck, J., 1995, "One Security, Many Markets: Determining the Contributions to Price Discovery", *Journal of Finance* 50, pp. 1175–99.

Hasbrouck, J., 2007, *Empirical Market Microstructure.* New York: Oxford University Press.

Hendershott, T., and A. J. Menkveld, 2011, "Price Pressures", Manuscript, VU University Amsterdam.

Kraus, A., and H. Stoll, 1972, "Price Impacts of Block Trading on the New York Stock Exchange", *Journal of Finance* 27, pp. 569–88.

Menkveld, A. J., 2011, "High Frequency Trading and the New-Market Makers", Manuscript, VU University Amsterdam.

Menkveld, A. J., S. J. Koopman and A. Lucas, 2007, "Modelling Round-the-Clock Price Discovery for Cross-Listed Stocks Using State Space Methods", *Journal of Business and Economic Statistics* 25, pp. 213–25.

Morley, J. C., C. R. Nelson and E. Zivot, 2003, "Why Are the Beveridge–Nelson and Unobserved-Components Decompositions of GDP so Different?", *Review of Economics and Statistics* 2, pp. 235–43.

Perold, A. F., 1988, "The Implementation Shortfall: Paper versus Reality", *Journal of Portfolio Management* 14, pp. 4–9.

Shumway, R. H., and D. S. Stoffer, 1982, "An Approach to Time Series Smoothing and Forecasting Using the EM Algorithm", *Journal of Time Series Analysis* 3, pp. 253–64.

Stock, J. H., and M. W. Watson, 1988, "Testing for Common Trends", *Journal of the American Statistical Association* 83, pp. 1097–1107.

10

The Regulatory Challenge of High-Frequency Markets

Oliver Linton; Maureen O'Hara; J. P. Zigrand

University of Cambridge; Cornell University; London School of Economics and Political Science

High-frequency trading (HFT) has become the norm in equities, futures and options markets, and is quickly becoming commonplace in foreign exchange and commodity markets. The influence of HFT goes far beyond simply "speeding up" markets, but instead changes everything from liquidity provision to order strategies to market stability. For regulators, HFT poses daunting challenges as to how best to oversee markets in which computers generate, route and execute orders. An added complexity is that HFT also ties markets together at lightning speed, meaning that regulatory frameworks cannot simply apply to particular markets or even to specific asset classes. From "flash crashes" to new methods of manipulation, regulators now face a host of problems.

In this chapter, we address the challenges of regulation in a high-frequency world. We discuss in detail regulatory issues created by HFT and how these differ from the problems facing regulators in the past. We provide some specific examples of the problems raised by HFT, and then turn to a discussion of the proposed solutions. Our premise in this chapter is that, just as markets have changed in fundamental ways, so, too, must their regulation and supervision. Two issues are particularly important. First, the speed of markets necessitates that regulation must move to an *ex ante* rather than *ex post* basis. There is simply not enough time to intervene effectively in markets after something has happened, so regulatory actions in the event of faltering markets must be pre-specified and applied concurrently. Coincident with this change is the use of technology to monitor markets in real time, in effect applying the same high-frequency technology to supervise the markets as is being used by traders in the markets. Second, regulatory structure must also explicitly address the role of uncertainty in affecting the behaviour and stability of high-frequency markets. Speed can induce uncertainty which, in turn, induces lack of participation. As we discuss in this chapter, regulatory policies designed to limit uncertainty can play an important role in limiting market instability.

In contemplating the new regulatory paradigm, it is useful first to consider what role regulation plays in security markets. Arguably, regulation should serve to make individual markets, and the capital markets as a whole, work efficiently and effectively. This is a complex task, as the role of individual markets is to provide liquidity and price discovery, while the role of capital markets is to facilitate risk-sharing for all investor classes and to foster capital provision. Regulators have to make sure that markets do the former, but they also have to ensure that in doing so the capital markets reach these larger goals. This is not always straightforward, as the interests of individual markets may conflict with the broader interests of the overall capital markets. For example, it is in the financial interest of exchanges to attract the greatest trading volume, and one way to do so is to design trading systems that are more attractive to high-frequency trading firms. If by doing so, however, market rules disadvantage small traders, risk-sharing in capital markets will be degraded. Similarly, a market may decide to allow particular trading practices that increase the potential for periodic illiquidity.[1] The nature of linkages across high-frequency markets, however, means that problems in one market can turn into systemic liquidity problems for all markets. The goal of regulation is to avoid these negative outcomes while still retaining the benefits arising from the enhanced HF technology. In the next section, we consider these trade-offs in more detail.

REGULATING HIGH-FREQUENCY MARKETS: GOOD NEWS AND BAD NEWS

Market quality is usually defined in terms of transaction costs and market efficiency. By these metrics, high-frequency markets today are "better" than markets in the pre-high-frequency era. Virtually every academic study of market quality has found that transaction costs are lower now than in the past, and often by a substantial amount.[2] Similarly, studies of market efficiency also conclude that markets now reflect information more quickly than in the past, resulting in prices more accurately reflecting underlying asset values (see, for example, O'Hara and Ye 2011; Hendershott *et al* 2011; Boehmer *et al* 2012; Hasbrouck and Saar 2013). Evidence from Brogaard *et al* (2013) and Hagströmer and Nordén (2013) also suggests that HFT is associated with lower volatility. From a regulatory perspective, these studies provide welcome news that the market structure appears to be working well.

A natural concern is whether studies based on averages (for example, average transaction costs or average variance ratios) fail to pick up negative impacts of HFT on the market. Two issues are relevant here. One is whether average effects mask negative effects on specific segments of the market. An intriguing study by Malinova *et al* (2012) looks specifically at how the introduction of message fees in Canadian markets affected market quality and trading costs for retail traders. High-frequency firms rely on the ability to submit and cancel massive numbers of orders, and message charges fall disproportionately on such traders. Malinova *et al* found that following the change HF traders reduced their market activity significantly. Using order level data, they also found the reduction of HF message traffic increased both overall spreads and trading costs, in particular, for retail traders. Their paper is provocative for giving hard evidence that high-frequency activities *per se* can enhance market quality for other market participants.

A second issue is whether measuring quality on average misses important negative effects arising from infrequent, but periodic, instability. Here concerns seem well founded, as markets worldwide seem to have been experiencing more episodic illiquidity. The US "flash crash" in May 2010 is instructive in this regard. The flash crash, so-named because the entire event took place over a 30-minute period, saw the E-mini S&P 500 futures fall by 8%, inducing a 1,000-point fall in the Dow Jones index, and then a subsequent recovery to near pre-crash levels. During the crash, prices in equity Exchange Traded Funds (ETFs) plummeted, in some cases to zero, while prices in individual equities both plunged and skyrocketed, reflecting that order books had emptied. The transmission of illiquidity from what

Figure 10.1 Flash crashes

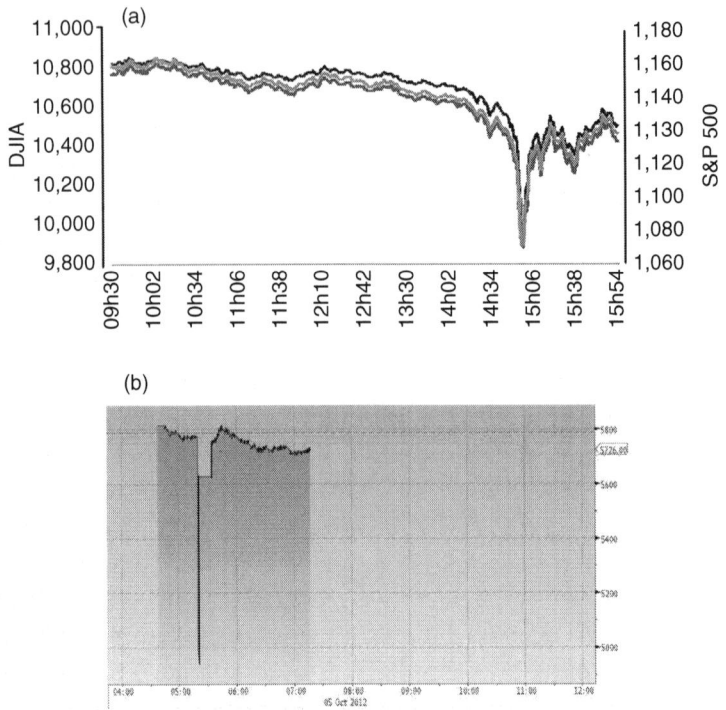

(a) US flash crash, May 6, 2012: black line (top), DJIA; mid-grey line (middle), E-mini S&P 500; dark-grey line (bottom), S&P 500 Index. (b) India flash crash, October 5, 2012.
Source: adapted from Bloomberg.

is the most liquid equity future contract to the equity market, as well as the speed with which this occurred, was a wake-up call for both markets and regulators. Figure 10.1 illustrates this US flash crash, as well as a flash crash in India.[3] Unfortunately, there have now been a variety of similar illiquidity events in settings around the world, raising serious concerns about the stability of the HF market structure.

How do we reconcile the apparent evidence of improved market quality with the equally apparent evidence of decreased market stability? The answer lies in recognising that the mechanics of high-frequency markets are simply different from the mechanics of markets heretofore. Liquidity provision, for example, results from orders placed on electronic limit order books, and not from specific intermediaries (specialists or designated market makers) standing ready to buy or sell. High-frequency traders place most of these passive orders and so are the new "market makers". But HF market making often arises as part of inter-market arbitrage, with computerised programs placing bids in one market and offers in another. There is no "intermediary" standing ready to buy or sell when liquidity is needed in a given market. Moreover, these limit orders are all placed (and cancelled) strategically in the book within milliseconds, meaning that liquidity can be ephemeral. From a regulatory perspective, how to ensure that markets consistently provide liquidity and price discovery is a problem.

The nature of trading has also changed, with algorithms now directing most order flow, and direct market access (combined with co-location) providing some traders with unprecedented ability to get to markets before others. Algorithmic trading can greatly reduce trading costs by timing and slicing orders both temporally and spatially to find dispersed liquidity. But the deterministic nature of most trading algorithms gives rise to new forms of market manipulation such as layering, spoofing and quote stuffing.[4] In particular, knowing that some traders (or, more precisely, computers acting for traders) are executing orders via particular strategies such as VWAP (ie, trading so as to achieve the volume-weighted average price over some interval of time) allows other traders' computers to take advantage of their order behaviour. While some of this behaviour is legal (for example, putting orders on the book to sell when algo-based buying is predicted to be high), other behaviour is not, and it raises new and important regulatory challenges.

Figure 10.2 illustrates one such manipulative strategy known as layering. As discussed in O'Hara (2010), the data show a market where a limit order to buy (shown by dots) is placed in the market. A computer then rapidly places multiple buy orders (shown by dashes) at prices just above the resting buy order, essentially raising the quoted bid price. These orders are not "real", as they are cancelled almost instantaneously, but the intent is to force the algorithm having placed the resting buy order to raise its price, essentially competing against itself. As the figure shows, this process continues, with the limit price gradually going up. The episode would normally end with the manipulative algorithm hitting (ie, selling to) the now higher priced limit buy order, thereby making a profit by selling at

Figure 10.2 Example of a layering strategy

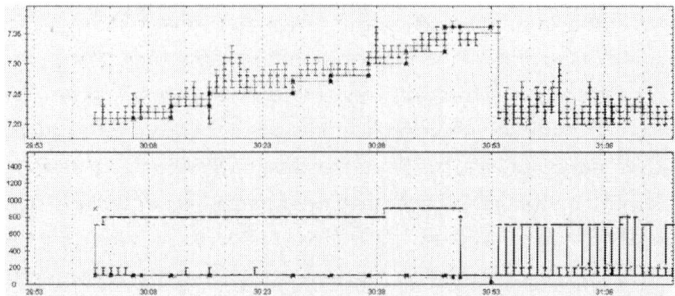

This figure shows what appears to be an automated strategy to induce an algorithm to trade against itself. In the upper panel, the vertical axis shows prices, and the horizontal axis time. The dots are limits orders to buy placed by an agency algorithm, while the dashed lines are limit orders to buy placed by the predatory algorithm. The predatory algorithm submits, and then immediately cancels, an order, replacing it with an order at a higher price. The intent is to get the agency algorithm to increase its bid, which in the example in the lower panel it does. The predatory algorithm makes money if it can sell to the agency algorithm at the higher price. In this example, the agency algorithm cancelled the order, and the predatory algorithm resets and trolls for a new victim.
Source: ITG data (O'Hara 2010).

an artificially high price. In this particular case, the algorithm cancelled the order, so no trade occurred, but the manipulative strategy simply reset to try to entice a new algorithm to trade against itself.

The incidence of such manipulative strategies is clearly on the rise, as demonstrated by a plethora of enforcement actions by the Financial Industry Regulatory Authority (FINRA, the US regulator), the Financial Conduct Authority (FCA, the UK regulator) and other regulators around the time of writing. But the difficulty of discerning such complex strategies in actual markets cannot be overstated, leading to concerns that regulators are catching only egregious cases. Moreover, new forms of manipulation emerge that are recognised only after the fact. A case in point is "banging the beehive", a colourfully named strategy in natural gas futures markets, where high-speed traders send massive numbers of orders to a market right before a scheduled data release, with the goal of creating large price volatility. This strategy is designed to create "synthetic momentum" and thereby take advantage of resting orders placed in anticipation of the data release.[5] For regulators, the challenge of how to monitor and police high-frequency markets is a daunting task.

Of course, another way that high-frequency markets differ from traditional markets is speed. Technological advances have always emerged that increased the speed of the markets, but with markets now already trading at microsecond speeds, recent innovations involve thwarting the constraints imposed by the speed of light in solid media. A case in point is a new joint venture of the Chicago Mercantile Exchange (CME) and the Nasdaq (Javers 2013). By using a network of towers to send microwave messages between their respective data centres in Chicago and New Jersey, this linkage shaves four milliseconds off of the time it takes ground-based cables to transmit orders.[6]

What is unique now is that ultra-high speed raises concerns about market failure due to technological glitches that can cause havoc in a matter of moments. The Knight Trading debacle, where an out-of-control algorithm caused a US$440 million loss in 43 minutes, is a case in point. But, so too is the chaos surrounding Facebook's opening on Nasdaq, or any number of computer-related malfunctions in which errant algorithms caused prices to spike or plummet in markets.

What is particularly worrisome is market aberrations occurring at, or near, market close. A market experiencing a liquidity event just before the close has no opportunity to remediate what can be a dramatic fall in prices before trading ends. This, in turn, can cause other markets to experience similar liquidity events, based on uncertainty about what caused problems at the first market. For regulators, the lessons of such market aberrations are clear: illiquidity contagion now poses a systemic risk for world markets.

As we discuss in the next section, to avoid this outcome there must be mechanisms in place that rapidly shut down faltering markets, or even close markets in advance if possible. Contingencies regarding end-of-day problems, such as allowing markets to reopen to allow a more orderly close, must also be specified. Moreover, regulators have to provide greater information to the markets regarding the nature of market disturbances. An errant algorithm in one market right before close, for example, should not result in worldwide market closures.

But when, exactly, should regulators "pull the plug" on markets? A case in point is the perplexing behaviour of the US equity markets on July 19, 2012. Beginning soon after the open, the transaction prices

Figure 10.3 Aberrant stock-price movements, July 19, 2012

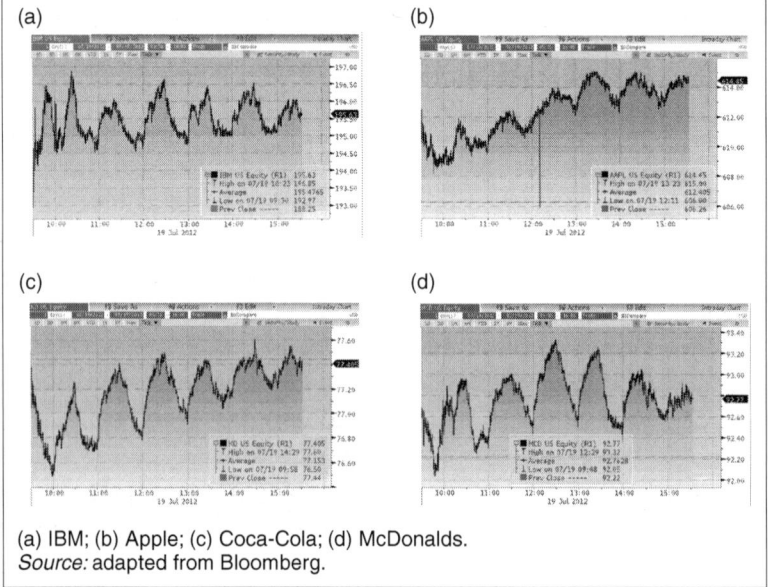

(a) IBM; (b) Apple; (c) Coca-Cola; (d) McDonalds.
Source: adapted from Bloomberg.

of Apple, Coca-Cola, IBM and McDonald's began exhibiting odd patterns. As illustrated in Figure 10.3, each of these highly liquid stocks began to oscillate, moving in what were clearly time-linked patterns with turning points every 30 minutes. These patterns persisted for several hours. Given that these stocks are among the largest in the US market, how is it possible that anything could move prices that way? And what trading strategy could possibly be in play that would make this a desirable outcome? In this case, subsequent investigation found the culprit to be a wayward agency algorithm, and markets quickly returned to normal.[7] But the lesson is clear: in today's high-frequency markets, even the largest stocks and markets are not immune to the influences of errant technology.

REGULATORY SOLUTIONS

What, then, should regulators do about high-frequency trading? Not surprisingly, regulators around the world are asking this very question. In the US, the "Flash Crash" Commission[8] recommended a variety of changes, including enhanced market halts and circuit breakers, increased information gathering and surveillance and changes to trading priority rules. The European Union, as part of its MiFid II analysis, recommended a host of changes, including market-maker obligations, minimum resting times, algorithmic trading restrictions and transactions taxes. The UK commissioned an extensive study, the Foresight Project, to evaluate many of these proposals. Germany opted not to wait on the EU process, and passed its own High-Frequency legislation.[9] Around the time of writing, Canadian regulators implemented sweeping changes with respect to pre-trade risk controls and off-exchange trading. The Australian Securities and Investment Commission undertook a six-month study of on the impact of high-frequency trading in Australia, concluding that HFT fears for their markets had been "overstated".[10]

The plethora of suggested reforms reflects the divergent views surrounding HFT. For some, HFT is a technological advance that requires adjustments to market surveillance and coordination. For others, it has distorted the functioning of markets, and new rules are needed to ensure proper market behaviour. Yet another group views high-frequency trading as inherently wrong, and thus should be removed from, or at least greatly reduced in, markets. A "middle ground" has yet to emerge in this debate.

While reviewing all of these various proposals would be a Herculean task, we now consider some of the more significant proposals.

Proposals for greater surveillance and coordination

Instability in markets has revealed two basic problems facing regulators: they do not have the technology needed to surveil the market, and they do not have the capability to ensure that technology used by firms and trading venues is not causing harm to the market. The nature of these problems defies easy solutions, but one thing is clear: regulators will have to adopt new methods and approaches for overseeing these new, technology-based markets.

The US Securities and Exchange Commission (SEC) has focused on developing new data and trading analytics. The foundation for these efforts is the Market Information Data Analytics System (MIDAS). In October 2012, the SEC commissioned Tradeworx, a high-frequency trading firm, to develop this platform, essentially to give the SEC the same analytical capabilities as the high-frequency firms. Thus, the MIDAS system collects data on all quotes, trades, orders and cancellations in "real" time. The system also allows for data analysis, providing the SEC with an ability to evaluate the market on a real-time basis. SEC Commissioner Elisse Walter argues that this will be revolutionary for regulators, likening it to "the first time scientists used high-speed photography and strobe lighting to see how hummingbirds' wings actually move" (Walter 2013).

A second, and related, initiative is the Consolidated Audit Tape (CAT), which will include both public and non-public information, such as the identities of traders submitting, cancelling or executing orders. The CAT will allow the SEC to see across markets, an ability surely needed given the fragmentation characterising the markets at the time of writing. MIDAS and CAT together should also give the SEC the ability to identify abusive trading behaviours (the spoofing, quote stuffing, etc, discussed earlier), as well as provide a means to identify incipient market problems.

Exactly how regulators accomplish this latter task is not clear. The challenge with HF markets is that illiquidity can develop in milliseconds, but predictors of market instability are not typically defined over such time scales. Researchers have begun to develop such tools, with volume-synchronised probability of informed trading (VPIN; Easley *et al* 2011) and quotation frequency measures (Madhavan 2012) both being examples of metrics that appear to signal market instability. But much more work is needed to turn the data generated by these new projects into the knowledge needed to regulate markets.

These new tools allow greater surveillance of market behaviour, but in high-frequency markets it is better still to cut off problems before they reach the market. This is the motivation for proposals in both the US and the European Commission for algorithm standards and oversight. The SEC has proposed Regulation SCI, a series of practices designed to improve system compliance and integrity. Regulation SCI would replace the current voluntary oversight with a compulsory system. Firms would be required to ensure that their core technology meets certain standards, as well as to conduct periodic business continuity testing. Firms would also be required to notify regulators of any problems, outages, or discrepancies.

The European Union has taken a stronger stand, proposing specific rules for algorithm notification. The Markets in Financial Instruments Directive (MiFid II, Article 17(2)) proposes that an investment firm engaging in algorithmic trading must provide annually to the regulator a description of its algorithmic trading strategies, details of the trading parameters and limits, the key compliance and risk controls it has in place and details of the testing of its systems. Professor Dave Cliff, writing in the Foresight Project (Government Office for Science 2012), argues that this is both conceptually and financially infeasible. Describing an algorithmic trading strategy requires not only all the programs that have been written to implement it, but also the full details of the code libraries used, as well as the software tools involved. The description must include the actual computations required, the algorithms that affect the computations and full details of how the algorithms are implemented. Regulators would then have to evaluate the algorithms and determine the risk they pose to the market. However, this would require substantial technical expertise, as well as considerable expense. Because algorithms are updated frequently, such notification and review would have to be done on a continuous basis. Germany has already adopted rules requiring that algorithmic trading firms provide information on trading algorithms to the regulators. It remains to be seen whether this proposed requirement will be implemented more broadly in the rest of Europe.

One area where changes have been made is to circuit breakers. Circuit breakers can take many forms: market-wide or single-stock halts; limit-up and limit-down rules; restrictions to one trading venue or coordination across multiple venues. The London Stock Exchange (LSE), for example, operates a stock-by-stock circuit breaker that, when triggered, switches trading to an auction mode in which an indicative price is continuously posted while orders are accumulated on either side. After some time, the auction is uncrossed and continuous trading resumes. The trigger points that determine the trading mechanism switching are in several bands depending on the capitalisation and price level of the stock, and are determined dynamically (relative to the last transaction price) and statically (relative to the last auction uncrossing price).

In June 2010, the SEC mandated the use of single stock circuit breakers that would halt trading in all markets when a stock price moved 10% in a five minute period. At the time of writing these circuit breakers were being replaced by limit-up/limit-down rules, which were rolled out across all US stocks from April 2013. Limit-up/limit-down essentially creates a rolling collar around a price, with trades outside of the collar being prohibited. Following a specified time period, the collar is adjusted and trading can resume within the new bounds. The advantage of such rules is that they prevent obviously incorrect trades from printing; the disadvantage is that they can slow the adjustment of prices to new equilibrium values.

A more daunting task is to impose market-wide circuit breakers. What became painfully clear in the US flash crash was that efforts by the NYSE to slow trading were neutralised by traders simply trading in other markets. Moreover, the linkages in high-frequency markets mean that problem in one market almost instantaneously spill over into other markets. That futures and equities were so interlinked was starkly illustrated when problems in futures turned into problems in cash equities, which turned into problems in ETFs, which turned into problems with futures.

The US had regulations requiring market-wide trading halts in equities and futures, but the bounds defining these price moves were so large that none of these were actually triggered during the flash crash. A new structure has been put in place, pegging halts to the S&P 500 Index (as opposed to the much smaller Dow Jones Index) and specifying smaller price movements to trigger a halt. Europe, with its much more decentralised exchange and markets system, has not yet implemented such a structure. Singapore planned to adopt market circuit breakers in the coming year, joining Australia, which already has such rules in place at the time of writing. Most equity markets have single stock circuit breakers.[11]

Proposals to change market rules

Concurrent with the changes discussed above, there have been calls for regulators to change features of market structure viewed as sub-optimal in a high-frequency setting. One such proposal involves the minimum tick size, which is the smallest allowable increment between quoted prices in a market. Tick sizes have important implications for transaction costs, liquidity provision and stability. A larger tick size, if binding, increases trading costs by widening the spread between bid and offer prices, thereby rewarding liquidity providers, whose trading model is to capture the spread. The tick size determines how easy it is for another trader to 'step ahead' of an existing limit order. In markets with a standard price/time priority rule, an order placed first executes ahead of one placed later unless the later order is posted at a "better" price. Smaller tick sizes make it easier for traders to post that better price, so smaller tick sizes push up the cost for liquidity providers and for those traders who are not able to react so quickly. Small tick sizes allow more price points for trades and quotes, and so lead to more cancellations and revisions and price movements, and hence perhaps longer times to execution.

There are important differences in minimum tick size policy between the US and Europe. In the US, Regulation National Market System requires that in all "lit" venues (exchanges and large Alternative Trading Systems) stocks over US$1 are quoted with a minimum tick size of 1¢, and sub-penny pricing is prohibited, except on dark pools, where midpoint crossing is common. In Europe, there is no mandated tick size and local exchanges are free to set their own tick policy. As a result, there are generally a range of tick sizes operating on any given venue (typically, there are a number of categories defined by the stock-price level[12]). In addition, a European stock may trade on different public venues under different tick size regimes, whereas in the US such differences can only currently happen in dark venues. Historically, the trend has been towards smaller tick sizes since US trading in "eighths" (12.5¢) yielded to decimalisation in 2000. Now, active stocks in the US typically trade at 1¢ spreads, leading to concerns that a 1¢ minimum tick may be too large, thus illustrating the above-mentioned trade-off between transaction costs and liquidity provision. In Europe, spreads at minimum levels are not as common, suggesting that the tick rules are not as binding on market behaviour.

The question is whether tick size policy can be effective in dealing with some of the ills of financial markets outlined above. Larger tick sizes might make for more stable markets but would increase transaction costs, especially for retail orders. They may favour some types of HFT strategies (such as market making) but disadvantage others (such as cross-venue arbitrage), and the net effect on this industry is uncertain. Mandating common price grids for the same stock on all public venues may reduce wasteful competition, but it also needs to be balanced against the competition with dark venues for order flow, where price grids are typically finer than in the public space.

How then to determine tick sizes that balance these potentially contradictory outcomes in an objective and transparent way? An important step in this process is the design and execution of careful studies to quantify the trade-offs in current markets (along the lines of the pilot study by the Federation of European Securities Exchanges (FESE)).[13] In 2012 the SEC published a report on decimalisation, advocating pilot programmes for further study of this issue (US Securities and Exchange Commission 2012).

At the time of writing there have been some regulatory developments. A report by the Australian regulators has found that for some stocks the tick sizes were too large and that this had been driving trading activity away from lit venues into dark pools with negative consequences for price discovery. They have been seeking industry views on lowering tick sizes for certain securities that are tick constrained. The Autorité des Marchés Financiers (AMF, the French regulator) has developed a new tick size regime approach that could be applied across the EU. Their proposal is based on both the price and the liquidity (the average observed spread of the stock, whereas the FESE tick size tables are determined solely according to the share price). The German High-Frequency Trading (HFT) Bill ("Hochfrequenzhandelsgesetz") requires that standardised minimum tick sizes be introduced on German trading venues.

Another important market structure issue is the role of price discrimination by trading venues through so-called maker–taker pricing[14] and volume discounts. Some argue that this pricing scheme encourages "rebate arbitrage", motivating trades that would not be profitable without the rebate but are marginally so with it. These trades are more likely to be associated with HF traders.

In electronic markets, liquidity is provided by limit orders posted by passive traders willing to provide an option to active traders. The more limit orders posted on a market, the more liquidity there is for other traders to execute against. If there are no frictions in the market, then the bid–ask spread settles at a level that exactly compensates the providers of liquidity with the value received by takers of liquidity. But real markets do have frictions (such as non-zero tick sizes), so fee and pricing models are not irrelevant. By paying those who make liquidity while charging those who take liquidity, maker–taker pricing has the potential to improve the allocation of the economic benefits of liquidity production. This, in turn, can incentivise potential suppliers of liquidity and lead to faster replenishment of the limit order book. Varying maker–taker fees with market conditions also provides a means to improve liquidity provision during times of market stress. A recommendation to have such time-varying fee structures was one finding of the "Flash Crash" Commission.

Maker–taker pricing can also be an effective way for new market venues to compete against established venues. Smart order-routing systems can direct order flow to venues with more aggressive pricing models. That can, in turn, put pressure on fees in other markets and lead to more competitive pricing. The success of BATS in the US is often attributed to their aggressive use of maker–taker pricing.[15]

High-frequency traders are generally better able to put their limit orders at the top of the queue, due to their speed advantage, their use of sophisticated order types such as "hide not slide"[16] and their use of "big data" to forecast market movements. The maker–taker fee structure may incentivise them to do so even more, with the result that institutional investors' limit orders are executed only if high-frequency traders find it uneconomical to step in front. It follows that institutional investors will hold back from submitting limit orders, leaving the market vulnerable to transient participation by high-frequency traders during times of market stress. This, in turn, could exacerbate episodes of periodic illiquidity.

It also follows that because institutional investors would then submit more market orders, they would face increased costs arising from bid–ask spreads, and taker fees. This problem of higher trading costs can be compounded if the routing decisions taken by intermediaries on behalf of clients are influenced in a suboptimal way by the fee structure offered by disparate venues. In particular, the broker may opt to send orders to venues offering suboptimal execution in return for rebates that are not passed on to the originating investor. This incentive will be even greater if these rebates are volume dependent. It may not be easy to monitor such practices.

A complex system of maker–taker pricing that is context and venue dependent can confuse market participants and lead to erroneous decisions. This may be particularly true if markets vary fees and rebates across time. Because spreads can vary, it is not entirely clear how much incremental effect on liquidity will arise from time-varying rebates.

There is little evidence in the academic literature that high-frequency traders have been "abusing" the existing fee structure.

Overall, the limited evidence suggests that maker–taker pricing improves depth and trading volume without negatively affecting spreads. In addition, the explicit trading fees on most venues have fallen substantially since around 2008, benefiting both makers and takers of liquidity (Chesini 2012).

A third area of market structure concern is whether orders sent to the book are too transient. Proposals to address this issue involve minimum resting times or the minimum time that a limit order must remain in force. While, in principle, minimum resting times could depend on factors such as trade side (buy or to sell), volatility or other market conditions, typically a uniform time span is proposed, such as 500 milliseconds. The impetus for imposing a minimum is that markets feature a large number of fleeting orders that are cancelled very soon after submission. This increases the costs of monitoring the market for all participants, and reduces the predictability of a trade's execution quality, since the quotes displayed may have been cancelled by the time the marketable order hits the resting orders.

The nature of high-frequency trading across markets and the widespread usage of hidden orders on exchanges are responsible for some of this fleeting order behaviour. However, frequent cancelling of quotes may also result from abusive strategies (the spoofing, layering and quote stuffing noted earlier), which can undermine market quality or, at the least, create a bad public perception, and a minimum resting time may allay concerns that the markets are "unfair".

Minimum resting times can increase the likelihood of a viewed quote being available to trade. This has two important benefits. First, it provides the market with a better estimate of the current market price, something which "flickering quotes" caused by excessive order cancellations obfuscates. Secondly, its visible depth at the front of the book should be more aligned with the actual depth. Quotes left further away from the current best bid or offer are less likely to be affected by the measure, since the likelihood of them being executed within a short time is small.

The drawback of minimum resting times lies in the fact that posting a limit order offers a free option to the market that is exercised at the discretion of the active trader. If an active trader has better or newer information, the limit order poster will be adversely selected, buying when the stock is going down and selling when the stock is going up. As with any option, its value increases with time to maturity and with volatility. Thus, forcing a limit order to be in force longer gives a more valuable option to the active trader, and consequently raises the cost of being a limit order provider. The expected result would be an increase in the bid–offer spread or decreased depth, as posting limit orders will be less attractive. Assuming limit order submission remained unaffected, the Foresight Report estimates that the cost of hitting such stale quotes may be as high as €1.33 billion per year in Europe.

This reluctance to post limit orders will be particularly acute during times of high volatility, when the cost of posting the option is naturally increased. This has the undesirable implication that liquidity provision will be impeded just at the times when markets need it most. It also suggests that there could be a feedback effect if increasing volatility triggers orders, further increasing volatility.

Another proposed market structure change is to put an upper limit on the ratio of orders to executions. The idea of such restrictions is to encourage traders to cancel fewer orders, thereby providing a more predictable limit order book. It is hoped that such predictability will improve investor confidence in the market. As cancellations and resubmissions form the bulk of market message traffic, this proposal would also reduce traffic and the consequent need for market participants to provide increasing message capacity in their trading systems. A number of exchanges have some restrictions on messages or the order/trade ratio. So there are sensible exchange-specific measures already in place that constrain the total message flow and price the externality those messages contribute. Germany has taken this further by requiring all exchanges in Germany to implement order-to-trade restrictions.

Receiving, handling and storing messages is costly for exchanges, brokers and regulators. Whenever an economic good is not priced there is a tendency to use more of it than if the user had to pay its actual costs. If the social cost of messages exceeds its private costs, an externality results; the standard solution is to tax messages. A ratio of orders-to-executions does this to some extent, and it can serve to align these private and social costs, thereby reducing the number of economically excessive messages and the temptation to slow down matching engines by quote stuffing markets. This, in turn, reduces the need for exchanges, brokers and other market participants to invest in costly capacity and it may also alleviate concerns of various manipulative strategies.

On the cost side, the nature of trading and market making in fragmented markets naturally implies order cancellations. Algorithmic trading, for example, seeks to reduce trade execution costs by splitting large orders into smaller pieces and sending orders both spatially and temporally to markets. As orders execute or languish, the execution strategy recalibrates, leading to cancellations and resubmissions. Such a trading approach reduces execution costs for traders and leads to greater efficiency in execution. Many HFT strategies (including HFT market making) involve statistical arbitrage across markets whereby movements in a price in one market (eg, in an ETF) trigger orders sent to other markets (eg, the potentially large number of ETF underlying stocks or bonds). Again, subsequent price movements in any of the markets will trigger cancellations and resubmissions as part of the process of reducing price discrepancies and enhancing market efficiency. Stifling such cross-market arbitrage trades would lead to inefficient pricing.

Many order cancellations result from searching for hidden liquidity on limit order books by "pinging" or sending small orders inside the spread to see if there is hidden liquidity. Because such orders are typically cancelled, a binding order-to-trade ratio would result in less pinging and, therefore, less information being extracted at the touch (the best bid and ask prices). As a result, more hidden orders will be posted, leading to a less transparent limit order book. A second effect on the book may arise because orders placed away from the touch have the lowest probability of execution. In a constrained world, these orders may not get placed, meaning that depth may be removed from the book away from touch. The Foresight Report investigated the effect of the introduction of an order-to-execution ratio (OER) penalty regime on the Milan Borsa on April 2, 2012. The preliminary findings (the authors of the report acknowledge some issues with their methodology, given the short time available) were that liquidity (spreads and depth) worsened as a result of this policy measure, with the effect more pronounced in large stocks. Similarly, anecdotal evidence suggests that the LSE message policy was not fully effective in that it gave rise to new patterns of trade in low-priced stocks.

An OER is a blunt measure that catches both abusive and beneficial strategies. It may not do too much harm if the upper limit is large enough not to hinder market making and intermediation, but to the extent that it is binding on those activities it may be detrimental to both spreads and liquidity. It is unlikely that a uniform OER across markets would be optimal, because it depends upon the type of securities traded and the trader clientele in the market.

Proposals to curtail high-frequency trading

A third direction for proposed regulation focuses more on curtailing, if not completely eliminating, high-frequency trading. At the forefront of these proposals is the Financial Transactions Tax (FTT). Such a tax has a long pedigree, having been proposed by a number of famous economists, including Keynes (in 1936) and Tobin (in 1972), at times of previous financial crisis. On September 28, 2011, the European Commission put forward a detailed proposal for an EU-wide FTT (European Commission 2011). The proposed tax covers a wide range of financial instruments. One of the stated objectives of the proposed tax is to create "appropriate disincentives for transactions that do not enhance the efficiency of financial markets thereby complementing regulatory measures aimed at avoiding future crises" (European Commission 2013). The Commission's targets here include short-term trading, particularly automated and high-frequency trading.

The UK has had a "stamp duty" on shares since 1694, with a rate of 0.5% at the time of writing. However, registered market participants are exempt from this tax, so it only falls on the beneficial owners rather than on the intermediary chain. Also, it applies to equities only, and not to close substitutes. The EU proposal is to apply the tax to all transactions. The figure of 0.1% is widely quoted in this regard. This should be compared with the typical transaction fees charged by trading venues across Europe, which seldom exceeds 0.005%, so that the magnitude of the tax rate is substantial and likely to be binding on behaviour.

At the time of writing became clear that the proposal would not achieve the unanimous support of EU Member States as required for it to be adopted across the EU. Numerous concerns have been raised, including: the potential negative effects on GDP, in part resulting from an increase in the cost of capital and hence a decline in investment; the susceptibility of the tax to avoidance through relocation unless it was adopted at a global level; and the uncertainty as to the bearers of the economic incidence of the tax. However, supporters of the proposal dismiss these concerns, and a number of Member States have been considering implementing a financial transaction tax through the enhanced cooperation procedure. Subject to a number of conditions, this procedure would allow a sub-group of Member States to introduce measures that only bind the participating states.

Apart from their revenue-raising potential, the perceived corrective function of these taxes is also often cited in their support. Proponents argue that such taxes can produce positive effects on financial markets by increasing the cost and reducing the volume of short-term trading. Crucially, this argument is based on a view of short-term trading as being mostly speculative (often supported by or based on trading systems) and unrelated to market fundamentals. This form of trading is thus viewed as having a negative impact on financial markets by contributing to excessive liquidity, excessive price volatility and asset bubbles. Furthermore, it is argued that the increasing ratio of financial transactions to GDP suggests considerable socially unproductive financial activity and hence a waste of resources. Financial transaction taxes are also seen as a way of compensating for the fact that many financial services are exempt from Value Added Tax (VAT).

In response it has been pointed out that:

- not all short-term trading is "undesirable";
- financial transaction taxes do not distinguish between long-term and short-term trading or between "desirable" and "undesirable" short-term trading;[17]
- such taxes might not affect volatility or might even increase it because they reduce liquidity in markets and create a random wedge between prices of identical securities traded across multiple venues;
- asset bubbles may also develop in the presence of high transaction costs, as documented by real estate bubbles; and
- it is neither obvious what the ideal ratio of financial activity to GDP should be, nor clear whether this ratio should increase or decrease over time, or how it should compare say with the ratio of health-care expenditure to GDP or legal services to GDP.

Finally, the VAT exemption of financial services reflects the difficulties of applying VAT to margin-based financial services. Financial transaction taxes cannot solve this problem for a number of reasons. Most importantly, financial transactions taxes do not tax value added in the financial sector.

There have been a number of academic studies, both theoretical and empirical, on the effect of financial transaction taxes, and transaction costs more generally. Overall, the results suggest that financial transactions taxes will give rise to significant relocation effects to tax havens, cannot be expected to reduce price volatility in asset markets and will bring about a sizable drop in market capitalisation that will be borne by the holders of the securities, including pension funds, whether or not they trade repeatedly or bear the FTT. For instance, a simple back-of-the-envelope calculation suggests that with plausible numbers such as an annual turnover of equity portfolios of 44%, an FTT of 0.1% and a dividend yield of 1.1%, the drop in market value is around 4.2%.

The experiences of France and Italy, both early adopters of an FTT, around the time of writing have underscored concerns with implementing such a tax. For France, tax revenues have been half of expected levels, reflecting the negative impact that such taxes have on overall trading. The paper by Haferkorn and Zimmermann (2013) on the French FTT find increased spread levels, and a strong decline in top order-book depth, resulting in additional transaction costs for market participants besides the tax. They also find that inter-market transmissions are impaired in that price dispersion between venues is significantly deteriorated and transient exogenous shocks create much slower reversions to fair value. Italy experienced a similar fall in volume (Fairless 2013). What have not been demonstrated are any positive effects on market quality, an issue that clearly warrants additional research.

A more direct assault on high-frequency trading is found in Germany's Hochfrequenzhandelsgesetz legislation. As noted earlier, the German Act on the Prevention of Risks Related to, and the Abuse of, High-Frequency Trading sets out a variety of restrictions on both high-frequency trading firms and practices. While the constraints on practices mirror the MiFID proposals discussed earlier, the constraints on HFT firms may be of more consequence. German law will require HFT firms to obtain a license for financial trading institutions and comply with the minimum capital requirements for financial trading institutions. This licensing requirement will apply both to HFT firms who are members of German exchanges and to those who simply trade via direct access to German markets.

How significant a constraint this will be remains to be seen, but the greater capital requirement and regulatory burden will surely raise the costs of high-frequency trading.[18]

Whether it will improve the markets is less apparent. Removing HFT firms will also remove liquidity. This would be expected to increase spreads and reduce depths, raising transaction costs for traders. It may also increase the cost of capital for firms, as traders require greater compensation to invest in less liquid securities, and newly listed firms find it hard to attract sufficient liquidity to sustain trading interest. A final verdict on the effectiveness of this regulatory approach awaits a careful study of its market impacts.

Jean-Pierre Zigrand acknowledges financial support by the Economic and Social Research Council (UK), Grant number ESRC/BSB/05.

1   For example, markets may allow certain types of orders (such as orders that immediately cancel under certain conditions or the "hide or slide" orders designed to game the US trade-through rules) that could cause large changes in the order book almost instantaneously.

2   Excellent surveys of the academic literature are Chapter 4 of the Foresight Project (Linton *et al* 2012) and Jones (2013).

3   The Indian flash crash is an interesting case in point. On October 5, 2012, trading on the National Stock Exchange (NSE) was halted for 15 minutes following a sudden drop of 920 points in the NSE Index (known as the Nifty). Subsequent investigation revealed that this flash crash was due to a "fat finger" problem arising from errant orders placed by a Mumbai-based brokerage.

4   As explained in the FINRA News Release, September 25, 2012, "Spoofing is a form of market manipulation which involves placing certain non-bona fide order(s), usually inside the existing National Best Bid or Offer (NBBO), with the intention of triggering another market participant(s) to join or improve the NBBO, followed by canceling the non-bona fide order, and entering an order on the opposite side of the market. Layering involves the placement of multiple, non-bona fide, limit orders on one side of the market at various price levels at or away from the NBBO to create the appearance of a change in the levels of supply and demand, thereby artificially moving the price of the security. An order is then executed on the opposite side of the market at the artificially created price, and the non-bona fide orders are immediately canceled". Quote stuffing involves sending and cancelling massive numbers of orders with the intent of taking all available bandwidth and thereby preventing other traders from being able to submit orders.

5   For details of this strategy see Dicolo and Rogow (2012).

6   Basically, due to the curvature of the Earth, sending the messages from towers reduces the distance travelled relative to sending the messages along the ground. This, combined with use of the microwave propagation (which is marginally faster than fibre-optic propagation), allows the messages to be received more quickly.

7 An agency algorithm is one that is executing an order on behalf of a client.

8 The Commodity Futures Trading Commission–Securities and Exchange Commission (CTFC–SEC) Task Force on Emerging Market Issues.

9 On May 15, 2013, the "Act on the Prevention of Risks Related to, and the Abuse of High-Frequency Trading" was enacted.

10 See "Australia finds HFT fears 'overstated' ", *Financial Times*, March 18, 2013.

11 See the "Markets Trading Guide", Crédit Agricole (2012) at http://www.cheuvreux.com/pdf/Markets_trading_guide.pdf.

12 For comparison, in online (one-sided) auctions such as eBay, the minimum bid increments vary with price level and are much wider than the corresponding tick sizes for similarly priced stocks. See http://pages.ebay.com/help/buy/bid-increments.html.

13 Since March 2009, FESE has been in negotiations with the London Investment Banking Association and some multilateral trading facilities (BATS, Chi-X, Nasdaq Europe and Turquoise) to harmonise the tick size regimes in Europe (which stood at approximately 25 across the EU) in the interest of achieving benefits to markets, users and investors by simplifying the complexity and number of regimes in place.

14 Maker–taker pricing refers to the practice in many exchanges and trading platforms of paying a small rebate to executed orders that were placed as passive limit orders (the liquidity makers) and charging a fee to active orders that hit existing limit orders (the liquidity takers).

15 Direct Edge operated the reverse taker–maker system back in 2008, before switching to maker–taker pricing.

16 This order type has been publicised by the "HFT whistleblower", Haim Bodek. See Patterson and Strasburg (2012) for a description.

17 Bloomfield *et al* (2009) analyse the distributional effects of security transactions taxes and find that, while successful in curtailing uninformed trading, these taxes have negative consequences for informational efficiency.

18 The HFT firm CIT announced plans to shut down, citing the potential for significant costs from new HFT regulations (Cave 2013).

REFERENCES

Boehmer, E., K. Fong and J. Wu, 2012, "International Evidence on Algorithmic Trading", Working Paper.

Bloomfield, R., M. O'Hara and G. Saar, 2009, "How Noise Trade Affects Markets: An Experimental Analysis", *Review of Financial Studies* 22(6), pp. 2275–302.

Brogaard, J., T. Hendershott and R. Riordan, 2011, "High Frequency Trading and Price Discovery", Working Paper.

Cave, T., 2013, "German HFT Is Early Casualty of New Trading Rules", *Financial News*, June 5.

Chesini, G., 2012, "The Effects of Competition on the Fee Structures of the Major Stock Exchanges", *World Review of Business Research* 2(6), pp. 100–8.

Dicolo, J. A., and G. Rogow, 2012, "Gas Market Stung by Rapid Traders", *Wall Street Journal*, October 18.

Easley, D., M. López de Prado and M. O'Hara, 2011, "The Microstructure of the 'Flash Crash': Flow Toxicity, Liquidity Crashes, and the Probability of Informed Trading", *Journal of Portfolio Management*, 37(2), pp. 118–28.

European Commission, 2011, "Financial Transaction Tax: Making the Financial Sector Pay Its Fair Share", Press Release, September 28.

European Commission, 2013, "Proposal for a Council Directive in the Area of Financial Transaction Tax", February 2, 2013/0045 (CNS).

Fairless, T., 2013, "EU's Trading Tax Takes Slow Road", *Wall Street Journal*, May 30.

Government Office for Science, 2012, *Foresight: The Future of Computer Trading in Financial Markets. An International Perspective*, Final Project Report. The Government Office for Science, London.

Haferkorn, M., and K. Zimmermann, 2013, "Securities Transaction Tax and Marked Quality: The Case of France", Working Paper.

Hagströmer, B., and L. L. Nordén, 2013. "The Diversity of High-Frequency Traders", *Journal of Financial Markets*, forthcoming.

Hasbrouck, J., and G. Saar, 2013, "Low Latency Trading", *Journal of Financial Markets*, forthcoming.

Hendershott, T., C. M. Jones and A. J. Menkveld, 2011, "Does Algorithmic Trading Improve Liquidity?" *Journal of Finance* 66, pp. 1–33.

Javers, E., 2013, "How High-Speed Trading Is about to Get Speedier", April 11. URL: http://www.cnbc.com/.

Jones, C., 2013, "What Do We Know about High Frequency Trading?", Working Paper.

Linton, O., M. O'Hara and J. P. Zigrand, 2012, "Economic Impact Assessments on Policy Measures", in *Foresight: The Future of Computer Trading in Financial Markets. An International Perspective*, Final Project Report, Chapter 6. The Government Office for Science, London.

Madhavan, A., 2012, "Exchange Traded Funds, Market Structure, and the Flash Crash", *Financial Analysts Journal* 68(4), pp. 20–35.

Malinova, K., A. Park and R. Riordan, 2012, "Do Retail Traders Suffer from High Frequency Traders?", Working Paper, University of Toronto.

O'Hara, M., and M. Ye, 2011, "Is Market Fragmentation Harming Market Quality?", *Journal of Financial Economics* 100(3), pp. 459–74.

O'Hara, M., 2010, "What Is a Quote?" *Journal of Trading* 5(2), pp. 11–16.

Patterson, S., and J. Strasburg, 2012, "How 'Hide Not Slide' Orders Work", Wall Street Journal, September 18.

Schwert, G. W., and P. J. Seguin, 1993, "Securities Transaction Taxes: An Overview of Costs, Benefits, and Unresolved Questions", *Financial Analysts Journal* 49, pp. 27–35.

US Securities and Exchange Commission, 2012, Report to Congress on Decimalization, July.

Walter, E., 2013, "Harnessing Tomorrow's Technology for Today's Investors and Markets", US Securities and Exchange Commision, Speech, February 19. URL: http://www.sec.gov/news/speech/2013/spch021913ebw.htm.

Index

(page numbers in italic type relate to tables or figures)

and trading signals,
construction of, 31–8; *see
also* trading signals
and types of client or market
agent, 22
European Exchange Rate
Mechanism (ERM),
sterling joins, 8
execution shortfall, and
information leakage,
164–6, *165*; *see also*
information leakage
execution strategies:
in equity markets, 21–41, *25,
29, 30, 33, 35, 37, 38, 40*
and fair value and order
protection, 38–41, *40*
and trading signals,
construction of, 31–8; *see
also* trading signals
in fixed-income markets,
43–62, *47, 48, 49, 50, 51, 52,
54, 55, 57, 58, 61*
and cointegration, 44, 53–9
and information events, 44,
46–53
and pro rata matching, 44,
59–62
and fixed-income products,
44–6
experimental evaluation, 133–40

F

fair value and order protection,
38–41, *40*
fixed-income markets:
execution strategies in, 43–62,
*47, 48, 49, 50, 51, 52, 54, 55,
57, 58, 61*
and cointegration, 44, 53–9
and information events, 44,
46–53
and pro rata matching, 44,
59–62
and short-term interest
rates, 45–6
and Treasury futures, 46
fixed-income products, 44–6

and short-term interest rates,
45–6
and Treasury futures, 46, *47,
48, 51, 52, 55*
see also fixed-income markets
flash crash, 2, 77–8, 207, 209–10,
210, 218
see also market stress
foreign-exchange markets:
and the currency market,
65–73
trading algorithms, 69–72
and trading frequencies,
65–73, *72, 73*
venues, 66–9
high-frequency trading in,
65–88, *66, 72, 73, 86*
academic literature, 74–80
and alternative limit order
book, 80–6; *see also main
entry*
Foresight Project, 215, 217, 224
futures markets:
microstructural volatility in,
125–41, *133, 134, 136, 137,
138–9*
experimental evaluation,
133–40
HDF5 file format, 127
maximum intermediate
return, 131–2
parallelisation, 132–3
test data, 126–7
and volume-synchronised
probability of informed
trading, 128–31

G

Goldman Sachs Electronic
Trading (GSET), 159, 160,
161, *163*, 166–80 *passim*,
167, 168, 169, 174–5

H

HDF5 file format, 127
high-frequency trading (HFT):
and "cheetah traders", 1, 13

and event-based time
  paradigm, 15
in FX markets 65–88, *66, 72, 73,
  86*; *see also*
  foreign-exchange markets,
  74–80
  and alternative limit order
  book, 80–6; *see also main
  entry*
  and the currency market,
  65–73
  and trading frequencies,
  65–73, *72, 73*
legislative changes enable, 2
machine learning for, 91–123,
  *100, 101, 103, 104, 107,
  108–9, 111, 117, 121*
  and high-frequency data,
  94–6
  and optimised execution in
  dark pools via censored
  exploration, 93
  and optimised trade
  execution via
  reinforcement learning,
  92
  and predicting price
  movement from order
  book state, 92–3
  and price movement from
  order book state,
  predicting, 104–15
  and reinforcement learning
  for optimised trade
  execution, 96–104
  and smart order routing in
  dark pools, 115–22
in market stress, 76–80
  central bank interventions,
  79–80
  flash crash (2010), 77–8
  yen appreciation (2007), 77
  yen appreciation (2011), 78–9
markets' operation and
  dynamic interaction
  changed by, xv
and matching engine, 3, *4*
and more than speed, 7–12

new paradigm in, 2–4
paradigm of, insights into,
  1–17, *7, 10–11, 14*
regulatory challenge of, 207–9,
  210, 212, 214
  good and bad news
  concerning, 208–14
  and greater surveillance and
  coordination, proposals
  for, 215–18
  and market rules, proposals
  to change, 218–25
  and proposals to curtail
  HFT, 225–8
  solutions, 214–28
statistics to monitor,
  developing, 15
and time, meaning of, 5–7
and volatility, heightening of,
  12
see also low-frequency trading

I

implementation shortfall:
  approach to, illustrated,
  192–203
  daily estimation, 195–9
  intra-day estimation,
  199–203
  shortfall calculations, 193–5
  discussed, 186–9
  with transitory price effects,
  185–206, *196, 197, 198, 199,
  200, 202, 203*
  implementation details,
  204–5
  and observed and efficient
  prices and pricing errors,
  189–92
indicator zoology, 27–8
information events, 44, 46–53
  and event microscope, 50–3
information leakage:
  and algorithmic execution,
  159–83, *176–7, 178–9*
  BadMax approach and data
  sample, 166–8, *168*